'Cauffman explores how solution-focused thought and practice may be applied to create diverse social contexts of change. He teases out the synergistic processes through which change emerges in solution focused client-practitioner interactions. Cauffman's discussion of professional mandates is particularly intriguing. It has important implications for understanding how professional authority is exercised in client-practitioner interactions. This is a coherent narrative linking early influences on solution focused pioneers with current themes in the field. Cauffman's accessible writing style makes the book appropriate as an introduction to the solution focused approach, and as an organizing framework for seminars involving experienced practitioners.'

Gale Miller, *emeritus professor, Department of Social and Cultural Sciences Marquette University, Wisconsin, USA*

'The solution-focused orientation is applicable in many human relation fields including coaching, psychotherapy, and team building in the business world. The approach has considerable depth although to those who only examine the surface it may seem pedestrian. We are blessed to have Louis Cauffman as a guide into the nuances of the method. Cauffman helps us bring out the best in our clients and helps us to bring out the best in our selves. *Creating Sustainable Results with Solution-Focused Applied Psychology* is an essential text for change agents of all types. Principles are clearly covered, and case studies provide background for those who will apply the methods. This book should be required reading for all those in human relations fields.'

Jeffrey K. Zeig, *The Milton H. Erickson Foundation, Phoenix, USA*

Creating Sustainable Results with Solution-Focused Applied Psychology

This practical, evidence-based guide details how professional practitioners and change facilitators can integrate a solution-focused approach into their daily work and practice.

While conventional therapeutic methods centre on the assumption that problems arise due to deficiencies, and therefore focus on diagnosis and subsequent treatment, the solution-focused approach is resource-based and operates on the assumption that human beings always have resources at their disposal to move forward. Free from the burden of detailed problem analysis, the solution-focused approach prioritizes clients' hope for change in their lives and taps into the opportunities and resources available to bring about such transformation. The solution-focused practitioner is able to design incisive interventions that are flexible enough to adapt to any situation clients might find themselves in, and this book provides a practical formulation that is immediately applicable to all professional fields of applied psychology.

Creating Sustainable Results with Solution-Focused Applied Psychology is important reading for therapists and coaches of all schools of thought, as well as anyone who practices as a professional change facilitator, including social workers, mediators, business leaders, and educators.

Louis Cauffman is a clinical psychologist and business economist with a wide range of therapeutic training, ranging from Systemic Family Therapy to Ericksonian Hypnotherapy through all possible directions within the solution-focused approach. One of the first to introduce the solution-focused approach in Europe, Louis remains passionate in his further development of the solution-focused approach as an epistemological tool. Louis is a highly praised international consultant, coach, and trainer. More information can be found at www.louiscauffman.com

Creating Sustainable Results with Solution-Focused Applied Psychology

A Practical Guide for Coaches and Change Facilitators

Louis Cauffman

LONDON AND NEW YORK

Designed cover image: Photograph taken by author. Private collection.

First published 2023
by Routledge
4 Park Square, Milton Park, Abingdon, Oxon OX14 4RN

and by Routledge
605 Third Avenue, New York, NY 10158

Routledge is an imprint of the Taylor & Francis Group, an informa business

British Library Cataloguing-in-Publication Data
A catalogue record for this book is available from the British Library

ISBN: 978-1-032-33539-1 (hbk)
ISBN: 978-1-032-33538-4 (pbk)
ISBN: 978-1-003-32010-4 (ebk)

DOI: 10.4324/9781003320104

Typeset in Times New Roman
by codeMantra

'If you don't know what you don't know, you're happy with what you already know.'

Prof. dr. C. Hange
Black Mountain University

'If you don't know what is right, go left'

Prof. dr. Diana Issolvante
Montenegro Universidad

In grateful memory of Steve and Insoo

Contents

Acknowledgments

Special thanks to Professor Dr. Mathieu Weggeman who helped shape this book and is the co-developer of SoFAP-P (Solution-Focused Applied Psychology, a Design Science Research Protocol (Routledge, 2023)) that scientifically validates and substantiates the solution-focused applied psychology approach.

Foreword

When you grow up with parents who develop a model of psychotherapy that ends up being used worldwide, that is taught in colleges and universities, that is the spark for new ideas across many disciplines, you would think that one would be impressed with their accomplishments. And while I am impressed, my upbringing was pretty normal with one exception. I got to meet the most interesting people from around the world. People who are extremely intelligent, creative thinkers, and people who are driven to help others. This was my normal.

I was fortunate to meet and know people such as Louis Cauffman along the way. Louis recognized that Solution-Focused Therapy could be applied to business, coaching, psychology, and management. He recognized that people in those fields are not that different than those who seek help in psychotherapy – they have a problem (or two) and need to find an answer or solution to that problem. And often people don't realize that they have the solution, so they seek out people to give them the answer. The Solution-Focused Approach posits that the client is the expert in their issues and the client already has the solution, they just need a bit of help in recognizing what has been working for them. Louis has done that exact thing for people in psychology, business, management, and coaching. He is here to help them recognize that the solutions they seek are there, they just need to be teased out and brought to light. Since then, it has not been uncommon for psychologists to find themselves working in courtrooms, boardrooms, schoolrooms, and community health centers. The common thread is people helping people through dialogue. Louis has taken the Solution-Focused model and is in dialogue with you, the reader, to use it in areas of applied psychology beyond its original scope.

Louis was originally a student of my mother and stepfather, Insoo Kim Berg and Steve de Shazer. They gave workshops worldwide on Solution-Focused Therapy and taught thousands of people the model they developed. Louis was among the first to invite them to Europe. Steve especially loved to discuss theory and philosophy with friends such as Louis. And both Steve and Insoo were excited by the ideas that their "trainees" brought to the table. (They never thought of the people attending their workshops as trainees but more as people who had not yet learned about the Solution Focus – more like people who didn't yet know where the path was and just needed someone to point the way.) Louis was one of their friends who had exciting ideas of using a solution-oriented model and rather than using it in just therapy, to apply it to coaching, business, and management. He has been ahead of his time!

You will find Louis's work thought-provoking, exciting, and well-worth studying. He brings insights and ideas to psychology that only a good practitioner can. I'm sure the reader will find this book useful, and it will become a favorite. Enjoy!

Sarah Kim Berg
Daughter of Insoo Kim Berg, Stepdaughter of Steve de Shazer
Former Office Manager Brief Family Therapy Centre, Milwaukee, USA

Note from the author

The current book *Creating Sustainable Results with Solution-focused Applied Psychology: A Practical Guide for Coaches and Change Facilitators* provides an in-depth practical guide to facilitate adding the intricacies of solution-focused thinking and working to the existing professionalism and expertise of practitioners.

Our goal and ambition are to extend solution-focused thinking and working to different application domains so that the epistemological tool used to cocreate alternative realities between involved parties enters the domain of applied psychology.

The companion book, *Solution-Focused Applied Psychology, a Design Science Research Protocol* (SoFAP-P, Routledge 2023) offers a scientific foundation of the solution-focused arrangement of interventions to facilitate change. It is mainly written for students and academics that are interested in discovering how evidence-based interventions can be developed by using the novel and innovative Design Science Research methodology.

Introduction

Simple is not easy

The Miracle Question, scaling questions, exceptions to the problem, and compliments are the icons in which the richness of solution-focused epistemology shines. But there is so much more!

Facilitating positive change is a co-creation of client and professional, in which care and well-being are two sides of the same coin.

The time when therapy was merely taking care of or providing care for people is over. From a solution-focused perspective, care is the creation of a context in which the client is helped to (again) help himself to achieve his goals. The Mother of All Goals in life that overarches all other life goals is the search for self-healing and well-being.

This book offers a look behind the scenes of the scientific developments that are the backbone of solution-focused thinking and working. The evidence-based efficacy of the non-specific factors is complemented by the innovative Design Research Science paradigm that acts as the scientific foundation. The goal of this book is to provide both state of the art practical solution-focused applications with a scientifically validated foundation based on Design Research Science methodology. Therefore, we "upgrade" the terminology from solution-focused thinking and working into Solution-Focused Applied Psychology (SoFAP). The terms SoFAP and solution-focused will be used intermittingly throughout the book. The careful reader will discover that SoFAP refers to the overarching and foundational approach that acts like an operating system versus the concrete interventions methods that are like applications. SoFAP as Windows or IOS versus solution-focused interventions that are like apps.

Add lightness!

In the mid-1960s, a journalist asked Colin Chapman, the owner of Lotus Sports Cars, how he, with such small budgets and with such a small company, managed to win almost all the races compared to his direct competitors that were far larger and richer. His answer was, "Add lightness!"

DOI: 10.4324/9781003320104-1

That statement could be a hologram capturing the essence of SoFAP. Add lightness to the interactions with yourself and your clients and thus help yourself and your clients to add lightness to life.

The image of mankind behind solution-focused thinking and working (SoFAP) assumes that all people always have resources at their disposal, albeit that these are sometimes hidden under the rubble of human misery. Resources can be defined as whatever it is that the client can use to reach his goal. That goal is: get rid of his complaints, learn how to solve them himself in the future and learn to do something else so that the mother of all goals, well-being can be accomplished, albeit tentatively and temporarily.

Treatment that focuses exclusively on solving the client's problems ignores the essence of what ultimately drives human beings: growth, well-being, and contentment. In this book, we provide tools to help the client and the professional to extend the step from mere treatment and care to self-healing (that in this view equals growth) and well-being.

There are only two kinds of therapy: good and bad. And it is the client who gives the definition. This premise puts the client at the center of the entire therapy process. And, thanks to research, we know what the discriminating factors for good therapy are, i.e., the non-specific variables that are common to all successful facilitation interventions, coupled to attention for the client's context and specific technical interventions.

The solution cube

Six chapters of this book form the six sides of a cube or better, a prism with six equal sides. The reality as we co-construct it with our clients can be viewed through each side of this prism. Each view offers a different perspective. All six different perspectives help co-create a coherent new reality for our clients.

Chapter 1 examines the basic axioms behind solution-focused thinking and working: the thinking behind the thinking.

Chapter 2 explains the factors common to all forms of helpful change facilitation, be it therapy or coaching.

Chapter 3 deals with the decision rules you can use to generate maximum effect with minimum energy, a.k.a. the minimax rules.

Chapter 4 explains that we have multiple mandates at the same time: change facilitation is more than just therapy or coaching. It also has to do with leadership and with a management mandate that guides the change process.

Chapter 5 offers the seven-step dance that you can use to dance with your clients toward solutions and greater well-being.

Chapter 6 contains the flow chart, a decision tree that helps you know, given the quality of the working relationship with your client, what to do when and what not to do to be maximally effective.

Beyond techniques

Too often, solution-focused work is reduced to the use of techniques such as scaling questions or the Miracle Question. These techniques have – rightfully – become icons of the solution- focused approach. Yet, they are only techniques. To put their importance in perspective, in Chapter 7 we will unravel the linguistic mechanisms behind these icons.

Your personal 3-D solution cube

We invite you to scan this QR code where you will find the full-size Solution Cube. To create your personal Solution Cube, simply print and cut it out.

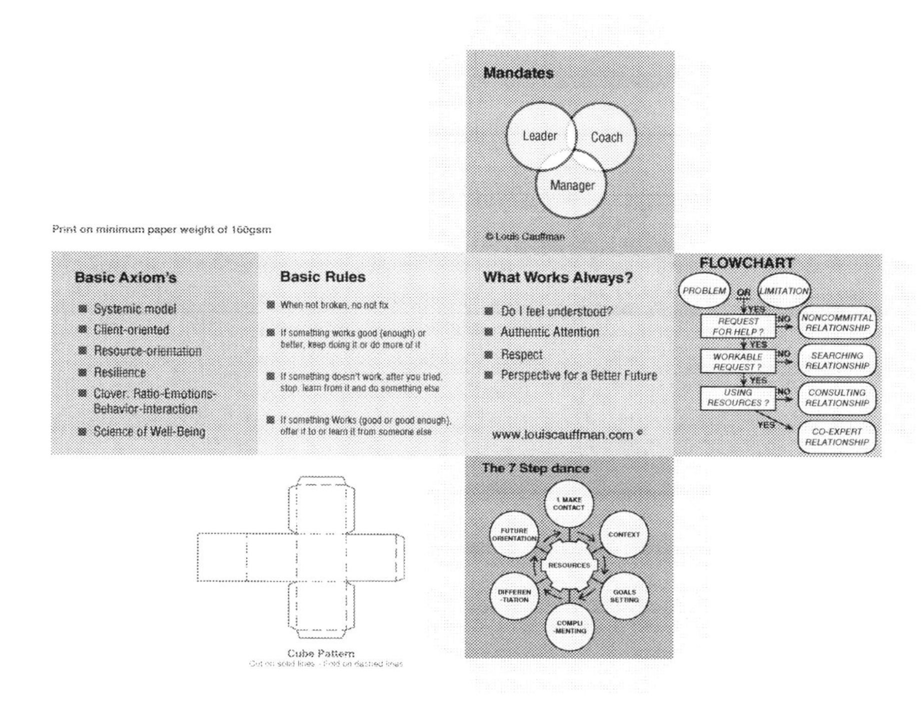

Gender, footnotes & readability

One can read "she" where ""he" is used and vice versa.

The many cross-links between chapters deepen and accelerate your learning process. To make reading easier, we move most of the cross-references to the footnotes.

We offer many examples, case studies, scientific developments in psychology and from other fields, subtle linguistic deconstructions, best practices, and overview lists to enhance your reading enjoyment and learning speed.

The founding father of modern therapy

Dr. Milton H. Erickson (1901–1980) was a famous psychiatrist and psychologist who was a pivotal figure in the development of the field of psychotherapy. His work sparked Steve de Shazer into developing the solution-focused approach. The Genius of Milton H. Erickson is our guide throughout this book who, through numerous quotations from his work, illuminates all the angles and insights of SoFAP.

* * *

The 10 SoFAP essentials

The following overview summarizes SoFAP as painted in broad brushstrokes. The chapters will then elaborate on all the essences and subtleties in the finest brushstrokes possible, so that the layered aesthetic will gradually become visible.

1 The Land of Possibilities

In the solution-focused approach, problems interest us mainly because they provide us with clues to the possible solutions. Although problems can be overwhelming, there are always moments when the problem is not there or when the problem is less severe or slightly different than at other times. In other words, there are always exceptions to the problems. These exceptions interest the solution-focused worker because they indicate that there are partial solutions that can be enlarged into broader solutions.

The solution-focused practitioner asks: "What still works in spite of the problems you are facing?" The working hypothesis of the solution-focused approach is that there are always things worth continuing with, that there are always things that still work and that – despite feelings of despondency – there are always possibilities.

2 The Solution-Focused Image of Mankind

The Image of Mankind behind the solution-focused model assumes that:

- Every human being and every human system come fully equipped to cope with life.
- Human systems (individuals, families, teams, companies etc.) always have resources at their disposal that they can use to achieve their goals.
- However dire the situation may seem, there are always things that are worthwhile to keep doing.
- There are always things that still work in spite of the problem.
- Change works best on a foundation of what already is there.

3 Resource Orientation

In solution-focused work, one continuously concentrates on the resources that the individual, couple, family, or larger system can use to move forward in their life. A resource can be anything, from your background, intelligence, work, relations, friends, family and environmental factors to convictions, experience, studies (whether or not at the "university of life"), financial situation, work, and so on. On the condition that you make proper use of it, anything can be a resource to draw strength from as long. A half full bottle contains exactly the same reality as a half empty bottle. Yet, seeing the bottle as half full is a resource that enhances your chances of survival in the desert.

Thinking in terms of resources is so pivotal in the solution-focused approach that it could've just as well been named "resource-focused working".

4 Future Orientation

Solutions belong to the future while problems belong to the past. The solution-focused model offers a wide range of interventions that channel your focus towards constructing possible solutions. Instead of concentrating on the (why of the) problems in the past, the solution-focused model concentrates on the desired outcome: "What do you want to accomplish tomorrow and next week?" "What could be the first little step towards this?"

5 Goal Orientation

The solution-focused approach focuses on the goals of the clients and not on the paradigm that the experts adhere to. In solution-focused work, the only goals that deserve our attention are the goals of the clients, as they need to be aligned with the restraints of legal-medical-deontological-ethical best practices.

Useful goals are practical, realistic, realizable, can be phrased in behavioral terms ("What will you do different if…") and they preferably go from small to large.[1]

6 Three Mandates

A mandate is the authority required to exercise a function. If we want to regulate traffic at a crossing, we have to make sure that we have a mandate as a police officer. In the perception of the rushing drivers, we are allowed to regulate the traffic because the (hired) uniform makes us look like a police officer. This means, you do not "have" a mandate. You "receive" a mandate by earning it from your clients' perspective. A mandate always results from interaction.

As a professional change agent, we always hold three mandates at the same time. We have a leadership mandate that allows us to take the lead in the interventions. At the same time, we have a stewardship or management mandate through which we apply our professional knowledge and make agreements with our clients. Our third mandate is the coaching or therapeutic, in general, facilitative mandate that uses our working relationship to create a context in which we help others to help themselves achieve their goals by making use of their resources.

Solution-focused work means that you must continuously switch between three mandates. The essence of your mandate as a leader, is to know precisely how and when to apply your mandates as a coach or as a manager. After all, it is you who decides – from your expertise, experience, and awareness of the current situation – whether you intervene as a coach or as a manager.

All three mandates drive and are driven by the quality of our working relationship with the clients.

7 Asking questions triumphs over giving statements

Questions elicit answers which in turn elicit questions which… and so on. Asking appropriate solution-building questions will uncover resources that can be used to build solutions towards the goals of the individual and his relevant system.

When offering suggestions or even specific directives that stem from your managerial mandate, it is best to phrase those in the form of a question. That way, the client who answers your suggestive question, becomes the owner of the answer, which enhances the chance that the client will actually do it.

8 Minimax decision rules

As a solution-focused professional, we are constantly aiming at obtaining maximal effects with minimal efforts. To reach this minimax effect, you can use the following decision rules:

Rule 1: if something is not broken, do not fix it.

Rule 2: if something is not, no longer, or not properly working after trying for a while, then stop, learn from it and do something else.

Rule 3: if something is working well, good enough or better, just keep doing it and/or do more of it.

Rule 4: if something is working well, good enough or better, learn it from someone else and/or offer it to someone else.

You can use this list of decision rules as a checklist. Whenever you feel a certain intervention does not work, you can go through this checklist, find what you missed or what you didn't pay enough attention to, add a difference, and then implement it.

9 Solution Talk

Language is our main instrument. Listening and talking are the main components of "languaging". The cooperation between the professional and his clients, aims at helping the clients create an alternative reality than their problem state.

Problem Talk: "What is the problem and why?"

Solution Talk: "What still works well in spite of the problem?" "What would you like *instead* of the problem?".

10 The Seven-Step Tango

What is it that you actually do in the relationship with your clients? Protocol-driven models follow a fixed script. The SoFAP approach is more like a dance. Since we never know what situations might pop up nor what clients will do or say, it is a far better idea to improvise creative answers that are adapted to the continuously changing and unpredictable conversations. We improvise on a theme that comes from the situation at that moment.

It takes two to tango. In the tango, a minimal number of steps can be combined into endless possible moves between the dance partners.

Solution-focused facilitation is like a tango with seven basic steps. Each step in the tango is an *activity* to be performed *together with* your client. Since the working relationship is the driver for change, it starts with making contact (step 1). After having explored the context (step 2), the client is asked for his goals (step 3), we listen for resources (step 4) and offer relevant compliments (step 5). When in trouble, people tend to think in black-white terms and, in order to not drown in a sea of misery, we offer differentiation (step 6). Problems per definition belong to the past. Problems that do not exist today are no problems (yet). Solutions on the contrary belong to the future. The future orientation (step 7) in SoFAP underlines this given.

The metaphor of the solution tango structures and guides the interaction process between yourself and your interlocutors.

Scope of applicability

The main theme of SoFAP is not to unravel the inner workings of a person or system, but rather to improve the mechanisms of influence. In this,

SoFAP takes a systemic view, specifically how parts of a system influence and are influenced by other parts of a system. These parts can be persons (ranging from individuals over families and groups to large parts of society, ranging from spouses over family members to coworkers and teams) but also immaterial agents (ranging from ideas, concepts, beliefs to values). SoFAP addresses how we influence and are influenced by the interactive behavior of people and intangible agents.

SoFAP is an epistemological meta-model in which interventions are contentless process drivers that are similar in all forms of human influence but differ in content based on the situation in which they occur. Therefore, SoFAP can be used in many different professional activities.

Terminology

This book covers the field of therapy, coaching, and all other professional activities aimed at facilitating positive change in and among people, regardless of area of specialization. To apply the principles of SoFAP to these diverse fields, we need broad terminology. Therefore, we use the terms change facilitator, coach, therapist, professional, and practitioner interchangeably. The most generic term is "change agent". Readers are invited to use the terminology that best suits their professional context.

Note

1 In Chapter 5, we will discuss the characteristics of useful goals and detail the similarities and differences of solution-focused goals with the well-known "SMART" goals.

Chapter 1

The basic axioms

The futile quest for a comprehensive theory

With the emergence of psychology as a science in the late nineteenth century, the quest for a comprehensive theory about the functioning of the human mind and ways to influence it had begun. A theory is defined as "a system of concepts that aims to offer a universal explanation for a certain field of expertise". Simply put: a theory (for instance about the functioning of the human mind) aims to tell us how things are or should be. Psychology has mainly concentrated on trying to understand what and why so many things go wrong in human existence. This "understanding" is embedded in theories and models. This soon led to the development of numerous theories with corresponding intervention models, each one pretending to be more all-encompassing, more profound than the competing models. All models have flaws and imitations that elicit lessons learned and lead to the next model.

Theories tend to reduce the complexity of the topic studied to phenomena that fit the theory. You may come across a phenomenon that does not fit the theory you adhere to. Often psychological theories are complicated and require that you learn a specific jargon. Both elements take time to master. One runs the risk of becoming so attached to the model that you had to learn the hard way, that the mind is blinded to other possibilities. How this blinding works is easy understood. The *Sunken Cost Fallacy* kicks in: you have spent too much time, energy, and passion to study this specific approach and it feels as a big loss to doubt the soundness of your beloved theory. On top of this, psychological theories are studied, taught, and therefore learned through schools of thought, faculties, associations, and training institutes. *Groupthink* kicks in. And to complete the blinding cycle, the *Confirmation Bias* kicks in: one sees what one believes. Consequently, instead of doubting and reviewing your theory, you may be tempted to research whether something is wrong with the phenomenon that should fit within the theory, and whether that specific phenomenon that does not fit the theory should be modified.

DOI: 10.4324/9781003320104-2

That's how we end up with our friend Procrustes, who used to have a rather painful habit for his guests who were allowed to stay at his inn for free on one condition. The condition was that they must fit the bed and if not...

> At the inn of Procrustes, the height of the guest was adapted to the length of the bed. If the guest was too tall, his legs were chopped off. If the guest was too short, he was stretched out on the rack.[1]

Because of their theoretical background, traditional therapy models tend to require clients to adapt to the model and the underlying theory. Diagnosis and assessment are necessary to verify if the client fits into the available "therapy model bed". If that is not the case, the client must look for another "therapy inn". If he does fit in but doesn't adapt himself to the therapy that is provided, we speak of "resistance". If everything goes well, the client will be helped, and the therapy will relieve him of his symptoms and complaints. However, the price of this exclusive focus on the reduction of the complaints is that the client needs to work on his growth and well-being on his own.

The image of mankind behind the solution-focused psychology

Each therapy approach falls back on an underlying concept of mankind. For the solution-focused therapist, a human being is a *unique* individual who functions in a *social network* and who, no matter how big the (temporary) problems may be or seem, always has the *resources* to achieve his ultimate goal: to grow as a person, lead a fulfilling life, and – ultimately – and become *happy*.[2]

Customization

The American psychiatrist and psychotherapist Dr. Milton Erickson, whose work is the foundation of solution-focused applied psychology, stated:

> Each person is a unique individual. Hence, psychotherapy should be formulated to meet the uniqueness of the individual's needs, rather than tailoring the person to fit the Procrustean bed of a hypothetical theory of human behavior.
>
> Milton H. Erickson[3]

Basic axioms

Solution-focused therapy originally does not result from big theories but from daily practice. de Shazer and his team strived to make the clients suffer less by eliminating all unnecessary detours like delving in the past, searching for root causes, or applying the diagnosis-treatment chain. Bypassing these classical routes and going straight for the solution-focused approach that you will encounter in this book saves time and energy. Even if it is not the goal but a welcome side-effect, the solution-focused approach works faster and produces more robust outcomes. That's where the original name comes from: Brief Family Therapy.

But SoFAP is not based on mere personal views and opinions. SoFAP is based on views from related scientific fields that we transform into axioms: unproven statements that are accepted as foundations.

These basic axioms support the way of thinking *behind* the solution-focused approach. They form the foundations on which we base our ways of thinking and are also an addition to, as well as a deepening of, the traditional solution-focused model.

From a theoretical viewpoint, these axioms enrich our way of looking at how we, together with our clients, co-create an alternative reality. From a practical viewpoint, the axioms offer us elements that we can fall back on when in doubt about the way to proceed.

The six basic axioms we are dealing with here are:

- resource orientation
- resilience
- the science of well-being
- working in a client-oriented way
- systemic approach and practice
- the four-leaf clover: cognition-emotion-behavior-interaction.

The axiom of resource orientation

A resource is a source that provides the strength a client can use to achieve his goal. A goal is not only the solution for a problem the client is struggling with. It can also be something the client strives for, what he wants to accomplish. It can be a concrete goal: I want to pass the next exam. It can also be something more diffuse like: I want to grow as a person, I want to find meaning in my life, I want to enhance my well-being.

A resource can literally come from anything: intelligence, family, friends, professional relations, world view and convictions, past crises. But resources can also come from difficult life events like loss of work, bereavement, a difficult financial situation. The crux is obviously what the client does to transform these events and emotions into a resource.

Let us take a simple example. Imagine your manager asked you to draw up an important strategic note about the operations of your department and do this within the next two days. The fact that the deadline is so close is a resource because it forces you to get straight to the point. Now imagine receiving the same task, but with a two-week deadline. That longer period is a resource as well, as you have more time to prepare the note in detail. In other words, whether something is a resource depends on the way you use it to reach your goal.

Some more examples: bereavement shows your sensitivity and is quite normal. A precarious financial situation forces you to be careful and helps you to stretch your funds. If you succeed, you can be proud of yourself, no matter how hard it was. Misery in the past indicates that – no matter how difficult it was – you have managed to somehow get through it. Being extremely intelligent can be tricky at times, but you can use your intelligence in a smart way to set yourself additional intellectual challenges.

Being less gifted is uncomfortable until you realize that keeping things simple can result in a satisfying life. It may be unfortunate that your family broke off relations with you, but if you are convinced that you have tried everything to make up to them, you can – temporarily – leave it for what it is. Seeing pain, grief, and loss as inconveniences requires a huge intellectual and emotional effort, but it will also give you a lot in return.

Traditional change models are often deficit-based and depart from the things the client cannot do and why he cannot do this. Solution-focused therapy is resource-based: What can the client still do *in spite of* the deficits? As you will learn in the upcoming chapters, the idea of resources is central to the solution-focused approach.

A common misunderstanding is that the solution-focused approach stands for positive thinking: if you look positively at everything and start from the conviction that humanity is beautiful, you can overcome all your problems. However, solution-focused thinking has nothing to do with positive thinking. It departs from reality as it is, but we see the same reality from a different perspective. We all know the metaphor of the half-empty and the half-full glass. Let's add some drama:

> A group of tourists is traveling through the Sahara. During a deep conversation about the meaning of life, two of them have lost track of the group. They struggle for hours through the desert when tourist A sees an oasis on the horizon. Tourist A: "Finally! Now we're saved." Tourist B has a look and says: "As long as it's not a mirage. I will never make it. My water bottle is already half empty." Tourist A: "Come on, don't give up now! We will make it; my water bottle is still half-full." Which of them do you think has the highest chance of survival?

Please note that positive thinking does not fill water bottles. In a half-full bottle, there is exactly the same reality as in a half-empty bottle. The Sahara example above does show that being focused on the resources (the amount of water) is a more useful basic attitude than being focused on what is not there (the half-empty bottle). Solution-focused thinking is no naïve optimism, but practical realism.

> I think one of his most important contributions was his idea that people have resources within them, the ability to heal their own pain and solve their own problems in ways they do not have to understand cognitively. It wasn't important to Milton that anyone, even the person, "understand(s)" how productive changes and growth occur – it was only important that it happened.
>
> Elizabeth Moore Erickson[4]

The lesson that the axiom of the resource orientation suggests to the practitioner is that it is wise to specifically pay attention to what goes well, despite all problems. In other words, the best way to help yourself and therefore your clients is to see beyond deficiencies and be alert to the possibilities that are always present. Obviously, seeing beyond the deficiencies is different from acting as if those deficiencies are not there. With "seeing beyond" we mean that we do not focus on them, accept them, and then look at what still goes well.

Change works best on a foundation of what is already there.

The axiom of resilience

There are cases that make everyone say: what those people had to go through is unbelievable. Losing your mother at a young age, with an illiterate alcoholic father who has been unemployed for years, with financial problems and with three kids having been placed under foster care ... And then – on top of it all – the eldest daughter, a mentally disabled girl, turns out to have been sexually abused by her uncle between the age of 10 and 15.

Such cases are hard for every therapist. You start brainstorming about the traditional psychological hypotheses. If you don't watch out, you will sink into a sea of misery. If you don't watch out, your heart will sink into your boots and you will give up all hope for the client's family. And with you, your clients will give up all hope as well.

However, there is a simple but difficult remedy to counter this. During your sessions, recognize the fact that they had a very hard time. If you then ask them how they managed to carry on in spite of all their problems, they will tell you that they had no other option but to persevere. If you ask them what has been the hardest thing and how they managed to overcome it, they will simply tell you. By starting off with showing recognition for the pain and miserable feelings, you show the clients that it is OK to talk about this and that you accept the situation as they tell you. Additional questions like: "How did you cope with all of this? What kept you going? How did you survive this avalanche of misery?" imply that the clients can handle it. Asking these questions give the family members the opportunity to talk about their resilience and therefore that there is hope that change is possible in the future. This way, you will be giving the family (and yourself) hope. Froma Walsh,[5] the international resilience expert, states:

Hope is to the human mind what oxygen is *to the body*.

Resilience is the ability to go through inevitable disrupting life experiences, to endure them and to recover from them, so that you learn from it and develop a pro-active response mechanism that will enable you to handle a next disrupting life experience somewhat better. This ability is forged *by* and not despite setbacks. As Albert Camus said: "In the midst of winter, I found there was, within me, an invincible summer."[6]

In our everyday lives, we all come across "disrupting life events". We were all born and we all die. Those are two inevitable life events that are quite disrupting. But life has more in store: loss, infatuation, illness, decline, adolescence, heartbreak, the joy at the birth of a child, layoffs, divorce, a young love, and so on.

Exercise

Think about your own life. How did you manage to overcome your worst experiences? What and who helped you the most? What did you learn from it? And how did these earlier experiences help you when you encountered similar difficulties afterwards? You can ask your clients the same questions. Their answers show their resilience in action.

The shape of a spring changes when you put a weight on it, but changes back to normal when you take away the weight. That is not how humans work. Some clients say: "Oh well, I wish it was all like at the beginning of our marriage. Back then, our relationship was a dream, everything went great. However, recently, it has become hell. Could you help us rediscover that dream relationship from back in the day?" The answer is simple: no. Nothing will become what it once was. Life is an unrolling spiral that starts with being born and ends with dying. The time between these moments of alpha and omega is best filled with as much well-being, meaningfulness, and joy as possible.

Our clients teach us – if we are willing to hear and see, that is – on a daily basis – that they are better off focusing on their own resilience instead of on their problems. Every relationship therapist knows couples that argue a lot during the therapy sessions and then leave arm in arm. They are capable of more than just arguing.

Every person has his own resilience. The areas in which individuals show the most resilience vary from person to person. It is a good idea to look for areas where the individual has a lot of resilience and see how this resource can be transferred to less resilient areas. Resilience is not limited to individuals. As we will later learn in the paragraphs about systemic thinking, resilience is also present in other human systems like a couple, a family, a club, a peer group, a company. A person's resilience will not disappear when someone encounters a problem. However, some people can get so taken up with their problems that personal competences fade into the background. At such a moment, it's the therapist's job to respectfully make the client (re) discover his own resilience and to help him use these hidden or obscured resources again.

The axiom of well-being

To the question "What's the meaning of life?", the most common reply is: "Being happy". But what does that mean? People have been pondering on this for thousands of years. Aristotle and Plato in the West, Confucius and Lao Tse in the East, and many other philosophers and authors throughout history have been ruminating on this question. All the major religions in the world have been contemplating the meaning of "a good life" and how to attain it.

In everyday language, the term happiness usually leads to misunderstanding and simplistic clichés. Happiness is no "happiology" and the pinnacle of happiness does not automatically mean a lifetime of sipping champagne on the sun deck of your private yacht with a view on your own tropical island. This lifestyle is bound to make the few people that can actually afford it really unhappy. Larry Allman, psychology professor emeritus at the University of Honolulu, has a practice on Maui, one of the most beautiful islands in the world. His waiting room is full of tycoons who, after the sale of their business, have moved to Maui to spend the rest of their lives in ultimate bliss. After a relatively short while when their villa is ready, the family has visited a few times, friends have come to enjoy paradise and the honeymoon of a lifelong vacation is over, they become bored and unhappy. Some of them come to Larry for therapy. According to Larry, as a result of his therapy, they forget about their dream, sell their property, return to where they came from and try to lead meaningful lives again.

Therefore, SoFAP no longer refers to "the science of happiness", but to "the science of growth, well-being, and satisfaction". We all want to grow as human beings and find meaning in each phase of our life cycle. We define "well-being" as: everything that makes life worth living, including accepting the fact that being unhappy is an inevitable part of it. Satisfaction stands for being content with what you have. A more common phrase is: count your blessings.

Well-being and satisfaction are linked to a combination of factors:

- positive emotions such as loving someone, feeling loved, gratitude, compassion, contentment, etc.
- a positive mindset such as a forgiving nature, perseverance, the ability to put things into perspective and to accept them, optimism.
- a meaningful and useful life beyond the material
- positive relationships with partner, family, friends, colleagues, social networks, etc.
- dedication to achieve what you really want, willingness to try, then enjoy what you have achieved and look for the next small step
- looking forward from today's perspective while carrying the lessons of the past with you.

Erickson's daughter Betty Alice bears witness to her father's vision of life:

> He believed the natural state of a human being was to be "healthy, wealthy, and wise", and to experience life as a joyous event. His basic philosophy was that life is joyous even though it is hard, unfair, filled with pain, and that every choice has both cost and benefit. Each of us is in charge of how we use what's in our minds and hearts.[7]

The axiom of client-orientation

> The most important thing in therapy is to speak the experiential language of the client. The most important thing to do in therapy is to put one foot in the client's world and leave one foot in your own.[8]
>
> Milton H. Erickson

If we paraphrase this statement, it becomes: "Therapy is not about techniques. Therapy is done in the language and experience of the client." This is reflected in the basic mindset of the solution-focused professional and constitutes a breach with the traditional therapy models. Within the solution-focused model, it is the client who is central not the therapist or his therapeutic theory.

The more client-oriented we are, the better we can understand the client's perspective. Also, the better we understand his language, the better we can connect with him. That way, the client becomes the central actor in his own healing process. It is the client who is the hero of the process, not the therapist. This client-orientation – or to say it with Duncan and Miller[9] this client drive – explains the effectiveness of therapeutic practice, as you will learn in Chapter 2 where we explain what always works in good therapy.

Therapists are facilitators, who create a context in which the client is helped to help himself. Any psychotherapy is in fact nothing more (but also nothing less) than "assisted" self-therapy.

> It is the patient who does the therapy. The therapist only furnishes the climate, the weather. That's all. The patient has to do all the work.[10]
>
> Milton H. Erickson

Health care stands for offering help: the client is offered help and it is up to the client to decide whether he can or wants to accept this offer and use it. In other words: therapists are midwives who help their clients give birth to their own possibilities.

Sometimes, solution-focused purists assume that the client is the expert of his own life. But in that case, why would they need any therapy? We fully agree with the statement that therapists can help their clients to (re)gain access to their own resources and (learn) how to use them (again). Clients therefore are experts that, as result of questioning, give the professional the necessary information so that the professionals can deploy their expertise to hand tools to the client.

By nature, therapists are interested in people and relationships. You can even say – a bit short of the mark – that therapists are professional "peeping Toms". Being a therapist may even be one of the most exciting professions: you hear, see, and experience things you could never have imagined. A therapist doesn't need to watch *reality TV*: after all, the reality he gets to know through his clients is far more exciting! Dealing with this requires professionalism and ethics and comes with great responsibility.

Two powerful tools to sharpen your client orientation:

1. *"Walk a mile in their shoes"*
   Always try to imagine how the things you say are coming across to your client. This helps you to meticulously adjust your language to the client. After all, we know from communication sciences that the way your message comes across doesn't always correspond to what you think you've actually said. It's possible that you may say one thing while your client hears something completely different. By walking in the shoes of the client and listening with his ears, the communicator keeps his focus on what the client hears and not on what the communicator thinks he says. By the way, it is good to realize that clients also tend to put themselves in their therapist's shoes. They arrive well prepared so they can talk about what they think the therapist wants to hear from them. They're often already familiar with therapy and they've "learned" that talking about the causes and details of their problem is very much appreciated by most therapists. We have to accept and respect this, but we also have to take the opportunity to show the client that we're more interested in

him as a person than in his problems. Therefore, we prefer to start our first session as follows:

Welcome. Is this the first time you have come to talk to someone like me? This is a courageous step forward that you have already taken. Congratulations. First, tell me something about yourself. How old are you? Married, engaged or single? Children? What do you do for a living?

These opening questions invite the client to give information, lead him away from his fixation with everything that doesn't work and clearly show that we're interested in him as a person.

2. *"My name is Manuel"*
   In a famous television series about a poorly run hotel, Manuel, the Spanish waiter, always said something along the lines of: "My name is Manuel. I come from Barcelona. I know nothing. You tell me everything please thank you."

One of the most important tools that the solution-focused approach uses to help the client articulate his goals, regain access to his resources, and finding ways forward, is asking questions. Solution-focused questions come in many types – this book is full of them. The types of questions can be subdivided into ten big categories that can be combined and experimented with.

1 Context-clarifying questions

- First of all, tell me something about yourself. How old are you, are you in a relationship, do you have kids, what kind of job do you have?
- Could you tell me something more about that?
- Could you give me a concrete example?
- What else can you tell me to make it easier for me to understand your situation?
- Is there anything I forgot to ask or you forgot to tell that is relevant for this subject?
- Are there any other things you should tell or ask me to make sure I understand what you are struggling with?

2 Goal-oriented questions

- What should we discuss to make this conversation useful to you?
- What do you want to achieve in your life?

3 Continuation questions

- In spite of all the problems, what are the things in your life that you would like to keep happening?

- What makes you so happy in life that you certainly do not want to lose this?
- What has to remain the same in your life?
- What are the things you enjoy, and you certainly would like to keep doing?

4 Change-oriented questions

- Have some things already changed in the period between the moment you made this appointment and today?
- Since our previous meeting, what have you done well and what has been difficult?
- How does your partner/colleague notice that you have gradually made progress?

5 Differentiating questions

- Are there moments the problem is less intense?
- What do you do differently then?
- How do others notice this?
- And how do they react to this?
- And how do you react to them?
- On a scale from 0 to 10, with 0 being "a disaster" and 10 "good enough to continue with", what is your current position? (Chapter 7, Icon 1)
- What do you do differently at moments you are feeling more contented?

6 Resource-based questions

- What is working in spite of the problems?
- What are you good at?
- What are your resources in your relation, family etc.?
- What would your partner say if I asked him/her what you are good at?
- Coping question: How do you manage to keep going?
- How much time between sessions would be useful for you?

7 Exception-seeking questions

- Have you experienced this before?
- What and who helped you best then?
- Are there any moments you are struggling less with your problems?
- Are there any moments when it is easier for you to be content?

8 Future-oriented questions

- How will you notice you have made progress? What will you think, do, and feel differently then?
- What would be the smallest step forward that will help you realize that you are making progress?
- Suppose your life were better, what would it look like?
- And what would be the next step forward?
- The Miracle Question (Chapter 7, Icon 2).
- What would you need to be able to hold on to this feeling of satisfaction and contentment in the future?
- And when you have achieved this goal, what *would* be your following smallest step forward?
- And when you have achieved this goal, what *will* be your following step?
- Imagine you are ten years older and wiser. How will you look back at this moment in your life? What will you have learned?

9 Triangulation questions

- How would others notice that you are making progress?
- What would your partner say you do differently when you are making progress?
- What would your deceased father/mother say if they knew how much effort you put into making the best of it?

10 Suggestive questions

- Have you ever thought of...?
- What would happen if...?
- Could it be that...?
- Suppose you tried to...?
- Would it help if...?

In dealing with our clients, we take the liberty of asking open-minded and open-ended questions, like Manuel. Asking questions helps us to listen more attentively to what the client has to say. In this way, we again show the client that he is the focal point of attention.

The benefits of asking questions

- To ask questions is to invite the client to the solution-focused dance
- Questions activate the working relationship
- Questions promote the client as the central actor in his own growth process
- Answering a question gives the client ownership of that answer

- Those who ask a question do not speak themselves but listen to the answers
- Questions orient the mental search process in the client toward alternative possibilities
- Journalistic questions that aim to gather as much content as possible are much less interesting than questions that support, orient, and stimulate the process of change in the client
- Solution-focused open-ended questions elicit answers that are building blocks for change
- Solution-focused closed questions are suggestions with a question mark behind them
- Each answer leads to the next question, which in turn leads to the next answer, which in turn leads to...
- We know the effect of our questions only through the client's response to them
- The cadence of question and answer promotes change and growth
- The questioner is the midwife who helps the client give birth to their own potential and corresponding possibilities

Open or empty minds?

A popular misconception among solution-oriented purists is: "You have to listen with an 'empty' mind." However, this is impossible unless you are in a coma or brain dead. Our brain is pre-programmed to always listen with filters, aka bias, assumptions, or even prejudices. There is nothing wrong with assumptions and prejudices, under the condition that you are aware of them. By asking questions, you can make sure that your own assumptions, or even worse, your own prejudices don't get in the way of the client. The same obviously applies to our client, but there's a slight difference: they have the right to be prejudiced about themselves and about whatever they consider possible or impossible. It's the change agent's responsibility to help the client open his mind by asking unprejudiced solution-focused questions.

Caveat

Client orientation doesn't mean that we blindly do anything the client wants us to do. The client is king does not mean that the therapist becomes his lackey. That is *not* the intention. Client orientation means that the client has a joint responsibility. Steve de Shazer used to start his interventions by making this clear to the clients. He frequently said: "My job is to do my best to help you. Your job is to do your best to help me." In this endeavor, it's not the therapist and his therapy model that play a decisive role. The decisive role is the shared effort.

Client orientation means that we help the client to look at the consequences of his choices and, if need be, that we confront him with those consequences.

Betty Alice, the daughter of Dr. Milton Erickson often told the following beautiful anecdote, which fully illustrates this:

> One day, Betty Alice (B.A. for the friends) was visiting her father, the famous Dr. Milton Erickson. He was sitting in the kitchen reading his newspaper. B.A. who thought she had gained too much weight after the birth of her second child, wanted to talk to her father: "Daddy, everyone says that you're a very important and famous psychiatrist, ..." No reaction ... B.A.: "Students come to you from near and far. Now, if you're such a famous and capable psychiatrist, you can certainly put me on a simple but effective diet." Erickson slowly lowered his newspaper, looked his daughter deep in the eyes and asked: "Are you sure, B.A., that you want a diet that really works?" After that, Betty Alice never raised the subject again[11].

The axiom of systemic thinking

Our concept of the image of mankind

The image of mankind on which solution-focused applied psychology is based states that every person is a unique individual who functions in a relational network. This implies that we are interested in the person, in the context in which the person lives and how he functions in this context. It's clearly "and-and-and" and most certainly not "or-or-or". In other words, we are interested in the intra-psychic structure of the person we are working with, as well as in his environment and how he deals with his environment. Consequently, when trying to help our clients, we can intervene in any of these three fields.

Every human is an individual with a unique intra-psychic structure

Even if we operate from a systemic point of view, we are still dealing with individuals. Having a good idea of what intra-psychic characteristics are, will enable us to help the client and his relevant system to help themselves more effectively and can help us avoid making mistakes.

An example where the individual features of the client can be used to help the client to help themselves (and each other). Suppose you are a youth care worker and you get a call from a mother who is very worried about her 12-year-old daughter Juliette, who transferred to secondary school a few months ago. You make an appointment and meet the mother and daughter together. Mother says that until a few months ago Juliette was a little angel: sweet, affectionate, playful, obedient, and diligent. But the last few months this has completely changed. Mother says:

> There is no way to live with her. She lies and cheats, is petulant, doesn't listen anymore. I have tried everything: from sweet talk over begging to letting her boil in her own juice. I have even become so angry a few times that it frightens me. Nothing helps. The only effect is that she locks herself up in her room. What's wrong with Juliette?

When you ask her to tell you more about the family, you find out that mother is a dentist and father is a professor of something complicated. There is also an older son, who at 17 is already studying at the university. So, this is an above-average gifted family. When you then talk to Juliette, you get the impression that her intellectual level is less high. An intelligence test confirms this and you find out that from the beginning of the school year Juliette cannot keep up at grammar school. Poor Juliette is constantly reaching for the moon, fails and translates her frustration into annoying behavior. A cautious and respectful discussion with the parents makes them decide to transfer Juliette to a school with lower intellectual demands that fit her skills. Within a few weeks, her "behavioral problems" are a thing of the past, simply thanks to the correct assessment of her intra-psychic capabilities and the fact that the clients have found out "by themselves" that a different school could have a healing effect. Thus, there was no need for family therapy, individual insight therapy or theories about possible loyalty conflicts within the family or "absent fathers and smothering mothers" and more of that kind of mythology.

More examples of when a correct reading of the intra-psychic variables is necessary to avoid professional mistakes.

Imagine a client telling you he has lost a few pounds in the past couple of months while he has not been on a diet, he's been sleeping badly and has been worrying a lot. He's been avoiding social contact and has gloomy thoughts. His appetite has decreased and his sex drive is completely gone. From our professional point of view, we know that we're (probably) dealing with a major depression. Telling that person to take it easy and take a little holiday will not only not help, but may trigger a medico-psychological breakdown. Best practice treatment consists of prescribing antidepressant medication with additional psychotherapy and structuring conversations. Overlooking a major depression can be dangerous for the client. The same applies to pseudo-dementia among older people, which can just as well be a masked depression. Failing to test this can be dangerous because the suicide rates among those suffering from a masked depression and pseudo-dementia are high.

Imagine you are a social worker and a client has been complaining about headaches, nausea in the morning, double vision and a severe fatigue that comes and goes. The client, who was recently promoted to an executive management position, is wondering whether it is work related, because lately things have been hectic. Instead of assuming the beginning of a work-related burnout, it seems best to *first* refer him to a doctor to rule out a brain tumor…

Clients complaining about being exhausted, having trouble concentrating, and having memory loss may suffer from severe sleep apnea. And that cannot be remedied with well-meant psychotherapy. Those people have to go to a sleep lab.

To make this point crystal clear: where a diagnosis exposes a specific cause, with unpleasant consequences, it is useful to use that diagnosis to provide the right care. That is especially the case in a strict medical setting and in situations where mechanical interference can immediately lead to a solution.

A famous case from the history of our field illustrates the importance of professionalism. We all know the lesson Sigmund Freud learnt when he was treating a high society lady for "hysterical nosebleeds" in Vienna around 1900. The lady in question loyally showed up for all her appointments and was very cooperative during her psychoanalysis. Unfortunately, the nosebleeds continued, and she got sicker and weaker each week. In the end, Freud decided to refer her to his friend Wilhelm Fliess, an ear, nose, and throat specialist. Dr. Fliess examined the lady and discovered that, during an earlier nasal septum operation, a nasal tampon of 20 centimeters had been forgotten in her nasal cavity … Freud hadn't noticed, because during his treatment, he was sitting behind the patient. Fliess, on the other hand, did the simplest thing: he looked inside her nose. The fact that Freud did refer his patient to a "real" physician is testimony to his professionalism. If he had clung to his hysterical theory (sic), the patient probably would not have survived this incident. This historic anecdote is a strong reminder for professionals with a psychological background and job, that it is *not* all in the mind.

The correct diagnosis can be an important tool in providing appropriate care, yet diagnoses can often lead to misunderstandings and create hidden pitfalls in which therapists can get stuck.

The context

Paying attention to the context or the system in which the client lives and functions, helps to focus on the resources of that relational network. Every human being is both an individual and part of a system: a couple, a family, an extended family, or a group of friends. The work environment, the church, the sports club, and neighborhood can also be part of this system. A system doesn't only consist of physical people, but also of immaterial contextual factors, such as convictions, faith, beliefs, (sub)culture, micro- and macro-economic circumstances.

It's remarkable that coincidences that happen in the client's life can be contextual factors as well. A lonely boy goes to Boy Scout camp during the holidays where he meets another boy from the same city. They take a liking to each other and the new friend introduces him to a new group of friends. A group of Moroccan youths, that has been causing trouble for a while, meet a new, young imam, who is less conventional and may be able to help them. And a young woman, who has been jobless for a long time, gets a new neighbor who offers her a job in a snack bar.

The key is to surf the waves of serendipity and turn chance happenings into a resource.

Working with the context

A systemic vision means that we are keeping the context in mind and use it, either by changing it or by using its elements as a tool (resource). Below are examples of both possibilities.

First, we give an example where a *change of context* is applied. Gerald, a 38-year-old intellectually disabled man, lives in a residential facility. During the day, he works in a workshop. Lately, Gerald has been quite agitated whenever he comes home from work. When his counselor asks what's wrong with him, he replies: "Leave me alone, you're always breathing down my neck." The counselor calls the sheltered workshop and finds out that Gerald's friend, with whom he has shared a table for three years, has stopped working there a few days ago. Gerald's new colleague is a very restless man, who continuously talks to him and keeps asking him question, while Gerald has been used to working in complete silence all day. After a short discussion, it is decided that Gerald will get another, calmer partner. The next day, Gerald arrives home in his residential facility and is back to his old sunny self.

In the second example, elements from *the context are used as a resource.* The parents of 15-year-old John make an appointment with a therapist because he gets bullied at school. When John and his parents arrive for their appointment, they say they're at their wits' end.

> We have tried everything. We have tried talking to John, and also to his teachers. The principal told John's class the bullying had to stop. That only worked for two days. We even had John take an assertiveness training and he has visited a child psychologist a few times. Nothing works. What are we going to do?

The therapist asks John and his parents if it's okay to discuss this with John and his classmates. They agree. The therapist starts a seemingly random conversation with John's classmates and asks them questions such as: "What courses are most fun?" "Who are the best teachers?" "What do you like to do in your spare time?" "How do you know if someone is a good friend?" "What bothers you most?" "Have you ever been excluded yourself?" "How did you solve that?" "What is the best way to become part of a group?" and "Who can help you to get more involved in the group?". It's clear that these questions are not random and that their order is important. The therapist is carefully trying to change the children's attitude toward each other, without discussing John's situation directly. The cruelty and wisdom of a group of 15-year-olds is best not underestimated. On the contrary, one should take advantage of it.

Systemic work with an individual

A popular misunderstanding is that systemic working always means that every member of a system must be present during the intervention. Although the presence of key members of the system involved often makes an intervention both more effective, powerful, and shorter, making this into an absolute requirement limits your possibilities. By asking triangular questions, absent members of the system can be involved by being virtually present. For example: some clients say they can't solve their issues, because they need to discuss something with their parents who are deceased. In such a situation, you can ask the following question: "What would you want to discuss with your parents if they were still alive, what would they tell you and how would that impact your current life?" Clearly you can use this intervention in different situations as well. "If we could ask your boss – what would he think of the situation, what would he say?"

By asking these triangular questions, you help clients to create a virtual reality that opens up the mind to ideas that are unthinkable without this elegant bypass. Asking follow up questions, you can help the client expand this new reality into ideas that have the power of transforming his perceived reality.

The treatment format

Working systemically also implies that we, as therapists, have the right (and sometimes the duty) to determine the format of the treatment. This involves our mandate as a leader as you will learn in Chapter 4 where we discuss our three mandates. After consulting with the client, we determine who to invite or involve in the treatment. Imagine having a conversation with an elderly couple. They are the grandparents of two lovely grandchildren, but they are having trouble with the way their daughter-in-law is raising the grandchildren. They think she is spoiling them, which, according to the worried grandparents, is leading to poor school results. The grandparents have tried to cautiously discuss this with their daughter-in-law, but she exploded with anger and threw them out. Meanwhile, the relationship has been restored, but now their son, the father, is telling them that he too, thinks his wife is spoiling the children. They don't know how to deal with the situation and ask for advice. As a therapist, you first ask at length what they have already tried, and you compliment them on their involvement. But after a while you're done talking. So, what's next? We can check if we get the permission to invite their son and daughter-in-law. The most elegant way to do this is by asking: "Wouldn't it be a good idea to bring your son and daughter-in-law in for the next session?" If the format of treatment is not broadened in such cases, where the parties are on opposite sides, this inflexible attitude can lead to many needless conversations with increasingly desperate grandparents. By initiating a broader discussion platform, you can probably help them solve their differences in a single session.

Multiple problems and multiple therapists

Using the systemic basic axiom is of the utmost importance in situations where multiple therapists are involved. "Multi-problem" families or rather, "multi-solution" families are often faced with different care organizations. Their efforts, no matter how well-meant they are, are hardly effective when they don't coordinate and cooperate with each other. In childcare, you can get assistance at home, some children get individual therapy, children can be taken out of the house and/or put under a guardian's supervision, one of the parents can have psychiatric problems that require a psychiatrist, other welfare workers can help with household and administrative problems, the extended family can be involved via network therapy, there may be problems in the neighborhood, which requires yet another social worker, etc. If all those professional instances don't coordinate their activities, the clients involved often have more trouble dealing with the overabundance of professionals than the overabundance of their problems.

Thinking out of the box

We can all remember the time when the therapy process was based solely on diagnostics and well-defined causal theories of pathology. Intake interviews were necessary to determine the indication for the appropriate treatment model and accordingly, the matching therapeutic interventions were assigned to different specialized therapists. In those early days of psychotherapy, we had a plethora of models and interventions available. There was a supporting and/or insight therapist for each individual family member, a couple therapist for the parents, a family therapist who talked to the family, a "play therapist" for the youngest son, a child psychiatrist for the eldest daughter with ADHD, and so on. In those days, when the indication for individual therapy was given after a thorough psychological and psychiatric evaluation, the result was that the partner, let alone the family, was never involved.

This approach is in stark contrast to the solution-focused approach, where, after consulting with the client, we invite all the concerned people and involve those contexts that can help our clients help themselves in the most meaningful, swift, and robust ways.

The four-leaf clover: cognition, emotion, behavior, and interaction

Based on recent scientific discoveries in the field of neurology, neuronal networks, and swarm intelligence, you could think of a human being as a neuronal network computer, wrapped in a biomechanical shell that functions in a network of social relationships with the characteristics of a self-learning and self-organized swarm.[12] This highly scientific definition can lead us astray from what's most important in everyday therapy: every human has thoughts and feelings and behaves in a certain way in the contact with other human beings and the environment. This four-leaf clover makes us human. Thoughts are constantly going through our heads; at the same time, we experience emotions, and we do something – even if that something is doing nothing. Moreover, we don't live in a vacuum, but are constantly interacting with others.

These basic insights increase our arsenal of interventions, as this can be made clear with some examples.

I'm stuck in my head

We see clients that complain about their constant brooding and getting stuck in a rut. Keeping the four-leaf clover in mind, you can ask them: "When you're brooding, what exactly do you do? What do you feel at that moment? How do the people in your environment notice that you are brooding?"

I'm all emotion

Just as frequently, we encounter clients who say they can no longer think straight because they are overrun by their emotions (for example, disgust, anger, rage, pity, or sympathy). In such case, you can ask "When your emotions are toying with you like that, what are you thinking? And what exactly are you doing?"

I run around like a headless chicken

We all know clients (especially teenagers specialize in this) who say they run around all day like a headless chicken and are trying to do everything at once, without really feeling that they're achieving something. The following questions come in handy:

> Would you like to learn how to become aware again of what you are doing, so it will be easier for you to think and plan? Would you be interested in trying to become aware of your feelings when you are running all over the place.

I am alone in this world

Some clients retreat to their own world, making them lose every form of social contact. Some of them say: "All people are bad and I don't want anything to do with them. They have done enough to me. I only trust my dog, Blacky." You could say: "Luckily you still have Blacky, otherwise you would be really lonely. Do you run into people that are walking their dog too?"

If you are conscious about the four-leaf clover of cognition, emotion, behavior, and interaction, you are less likely to get sucked into the overpowering despondency of the client and this awareness makes it easier to intervene in order to help him get balanced (again).

Conclusion

These basic axioms are no Nobel Prize winning truths. They are assumptions and working hypotheses that form the basis of our solution-focused interventions. Becoming aware of these basic axioms helps to connect the solution-focused practice to the complexity of life. When we intervene with our clients, the basic axioms help us see beyond mere solution-focused techniques. They help us create a rich world of ideas from which to draw incisive interventions.

Notes

1 See Diodorus (± 50 a.c.), *Βιβλιοθήκη ἱστορική*.
2 We explicitly mention "becoming happy" and not "being happy", because the continuous quest for happiness often results in the opposite: frustration, non-satisfaction, discomfort, and the feeling of "not quite". We prefer the concept of well-being. Moments of happiness are side-effects of the quest for well-being. Experiencing moments of happiness is not an esoteric activity reserved for holistic new-age characters in white garments, but a practical way of holding a philosophical view on life.
3 Personal communication from his daughter Betty Alice Erickson, 2013.
4 Mrs. Elisabeth Erickson Moore, spouse of Dr. Erickson, cited in Erickson, B.A. & Keeney, B. (2006). *Milton H. Erickson, an American healer*. Sedona, AZ: Ringing Rocks Press.
5 The standard work about resilience and normal families is the opus magnum of Froma Walsh *Normal Family Processes (2003)*.
6 Camus, A. (1989). *The Stranger*. Random House.
7 Erickson, B.A. & Keeney, B. (2006). *Milton H. Erickson, an American Healer*. Ringing Rocks Press.

8 Short, D., Erickson, B.A. & Erickson, R. (2005). *Hope and Resiliency: Understanding the Psychotherapeutic Strategies of Milton H. Erickson, MD.* Crown House Publishing.
9 Hubble, M., Duncan B. & Miller, S.D. (2009). *The Heart and Soul of Change.* APA.
10 Zeig, J.K. (1980). *A Teaching Seminar with Milton H. Erickson.* New York: Brunner-Routledge.
11 Erickson, B.A. & Keeney, B. (2006). *Milton H. Erickson M.D. An American Healer.* Sedona: Ringing Rocks Press.
12 Cauffman, L. & Kennedy, J. (2007). *Keynote SOL Conference.*

Chapter 2

What always works in good facilitation?

What is it that makes human change? How can one influence the way people look at life, himself, others, and reality? Is real change possible? What is real change? Are some people better equipped for change than others? How come? Is this nature or nurture?

These kinds of questions have kept philosophers busy for centuries. They have to do with the existential Question or is it Quest of what it means to be human?

Reading these sentences will make you involuntarily think about your own life, your own issues, and the nature of the work you do as a change agent. Who of us in our profession never had the question pop up "what on earth am I doing?" At the end of the day, besides listening, asking questions, nodding, looking at them, in short "be there for them", we don't do anything much. How come my clients keep coming back and testify that they find it meaningful to talk to us?

A full analysis of these important existential and fundamental questions is way out of the scope of this book. Yet, we will present an overview of the developments in our field that are relevant to these questions. After all, to be better change agents, we need to understand how we create impact, which are the mechanisms operating behind the scenes of our seemingly simple conversations and how do we need to act if we want enhanced effectivity for the sake of our clients.

Our professional field is – generally speaking – about the what and the how to interact with people by means of language to co-create a new meaning of what they encounter. Depending on the specific field, we call this therapy or coaching. In this book, we will use the term "facilitation" and even more broadly, the denominator "change facilitation".

Of course, there are important differences that need to be considered between the different fields of application, but these differences are on the level of content, as you will learn later in this book. Because it is a process-based approach, the "change technology of SoFAP" is widely applicable, across many content application domains.

DOI: 10.4324/9781003320104-3

Change agents and coaching

Let us start with analyzing what a change agent exactly is by digging up the etymology of the words in Merriam-Webster.
Change:

> Middle English, from Anglo-French *changer*, from Latin *cambiare* to exchange, probably of Celtic origin.

Agent:

> Middle English, "force capable of acting on matter," borrowed from Medieval Latin *agent-, agens* "something capable of producing an effect, person authorized to act for another," going back to Latin, present participle of *agere* "to drive (cattle), ride (a horse), be in motion, do, perform, transact,"

Coaching:

> Curiously, Merriam-Webster refers in the etymology of the concept of agent to horses. If we dig up the etymology of the term "coach", we find: Middle English *coche*, from Middle French, from German *Kutsche*, from Hungarian *kocsi* literally, wagon from *Kocs*, Hungary. For the activity of coaching, we find: 1610s, "to convey in a coach," Meaning "to tutor, give private instruction to or prepare (someone) for an exam or a contest" is from 1849. The first use of the term "coach" in connection with an instructor or trainer arose around 1830 in Oxford University and is slang for a tutor who "carried" a student through an exam. The word "coaching" thus identified a process used to transport people from where they are to where they want to be.
>
> Isn't that what we professional change agents do? To help transport the client from one interpretation and rather obstructive vision on his reality to another, more constructive and liberating view?
>
> Coaching as transporting a client by coach, is a straightforward activity, and the result is visible with the naked eye. When coaching someone towards another way of giving meaning to his life, that is not so straightforward or visible with the naked eye. So, how does this work?

In the chapter, we will coach (sic) you from a personal experience of the author, through a personal exercise for the reader to feel how it works, over the different historic waves in the thinking about change as guided, facilitated, provoked, or whatever term you prefer, by a professional change agent. We end the chapter with revealing the active ingredients for true change and provide the reader with five concrete tools to enhance the efficacy of his practice.

Clients are the best teachers

When a young therapist, full of ambition and theories, but unhindered by practical experience, I had a therapeutic conversation with a young woman. After she had given me her address, she started sobbing. It was clear that this woman was carrying a heavy burden and during the first session I used all my techniques to support her: "... it's okay to cry. ... I understand you are having a hard time. Take a deep breath, try to tell me what the problem is". Result: zero. The woman kept crying heartbreakingly and I had no idea what was going on. She couldn't put it into words. At the end of the session I still didn't understand what the problem was and even less what I should do. So, I kindly asked her if she wanted to come back. She could only nod "yes" and we made a new appointment. For the second session, I had prepared a whole series of questions. I had to find out what was going on with her. But the second session went according to the same scenario: tears, sobs, and despondency, but no words. I didn't know what else to do and I was starting to get very worried about her, so I tried a more direct approach: "Try to say something... Take a deep breath and tell me... Is there something wrong with your relationship or with your child... or with your work? What is going on? Calm down." No result, the woman kept crying and I seriously started to doubt if the profession of psychotherapist was something for me. The client wanted a new appointment; at least that was what I could make out of her head nod. But in planning that next session, she told me that it could only be in six weeks. I was flabbergasted, worried and, being convinced that she was on the verge of a mental breakdown, I insisted on an earlier appointment. She told me she would be visiting her parents who lived abroad. I accepted of course but, in my heart, I was truly worried about her. For our third session, I again had well prepared and even made a written scenario of "how I would deal with it to finally get results": "it's now or never. It must work this time!" However, my surprise was great when I let the woman in for the third interview. She looked different, was cheerful and told me, "I'm cured. I've come to thank you for what you've done for me." I was speechless. Slightly struck, I asked her what she meant exactly, to which she said: "I've never felt better understood than by you. You've been so patient with me. In our conversations, I could finally be myself."

To this day, I still don't know what was going on with this woman...

> 'The therapist's permissive attitude, of being willing to let his patient know but without himself knowing until and unless the patient is ready and wishes him to, serves to make it possible for some patients to place whatever meaning to their symptoms seems to them at the time therapeutically necessary.[1]
>
> Milton H. Erickson

Making the client feel understood is obviously different from understanding him.

It took me a long time of reading, thinking, taking training courses, consultations with more seasoned colleagues, hundreds of sessions with clients of all sorts and maturing as a person before I gradually got a handle on the phenomenon of change. Studying the work of Dr. Milton Erickson gave me corroborative information that supported my learning process. With my then-team, we had the honor to invite Steve de Shazer and Insoo Kim Berg as of 1987 to give workshops in Europe. Until their passing, Steve and Insoo came several times each year to teach for our training institute. During many workshops, but especially in the non-workshop hours that we spent together over many years, they took me under their umbrella.

I do not dare to say that today I know exactly what happened in the case I just shared with you, but I have some inkling.

Before we present an overview of the wave-like development of the ideas and working hypotheses that underlie our work as change agents, allow us to take you on a little personal journey so that you can experience for yourself what all of this means.

Know thyself

> Think about what you, as a therapist and coach, with your current experience and knowledge, are doing that works so well that you will keep doing these things, whatever the future may bring.[2]

There's a big chance that you will think of things like humor, contact, optimism, attention, giving and taking time, putting things into perspective, giving information, being open to the other's individuality, being understanding, offering clarity, showing empathy.

Over the years we asked this question to hundreds of trainees and most students respond alike. Some throw in a model-specific technicality but they are a minority. How come that most people answer this question in similar terms? Simple. Because they describe what it is that they think and feel to be the important factors that support their work as change agents.

These responses show that there are more similarities among the various psychological models of change than the differences in theoretical explanations and practical interventions might suggest.

The similarities of what all schools of change share as active ingredients of successful facilitation, whether psychotherapy or coaching, are called the common factors.[3]

Waves of development

To get an idea of the evolution of thinking behind the thinking hidden behind the developments in our field, one can surf the waves of that historical evolution.

Vladimir Nabokov describes exactly what we need here when he compared the transitions in Charles Dickens's book *Bleak House* with the fluid and elegant transitional movements in Flaubert's Madam Bovary: "If the transitions in *Bleak House* can be compared to steps, with the proceeding *en escalier*, here in *Madam Bovary* the pattern is a fluid system of waves".[4]

In contrast to a development in phases or stages, transition in waveform is not linear (in one direction from a to z), not unambiguous in the sense that phase a is strictly distinguishable from phase b, not chronological (c always follows b after a) and is asynchronous (a, b, and parts of c can happen at the same time). On the contrary, evolution in waves implies the opposite of these stage characteristics. Waves imply motion in all possible directions (sideways, forwards, backwards, upwards, or downwards, or a combination), waves run into, across, along, and parallel to each other, ... In short, wave-like evolution takes place in a complex chaos that is both structured and aleatory resulting in a never-ending aesthetic.

The developments each wave brings are iterative: each subsequent step leaves behind the limitations of the previous step and adds the lessons learned to the next wave of evolution. Implementing the consequences of the lessons learned creates a continuous improvement of the approach. The various iterative steps culminate in the SoFAP approach that incorporates all the lessons learned from the iterative steps.

You will notice that waves 1 to 5 are strictly about psychotherapy. It is only from wave 6 onwards that the scope is broadened to the general area of process-based change facilitation and applications to management and organizational issues are also discussed.

Overview of the waves

1. The pathology or problem-centricity
2. The therapeutic model or model-centricity
3. The person of the therapist or therapist-centricity
4. The common factors theory or non-specific variables-centricity
5. The client or client-centricity
6. The client-therapist cooperative alliance: SoFAP

Wave 1. The pathology or problem-centricity

Following the lines of the medical model where the pathology and the (presumed) causes of that pathology act as guidelines for the medical interventions, many psychotherapeutic schools followed suit. Two consequences stem from this premise. The first consequence is the focus on the problem and – if possible – it's root cause. The person or the context surrounding that problem is less important than the problem itself. Taking away the root cause solves the problem. The second consequence is that interventions need to be geared to the specific problem at hand. Logical overall consequence is that for every problem there exists an appropriate therapeutic intervention.

So, many psychotherapeutic schools started to develop so called eclectic approaches: for every problem, a fitting intervention protocol.

Limitations: the exclusive focus on the problem and its background leads to digging into ever-deeper problems, particularly when dealing with socio-psychological issues. Therapy becomes an almost mechanical cookbook in which, depending on the problem, you use ingredients from whatever method or approach seems suitable. This problem-oriented approach carries the risk that the client must adapt to the chosen intervention because the intervention theoretically fits the problem, even if the client has goals that do not fit the problem nor the corresponding therapeutic intervention. The Bed of Procrustes[5] resurfaces.

Lessons learned: From the development of early psychotherapeutic thinking, psychological problems are assigned more to external factors (possession, inner evil, punishing God…). Human problems, psychiatric symptoms are seen as self-contained phenomena that enter "into" the human being and can be addressed, albeit initially only prophylactically. Some useful strategies were developed.

Wave 2. The therapeutic model or model-centricity

Since the birth of psychotherapy there have been constant upgrades in the underlying theory. It became an industry in which two elements tended to dominate the developments. One theme was the continual refinement of one's own therapeutic model into an ever more sophisticated, sometimes even labyrinthine construction. Second was the quest to prove, or at least try to show, that the own model was better and more effective than the competition. Anyhow, the focus was on the model itself.

Limitations: this leads to a proliferation of therapy schools, which today number 400-and counting – different models. With the rare exception of a few (rather sectarian) "schools" that are more interested in their own benefit than in the good for their clients, most models contain useful tools that professionals use in their daily service to clients. Models converge, amalgamate, adopt elements from other models to integrate in their own work, retire older insights, etc. In short, these models exhibit the classic pattern of evolutionary behavior that allows for diversity. However, this diversity tends to focus primarily on evolution within its own paradigm.

Lessons learned: This approach engendered the proliferation of numerous therapy schools that provide a multifaceted view on the functioning of the human mind.

Wave 3. The person of the therapist or therapist-centricity

In much of the classic literature on psychotherapy, the all-powerful therapist and his mastery of technique are seen as the prime actors that generate change within the client. Bickman and Salzer[6] call this "professional centrism". One recognizes it even in the language that is used. What therapists do or say is called an intervention. What the clients do or say is called a response. In addition, the personality, experience, and specialized training of the therapist are seen as the determining ingredients that enhance the effect of the interventions. The client is seen as a passive recipient of the therapist's powerful interventions.

Limitations: the client is seen as a passive receiver and not an active participant in his healing whereas the professional is deemed to have the transformative power. The client is believed to have organized his life around his problems and is therefore sometimes considered to be resistant to change.

Lessons learned: the therapist becomes a professional in his own right, rather than the mere representative of a specific model or "school". The combination of training, continuous reflection on his practice and professional development (including supervision, intervision, and feedback sessions) during as many therapy hours as possible create a deep knowledge in the practitioner.

Wave 4. The common factors theory or non-specific variables-centricity

In a 4-page opinion article, published in 1936 (!) and afterwards forgotten for 40 years,[7] Saul Rosenzweig claims that the different therapy models he researched were just as effective as the next. This is the first time Rosenzweig mentions "common factors" in different models of psychotherapy. His theory was: "Since all methodology has similar results in terms of effectiveness, there have to be common 'pan-theoretical' factors in play that overshadow the differences in these methodologies." In his opinion article, Rosenzweig compared *"psychoanalysis, treatment by persuasion, Christion Science, and any number of psychotherapeutic ideologies"*. This, of course, was way before the birth of psychology as a scientific field and the article today holds no more than anecdotal value. The historic value of Rosenzweig's article, however, is that it foreshadowed the debate about what the active ingredients in successful therapy are.

The hypothesis today is that the outcome is more the result of factors common to the different therapeutic models than of school – or model-specific interventions. These findings and the consequences thereof, remains remarkably undiscussed in many publications on psychotherapeutic models.

Frank and Frank (1991[8]) name four factors which all effective therapy forms have in common: 1. an emotional and confidential relationship with a person who is trying to help you, 2. which takes place in a setting of which the client believes that the help offered is professional in which 3. the therapist gives a credible explanation for the client's symptoms 4. and offers reliable procedures to cope with these symptoms. Lambert[9] further details that four non-specific factors are responsible for changes caused by psychotherapy. The percentages he mentions are not mathematically measured realities, but they are the result of a deliberate and reasoned assessment.[10]

*40% client factors and extra therapeutic variables
*30% therapeutic relations
*15% the client's hopes and expectations
*15% model specific interventions

No less than 40% of the change caused by therapy sessions is ascribed to client factors such as openness, perseverance, trust, optimism, a warm family on the one hand and extra-therapeutic elements on the other, which are events, in which the client links his inner strength to coincidences, such as a colleague at a new job, moving to another town, a prize in the lottery, new neighbors, and so on. In short, 40% of the results are provided by factors that are completely outside the control of the therapist.

30% of these results are attributed to the therapeutic relationship and more specifically to the positive perception of this relationship. The therapist can enhance this by inviting the client to play an active role during therapy.

Fifteen percent is attributed to the clients' expectations about the outcome of his treatment: i.e., the placebo effect which occurs because the client's self-healing capacities are activated by hope, just like the trust he has in the treatment and his therapist.

Finally, 15% of the results are attributed to model-specific techniques.

In summary, these studies show that 70% of the changes attributed to therapy have something to do with factors the therapist has little or no influence over: 40% of extra-therapeutic variables + 15% being half of the therapeutic relationship + 15% client's expectations and placebo = 70%. Of the remaining 30%, 15% can be assigned to model-specific interventions and the other half to the therapeutic relationship. When we consider that a huge part of the 15% of the model- specific varieties is attributed to the trust the therapist has in his own actions and when we link this to the client's perception that the therapist knows what he's doing, then the contribution of the model-specific techniques is almost negligible.[11]

Wampold concludes:

> Decades of research in psychotherapy haven't given us the slightest evidence that any specific ingredient is necessary for change.

BUT BE NOT MISTAKEN!

- Is the use of common factors enough in itself?
- Does this mean that the study of any therapy model is a waste of time?
- Does this mean that professional training isn't necessary?
- Does this mean that the results of specific psychotherapeutic endeavors are flukes?
- Does this mean that becoming a "good" therapist is innate rather than the result of training?

NO!

You will become a danger to public health if you do this. The findings of the research on the common factors can be applied to make client cooperation more effective. We can help our clients do great things, but only if we are modest about our own knowledge, skills, and contributions to their change process. And – more importantly – when we can teach our clients *not* to be modest about their own knowledge and skills.

Limitations: Declaring the primacy of the common factors as a counter-reaction to the omnipotence of therapist and/or model-centrism leads to the naïve idea that if the common factors are activated, then everything one does in a psychotherapeutic encounter is okay. Building a nice relationship with ample room for common factors, however important and even vital if you want results, is just not enough.

If change is fueled only by the common factors, a reduction ad absurdum could lead to the conclusion that it is no longer necessary to talk to the client about what brings him into therapy or what the practitioner has to contribute as a professional. Such an attitude would strip the practitioner of his professional content expertise.

Lessons learned: This knowledge of the influence of the common factors helps to use these non-specific factors in a specific manner. You do this by paying attention to the client in his context, by using (exploiting is a better word) the therapeutic relationship to give the client hope that his expectations are achievable, and by occasionally using model-specific techniques to show the client that we know what we are doing.

Promoting common factors as resources rather than byproducts are the first steps toward a solution-focused approach.

Wave 5. The client or client-centricity

How Steve de Shazer came to put the client in the center of the therapeutic endeavor, was a direct consequence of his fascination with the work of Dr. Milton H. Erickson.

According to a probably – si non e vero, e ben trovato – apocryphal story, the young Steve de Shazer had to see his boss one day to discuss the progress of his Master's thesis.[12] The secretary told him that his boss was a bit late and de Shazer could wait in the library. There he picked up a random book and started reading. It turned out to be a book by Milton Erickson and Jay Haley. de Shazer says he got fascinated by this book, because it was filled to the brim with all types of clinical examples, was well-written and "the authors weren't guilty of using all types of mythologies and poetic inventions."[13]

Subsequently de Shazer and his colleagues studied hundreds of Erikson's case studies in the early 70s[14] hoping to find out which theory he used as a starting point. Erickson had written "I know what I'm doing, but I find it too difficult to explain what I'm doing".[15] de Shazer, researcher in heart and soul, split up all cases in five categories, each containing a certain sequence of interventions. There was also a sixth category, in which the remaining cases were put, called the "unusual interventions". Unfortunately, the sixth category grew much faster than the other five. For years, de Shazer was trying to find out the underlying theory of this sixth category, but without any success. Then he decided to go through all cases from a completely different point of view. He no longer read them as cases in which the magic of Erickson was hidden but instead, he read them as stories. Keeping his great example Sherlock Holmes in mind, he no longer focused on the main character, the therapist Milton Erickson, but on the other protagonist: the client. What did Steve discover? "It's the client, stupid!" de Shazer was amazed by the intelligence of the clients. Most of the ideas for the unusual interventions in the cases of the sixth category came from the clients themselves. Erickson had been smart enough to use them. Later this approach became known as the "utilization principle". Jeff Zeig, founder-president of the Milton Erickson Foundation[16] teaches: "Whatever you get, use it".[17] Closer study of this saying reveals that Erikson's cleverness does not rest solely in his clever mind, but that it is primarily the client's clever way of using the resources from his life context that bring about positive change. And it was de Shazer's cleverness to notice this.

> Most simply put, therapy is a conversation between at least two people (minimally one therapist and one client) about reaching the client's goal. When as a result of this conversation clients begins to have doubts about their immutable framing of their troublesome situation, the door to change and solution has been opened. This is the essence of brief therapy.[18]
>
> Steve de Shazer

The client and the therapist are actors in the conversation that focuses on the goals of the client, and therefore puts the client in the center of the conversation. In addition, the client brings the "sixth category" into the conversation, namely the unusual elements. This once again places the client at the center, ergo client-centrism.

Limitations: the client centrism puts the pressure on the client who is supposed to know what he wants for change and to have all the necessary resources to do so. In the early thinking of de Shazer et al.[19] the professional's task is limited to "help make these flukes" or "differences that do not make a difference [LC: flukes are moments when exceptions to the problem occur without the client being aware of them as important] into differences that make a difference".[20]

Lessons learned: while the client is finally put in the spot he deserves namely the center of the action, the therapist becomes the professional who's task it is to help the client un- or discover his resources as means to help himself. The phenomenon of resistance[21] is redefined as additional information with which the client helps the professional to do a better job of helping the client. Where resistance used to be an impediment, it becomes a stage direction that shows the way forward.

Wave 6. The client-therapist cooperative alliance: SoFAP

In 1991 de Shazer calls the next iteration of his thinking about change, "interactional constructivism" by which he stresses the idea that therapy is a cooperation between two equally contributing partners who co-construct a new reality.[22] This iteration is the logical step-stone to the development of SoFAP. Now, professionals and clients have a shared task and responsibility to develop a co-constructive working relationship that adds new insights to broaden and deepen the solution-focused approach. This wave culminates in an interactional structure that responds to the complexity of our existence, to the demands of supporting clients in their quest for sustainable change, and that integrates all the learning from the previous waves. Moreover, this development allows the application of the solution-focused approach to be extended to all domains where interpersonal influence is involved.

The basic axioms (Chapter 1) form the background for solution-focused thinking behind the thinking, i.e., they hide between the lines of practitioner-client interactions.

In the SoFAP wave, the following aspects are added:

- Decision rules support the minimax motto: eliciting maximal results in the client while using minimal energy as professional (Chapter 3)
- The practitioner always has three mandates at his disposition: leader, coach, and manager (Chapter 3)
- Formula-P helps translate problems into challenges (Chapter 5)
- Formula-GRC connects the client's **g**oals with their **r**esources and invites them to do more of what works by giving them appreciation (**c**omplimenting) for using those resources that help achieve their goal (Chapter 5)

True change

What is true change?

> When you enter the world of communication, organization, etc., you leave behind that whole world in which effects are brought about by forces and impacts and energy exchange. You enter a world in which "effects" – and I am not sure one should still use the same word – are brought about by differences.[23]
>
> Gregory Bateson

Gregory Bateson defines real change as a difference that makes a difference. If the difference does not have this quality, change is trivial, fleeting, and unsustainable. The quote implies that change – in our context – has nothing to do with the world of things or thing-like objects. Real change occurs as a shift in meaning and is the result of collaborative language interactions between a service-providing and a service-receiving party that co-construct an alternative, and preferably better working and growth-promoting alternative reality.

Who decides what true change is?

Just as beauty is in the eye of the beholder, real change is in the perception of the client. It is the receiver of services that defines if the service is good, good enough or bad and it is not the provider.

The active ingredients for true change, an overview

A client factors, systemic factors, and external circumstances

B the working alliance

→ B.1 Do I feel understood?

→ B.2 authentic attention

→ B.3 respect

→ B.4 Hope = perspective on positive change

→ co-constructive alliance

C credibility and expectations

→ C.1 Credibility of change process

→ C.2 Credibility of change agent

→ C.3 Expectations of the client

→ C.4 Expectations of the change agent

→ induce hope

D model-specific interventions

→ D.1 Solution-focused techniques

→ D.2 Interventions from other models

→ Crux & Caveat

Active ingredients at work

Client and systemic factors and external circumstances

By client factors we mean factors *inherent in the person of the client*, such as intelligence, introspection, insights and beliefs, convictions, openness, commitment, compassion, sadness, optimism, or appropriate sadness, perseverance, resilience, etc.

Client factors are also available *in the client's system*. Is his marriage sound? Is the family system supportive? How does the client deal with a difficult relationship? How does the individual flourish despite the tensions in the family? Are friends available? Does she belong to a church, club, or any other association? Does he work? How is it going in his business? How is his health and financial situation? Etc.

Circumstances are external to the change process but can be used as resources. When you ask a client what she does for a living and she tells you that she is an independent entrepreneur, it will be useful to ask for a detailed description. Who knows, you may be talking to a business owner who built up her business all by herself and has many people working for her. This entrepreneurship and resilience will surely be a resource! The resources she has used for this purpose can probably be used during the change process.

A quarrelsome couple tells you that they have been arguing less lately. If you ask them what has changed, they both reply that nothing has actually changed and that they don't know why their relationship has suddenly gotten better. But if you ask further (persistence is a virtue for a change agent), they might tell you, "The Champions League has started, and we are both soccer fans." So at least they have one thing in common and can put their bickering aside, even if it is for the duration of the tournament. Your logical next question then is, "What do you need to have a more satisfying relationship when there is no soccer on TV?"

While external circumstances may be mere coincidences, they only become useful if you help the client see them as resources that can be used. A change agent must help his clients link these external factors to whatever happens – by chance or by accident – that can be employed in the facilitation process.

When you put "resource detective glasses" on, countless factors can be found in every client, his system, and the external circumstances.

In the following case study, Steve de Shazer beautifully illustrates how to use client and system factors coupled with external circumstances in practice to help the client help himself.

The woman who got irradiated

A 50-year-old woman consults with Steve de Shazer. She looks pale and downcast. She tells him that she has been living under great stress for the past few months and is exhausted. She says she knows the reason for her exhaustion.

CLIENT (IN A CONSPIRATORIAL TONE): It all started to go wrong when my upstairs neighbor moved into our building. I am temporarily living in a luxury apartment owned by rich friends who are traveling the world for a year. I have a very small apartment that I sublet to make some extra money. But then this obnoxious upstairs neighbor started tormenting me from the first night he moved in. I haven't had a good night's sleep since. He irradiates me with some device. I don't know how he does it, but he does it. I know I sound crazy telling you this, but it's true.

DE SHAZER: Hm.

CUSTOMER: I've tried everything, but nothing works. I've even tried going to bed with a lot of noise and then sneaking into the living room to sleep on the couch. Without success: his machine seems to know exactly where I am.

DE SHAZER: Hm.

CLIENT: I spied on him once and when I was sure he was gone for the weekend, I thought I could finally sleep. And again: no result. The machine works automatically, he doesn't have to operate it.

DE SHAZER: Hm.

Dear reader, do you feel the urge to use your psychopathological expertise to diagnose this woman? Can you find a DSM-diagnosis and matching prognosis?

CLIENT: Other than that, I'm doing well, but at work the situation is starting to take its toll on me. I'm exhausted and I'm making mistakes. But I'd rather drop dead than move back into my own little apartment. I'm not going to let this guy scare me off.

THE SHAZER: Hm, so if I understand you correctly, you suffer from a sleep disorder. Would you like to see if there's anything you can do about that?

CLIENT (PUZZLED, SILENT): If you think that might be possible, sure.

They have a long conversation in which he asks her at length if there are times when she sleeps a little better, if there are degrees/levels of how well or poorly she sleeps, and what would be different in her life if the problem miraculously disappeared. Finally, Shazer asks if the therapy session was helpful, and the client says she doesn't know but will find out soon enough.

A few weeks later, the second therapy session takes place. The client looks a lot better and comes in smiling.

DE SHAZER: Good morning, what is different?

CLIENT (ENTHUSIASTIC): I've got him! He can no longer hurt me.

DE SHAZER: Hm.

CLIENT: After our first meeting, as I drove home, I was rehashing everything we had discussed. I was a little confused, and I took the wrong way home. Suddenly I was at a red traffic light and saw a store selling camping equipment. I stopped to buy a new sleeping bag because I'm going camping with my daughter in a few months.

DE SHAZER: Hm.

CLIENT: When I got home, I was pleased with myself. I was proud that I final got some help, and I had the feeling that you understood the problems I had been facing.

DE SHAZER: Had been facing? Past tense?

CLIENT: I've told you already: I got him.

DE SHAZER: Hm.

CLIENT: That night I decided to catch up on my sleep. It's impossible to fall asleep at home because of that guy and his machine. Don't worry. I'm an executive secretary and I have the keys to the company. My boss was going abroad for a few days that week and he has a small apartment behind his office. I was going to sleep there for a few nights. I went home and around bedtime I went back to the office. My upstairs neighbour couldn't possibly know where I work, but just to be safe, I drove around anyway in case he was following me. I didn't tell anyone, not even my boss. You never know. I even used my new sleeping bag so my boss wouldn't notice I was sleeping in his apartment. I made sure to leave the apartment early in the morning before my colleagues arrived. I treated myself to a nice breakfast at a hotel in town for a few days. It was delicious and best of all I was able to catch up on my sleep.

SHAZER: Hm.

CLIENT: But let me tell you something.

DE SHAZER: Hm.

CLIENT: There's more. One night I was watching National Geographic. I love that program. There was a documentary about thunderstorms, and they explained that when you are surprised by thunderstorms in the countryside, the safest place is in your car. Your car has rubber tires and the body acts like a Faraday cage.

DE SHAZER: Hm.

CLIENT: And then this camping gear store came to mind. They also sell all kinds of do-it-yourself materials there. The next day I went there again, and I bought a big spool of copper wire. My friend's bed in the apartment is very fancy and has those copper styles. On each corner is a copper ball that can be unscrewed, and that's what I did. With the copper wire, I turned the bed into a Faraday cage. That's how I got him (looks at the ceiling and gives him the finger). His machine doesn't work anymore.

Exercise

> What are the client factors, the systemic factors, and the external factors in this story? How did the Shazer, a master of minimalism, use the information the client gave him? Besides a lot of hm's, he only brought in the term "sleep disorder," nothing else. The client did the rest. How would you handle such a case?

The working alliance

In any (change-facilitating) relationship, there are three parties involved, A, B, and C. What the professional (A) offers, what the client (B) perceives, and what happens in their collaboration (C) In a relationship, these three components are merely related.

An alliance is more than just a relationship; it is an active connection between parties who have a common goal, i.e., progress toward a solution and growth for the client.

Two introductory remarks are helpful here: 1. The four components are a coherent whole. If one of them is present, but the others are missing, the intervention will probably not work (well or well enough). 2. The professional's belief that he is applying the four components is of less importance than the client's perception that they are present.

Do I feel understood?

The feeling of being understood arises from the interaction between the therapist and the client. It is *not* about the scientific understanding of objective truths! People live and function in a "thing-like" world where what one encounters, is seen as reality and this reality can be interpreted as truths. When it comes to dealing with meanings, we are confronted with unavoidable interpretative ambiguity. So, in reality (sic), in the world of meanings, every person must muster the courage to accept intellectually and emotionally that "the" truth does not exists, that there only exists "your" truth. Or more pointedly, there are more ways to look at the same phenomena and yet come up with a different "truth" about them.

Think of a quarreling couple. The husband makes an appointment with a therapist and gives him his point of view. Afterwards, the wife tells her story. Both partners are discussing the same problem from their own point of view. Who is right? No one and both. It is completely useless and even counterproductive to make statements in such cases about the "truth" of either vision. After all, everyone has his own truth. Recognizing those personal truths, without participating in the "who is right and who is wrong discussion", paves the way to see what both partners are willing to do differently to make their lives as a couple easier.

The job of a change agent is not to seek the truth, that is work for the professionals whose job it is to make expert statements. The job of the change agent is to make sure that both partners get the feeling that their truth is being heard, understood, and accepted for their truth. Arguing and/or trying to convince one side that his or her truth is truer than the other's view is counterproductive, unhelpful, and risks leading to the adoption of increasingly rigid positions against each other. However, if each partner feels that his truth is accepted as his view, which does not mean that he is right, then it becomes possible to accept that your truth may not be the only possible view of the matter and that the other may have an equally valid point, so that a constructive conversation can occur.

The basis of feeling understood lies in the ability of the professional to listen both unbiased and with equal attention to all parties involved. For that, the professional must be aware that we all have prejudices or filters with which we listen to and interpret reality so that it becomes our reality. Therefore, the change agent must (at least try to) turn off the filters of his prejudices and empathize with the other person's experience. The safest way to do this is to refrain from making statements and instead ask as many questions as possible. Asking useful questions will get you useful answers. An additional advantage of asking many questions is that the practitioner obliges himself to listen carefully instead of talking.

In a remarkable study,[24] clients – in their fifth therapy session – were asked to what extent they felt understood. They had to give a score on a scale of 0 (my therapist doesn't understand me at all) to 10 (my therapist knows exactly what my predicament is and how it bothers me). If the score was below 6.5, the therapy might as well be stopped because the chance it would achieve the desired results was close to nil. That shows how important the feeling of being understood is.

The non-specific factor of feeling understood is perhaps one of the most necessary aspects and a prerequisite, for a successful intervention.

Do I receive the appropriate amount of authentic attention?

When we dissect the triple term "appropriate authentic attention", we get the following:

The Oxford dictionary explains *authenticity* as: "Of undisputed origin and not a copy; genuine" and "Based on facts; accurate or reliable". The second explanation can be used for our purpose: real and therefore reliable. Authenticity is in stark contrast to artificiality and fake. Authenticity is not the same as spouting your opinions about the client and/or telling him everything about your personal life. As a change agent, you must be aware that you as a person are a tool for your clients, no more and no less.

The Oxford dictionary defines *attention* as: "the act of listening to, looking at or thinking about something/somebody carefully; interest that people show in somebody/something'. Analyzing this definition, "attention" means showing the client in word and deed that we are fully present with our client and that we are fully attentive to what the client has to say. To do this, empty your own mind of all preconceived ideas that will only get in the way of your unbiased view of the client. Attention also means that the therapist makes and takes time for the client to tell their story.

Attention has a volume knob. Too much attention and the client will get the uncomfortable impression that you are all over him. Too little attention, and the client will feel neglected as if he is not interesting enough for the change agent. Appropriate volume means not too much, not too little, but well matched to the client and the occasion.

Do I feel respected as a person?

Respect stems from the Latin word "respicere" which means "to look after" and which in contemporary language means: to take account of the other. That is why we read in the dictionary that respect means: to revere out of esteem or fear, with the synonym: to respect.

Although one may think of oneself as being very respectful of the other, it is the other who must decide whether that is the case. Strictly speaking, one cannot respect the other unilaterally, but one can only offer respect to the other so that it becomes bilateral. So, we turn respect into showing respect. By treating someone with respect, we honor their dignity. Every person deserves respect, and every person wants to be treated with respect.

If we fail to do so, we usually get a fierce reaction.

Martha

Even the best intentions can be felt as disrespectful. Martha T., 82-year-old, was recently transferred from a mental institution to the psychogeriatric ward. The nurses on that ward are all very nice people with their hearts in the right place. They treat their clients very kind-heartedly.

From day one, however, things went wrong with Martha. The nurses report that she is very aggressive – not only verbally but also physically. Martha's medical history is fully described in her medical record. After her divorce fifty years ago, Martha lost contact with her only child. After that tumultuous period, she has been admitted to ever possible institution and hospital. The series of diagnoses and treatments provides a nice overview of what has happened in the development of psychiatry over the past few decades.

A brief note at the very back of her thick medical file reveals that Martha studied medicine in an increasingly gray past and worked as a family physician for several years. When we visit her in her room

> together with a nurse, the colleague sits on her bed and says: "Good morning, dearest Martha. How are we feeling today? Did our Martha sleep well? Is our mommy feeling better today?" And before the nurse has a chance to introduce us, Martha gave her a cuff on the ears.
>
> Then the elderly lady starts screaming. At that moment, we take over the conversation saying: "Nurse, would you be so kind as to leave us alone with doctor T for a moment.? Good morning, doctor T., do you have a moment for us? If you agree, we would like to discuss some things with you." Martha T. becomes very quiet and looks surprised ...

Showing respect means seeing "the person in the client" and accepting his complaints, symptoms, idiosyncrasies and "quirks." Showing respect also means showing interest in the client's factors and resources (see point A above), which, as we could read in Dr. T.'s story, have been overlooked or forgotten.

Everyone has biases and so does the change agent. But showing respect becomes easier when you can set these biases aside. Perhaps it is easier, to see Martha as an aggressive old lady with a long psychiatric history and no sense of decorum, but this would not be very respectful, nor would it help her.

It is important to show respect for the client's complaints and symptoms because his perception of the world (temporary or otherwise) is often based on his problems. The change agent must acknowledge the client's problems and show respect for the way the client manages to cope, despite his difficulties. In this sense, SoFAP is different from solution-focused drivenness. It is inappropriate to say bluntly to a client, "I am a solution-focused therapist; I am not interested in your problems. What is going well in your life?"

All people need acknowledgment, and so that is the most universal human currency to exchange when we meet people inside or outside our office.

Three caveats to avoid potential misunderstandings:

- Every person deserves respect, but not all human behavior is respectable.
- Respecting someone is different from uncritically accepting whatever the other person does or says.
- The one who receives respect must also do something, namely accept the respect, and (try to) feel respected.

Finally, the more respect you show, the more you yourself will be respected.

Do I get hope that change for the better is possible?

Clients do not ask for help the moment they are faced with a problem, but only when they feel they cannot get out of it without help.[25] Then you hear them say: "It doesn't work, I can't do this anymore. I'm stuck, I've had enough, I'm going round in circles. I have tried everything, and nothing works". In other words, clients contact a change agent when they (or someone else in their place) have lost hope and have stopped believing that they can solve their problems themselves. When that happens, it is important that as a practitioner you offer them hope by helping them discover that there are options other than making fruitless rounds in the cycle of symptoms. Hope that changes for the better are possible emerges from a constructive working relationship that focuses on achieving the client's goals without minimizing his problems. You can do this by encouraging the client to focus on current and future possibilities rather than remaining fixated on the problem.

Froma Walsh's motto again offers guidance

> *"Hope is to the human mind what oxygen is to the body".*[26]

To begin this hope building process, the professional can say, "Good for you to have the courage to come. The first step to change is always the hardest. Congratulations, you've already taken that step. Can I ask you some questions?" From there, you apply the seven-step dance interventions described in Chapter 5.

Caveat: Raising hope that change is possible is not the same as saying to the patient, "It's good that you came. You're lucky. You have come to see the best therapist in the Western Hemisphere, 'me'. But first I must give an important piece of advice to the Nobel Committee, which is now on the phone. This will only take a few minutes. In the meantime, please start healing yourself".

Such an attitude is not professional service, but quackery and ego-tripping.

CO-CONSTRUCTIVE ALLIANCE

The very decision to seek help creates a virtual and symbolic relationship between the client and the yet unknown person of the change agent.

Once the client enters the room, this virtual relationship turns into a triangular relationship between the client, the change agent, and the client's goals, as indicated in Wave 6. From there, an alliance can be forged that creates a context in which the client is helped to help himself.

> Anything that can effect good cooperation between patient and physician in achieving an important goal is worthy of consideration.[27]
>
> Milton H. Erickson

Indeed, the relationship between the client and the change agent is only relevant in the context of the client's goals for change. Without those goals, the facilitation process is nothing more than a cordial and sympathetic but noncommittal conversation between friendly people. A change provoking alliance develops in a different, ritual context than a conversation at home on the couch.[28] Change agents had better not underestimate the power of this ritual context; they should make use of it.

The change agent and his expertise are no more (and no less) than a tool to help the client achieve his goals.

Credibility and expectations

To be useful and successful, clients must find the change process and the person of the change agent credible. Imagine going to your family doctor; you explain to him your baby's symptoms and anxiously ask him if he knows what is wrong. Imagine that the doctor replies "No idea, I'll have to Google that" ... Or worse, when the doctor takes a picture of the baby and then pours salt over the picture to get the disease out via osmosis.

When clients form a virtual and then a real alliance with a professional, they have expectations of what the process could and/or will bring them. The change agent also has expectations about their profession. The expectations of client and professional, although different for each party, must be aligned in the best interest of the client.[29]

Credibility of the change process

When clients seek help, they often have no explanation for their problems: "I don't understand why I've been feeling so bad lately. I feel ashamed and angry/sad/unhappy about not being able to handle the normal things in life anymore. I'm just not able to keep up with my work anymore..."

Sometimes, the more clients feel that they are in trouble, the more they tend to cling to their own explanations – even if they are incorrect and crippling: "It's probably my own fault that everyone hates me. I am a bad father/mother because I can no longer handle the challenges of my family. I've recently discovered that, compared to my peers, I'm just too stupid and lazy for this job..."

In most cases, it is not smart to bluntly go against these beliefs. It is better to come up with an alternative but credible explanation.

Clients who complain that they can do a mountain of work one day, while the next day they are so exhausted that lying on the couch all day is all they can muster to do. Instead of allowing the client to disqualify himself as a lazy loser with no strength of character, the explanation that he is managing his energy levels in the wrong way is more true, accurate, acceptable, and therefore more credible. These clients can be advised to manage their energy more efficiently by breaking their workload into small chunks, taking small steps at a time, and taking frequent breaks.

Parents whose adolescents are on the "hormonal warpath" are often helped by providing information about adolescent behavior: "As difficult as it may be, it is in fact normal for adolescents to try to develop their own identity by pushing everything and everyone away. This temporary phenomenon is called "counter-identification". Such an explanation may not be the most scientific, but it will make parents less likely to give in to flaring conflicts and make it easier for them to discuss problems in a calm manner. In this way, both parties will benefit: the adolescent feels acknowledged in his search for identity and the family members can negotiate compromises.

Alternative explanations and metaphors can be helpful. Of course, we must not talk nonsense. To my knowledge, it has never helped anyone to tell a client that his chakras should be aligned, preferably on a full moon…

> This is healing: it doesn't matter how you get well. It is the result that is important.[30]
>
> Betty Alice Erickson

Credibility of the change agent

If the client finds the alternative explanation credible, the change agent will also become more credible in the eyes of the client. In that case, the probability of success increases exponentially. There is nothing new under the sun. In the second century AD, Galenus[31] already knew: "He who is most trusted by the people cures best."

Insecure clients do not benefit from insecure practitioners: they already struggle enough with themselves and do not need to be bothered with their practitioner's uncertainty. The professional attitude of the change agent shows the client that he is competent and that he knows what he is talking about. Lerner and Fiske[32] have shown that the therapist's belief that he can really help the client is a better predictor of therapy outcome than the client's characteristics, as was thought in the early days.

Clearly, a delicate balance is needed between taking charge in the face of the client's uncertainty and being inclined, albeit with the best of intentions, to take over the client's life. The credibility of the change agent is more emotional than rational. The client must feel that the expert, in his perception and expectation, will take charge without hesitation, while rationally knowing that the expert does not know everything and will not solve it for him.

The change agent is not the Pied Piper of Hamelin who entices clients to go where he wants them to go, even if it means plunging them into a ravine of ever-deepening misery. On the contrary, the change agent is a well-accredited tour guide who helps clients safely get where they want to go (aka. achieve their goals).

> Favoring the therapeutic result was the prestige of the writer as a psychiatrist and a hypnotist well-spoken of by their friends, the medical students. This undoubtedly rendered them unusually ready to accept what I have to offer.[33]
>
> Milton H. Erickson

Expectations of the client

All clients have expectations when they first come to therapy, even the ones who do not want to be there.

One person says: "I don't think you can help me, because I'm beyond saving. Therapy won't have any effect on me". Another one says: "I don't know what else I could do differently, but I trust that you as a therapist will know what to do". A third client may say: "I do not want to be here, but I have to". And yet another may say: "I'll wait and see for the result of this therapy. It can't get any worse".

Once the conversation has started and he has explained what he is struggling with, the client may ask: "Can you help me?", there are three possible answers.

- If you think you can be of some use to the client, you say: "Of course I will do my best to help you. I can't do the work for you, but if you help me, I can help you".'
- If you are not sure you can be of any use, you say: "I'm not sure. Shall we try to find out together?"
- However, if you are of the opinion that you can't be of any use, you'd better be honest and say: "I'm afraid I can't help you. Is it okay to refer you to a colleague who is more experienced with this type of problem?"

Not giving an honest answer, for whatever reason, be it that your ego does not allow you to be open about your abilities, be it that you think with the best of intentions that you have a duty to save everyone from distress, such an attitude is like choking the client by depriving his mind of "oxygen."

Regardless of the situation presented by the client, each honest and appropriate response from the practitioner opens a hopeful perspective for the client.

Expectations of the change agent

Until proven otherwise, change agents want to do the best for their clients, or they would have chosen a different profession. They strive to be successful in their service to their clients, just as they want to be successful as individuals. This is expressed on the one hand in the form of satisfied clients who provide positive feedback that increases the professional's job satisfaction and self-confidence, and on the other hand, in the form of financial and prestige-related rewards. Professional pride goes hand in hand with their sense of meaningfulness, so they enjoy the intrinsic motivation to continually learn.

Caveat: The practitioner may have his own expectations about the work and its outcome for his clients, and therefore stick to his working methods. This is not a problem under two conditions: 1. that he does not unnecessarily bother his clients with his expertise, and 2. that he has the intellectual correctness to adapt his working methods to the needs of the client rather than trying to squeeze the client into the straitjacket of his methodology.

Induce Hope

When the clients meet a credible change agent who offers the client a credible approach that helps him achieve his goals, it further strengthens the hope for positive change. Being confronted by a practitioner who demonstrates in word and deed that he knows what he is doing helps the client to relax and put his full energy into his healing process.

Model-specific interventions[34]

In the classical models, the non-specific factors common to all change approaches were a byproduct and epiphenomenon of successful change processes. In Wave 6, SoFAP, these common factors are an intrinsic part of the approach itself. The more technical interventions are simply useful tools for putting the common factors and all the SoFAP additions to work in a practical way.

Solution-focused techniques

The scaling question and the Miracle Question, the iconic hologram-like techniques of the solution-focused approach, imply that the client can design an alternative reality using the change agent as the midwife who helps him give birth to his own possibilities.

Interventions from other models

All interventions that are described in the Big Book of Knowledge of Psychology and Common Sense, all conceivable interventions, and techniques that we derive from other change models can be used, up to and including "Golden Tips & Tricks". They only must be made fitting to what the client needs at this specific moment when he deals with that specific situation.

CRUX AND CAVEAT

Crux

All the technical interventions from the SoFAP model are practical ways to activate the client's independence and – at the same time – offer the therapist a coherent frame through which he helps to help himself. When the change agent is in full control of the underlying ideas, epistemology and techniques that facilitate robust and sustainable change, experienced practitioners will no longer need techniques. The solution-focused basic attitude will then be sufficient: more becomes less.

Caveat

If you reduce the rich epistemology of the SoFAP to mere techniques, without embedding them in a broader mindset, you will end up with a bag of tricks.

Seven tools for true change

From the client's point of view, real change, and again we define this as a difference that makes a difference, takes place when the client feels:

1. acknowledged for all the factors I bring to the change process
2. understood
3. treated with the right amount of authentic attention
4. respected as a person
5. hopeful that a new perspective in my future life is possible
6. receives credible help from a credible professional who meets my expectations
7. he gets access to model-specific techniques, tips, and tricks

Conclusion

The knowledge of the iterative waves of development, combined with all the defining elements necessary for real change, underlie the SoFAP approach which is more of a basic attitude than a collection of technical details.

Leaving aside the technical language, one can simply say that what always works can be summarized as "faith, hope and love. Faith in the power of the client's resources, hope that alternatives are always possible and love that powers the therapeutic alliance.

Notes

1 Erickson, M.H. & Rosen, H. (1954). Hypnotic and hypnotherapeutic investigation and determination of symptom function. *Journal of Clinical and Experimental Hypnosis, 2*, 201–219.
2 A practitioner can ask a similar question to his clients: "Despite all your problems, what are the things that are (still) going so well that you most definitely want to keep them? This can be anything: your health, your family, your job, your house, or even seemingly small details like your favorite brand of cereals". We detail this "continuation question" in Chapter 6.
3 This important topic deserves a book in itself, but we limit it here to a brief overview of the developments that help us understand how SoFAP came to be. For a great historic overview of the common factors, we refer to Duncan, B., Miller, S., Wampold, B.E. & Hubble, M.A. (2010). *The heart and soul of change: Delivering what works in Therapy*. 2nd edition. American Psychology Association.
4 Nabokov, V. (1983). Lectures on literature: Austen, Dickens, Flaubert, Joyce, Kafka, Proust, Stevenson. London: Picador Books.
5 See Chapter 1, p. 10.
6 Duncan, B., Miller, S., Wampold, B.E. & Hubble, M.A. (2010). *The heart and soul of change: Delivering what works in therapy*. 2nd edition. American Psychology Association, p. 94.
7 Rosenzweig, S. (1936). Some implicit common factors in diverse methods of psychotherapy. *American Journal of Orthopsychiatry, 6*, 412–415.
8 Frank, J.D. & Frank, J.B. (1991). *Persuasion and healing: A comparative study of psychotherapy*. 3rd edition. Baltimore, MD: John Hopkins University Press. The first edition of this book was published in 1961 and the second book in 1973. Frank's research covers a 30-year-period. The fact that he wrote the last edition together with his daughter is a nice detail.
9 Lambert, M.J. (1992). Psychotherapy outcome research: Implications for integrative and eclectic therapists. In J. C. Norcross & M. R. Goldfried (Eds.), *Handbook of psychotherapy integration* (pp. 94–129). Basic Books. Yet, therapists are spending so much time, energy, and money on acquiring these model-specific techniques. Many academics and therapy gurus make it their life's work to (further) specify their own model. An undefined part the effect of these model-specific techniques can probably be traced back to the previous factor, namely the active placebo effect it has on the client, caused by the trust the therapist has in his own model.
10 Personal message from Alasdair McDonald to the author, 2010.
11 In his meta-analytical study, which is highly esteemed in scientific circles, Wampold (2001) states that the best-case scenario is that only 8 (read: eight) % can be assigned to model-specific contributions. See: Wampold, B.E. (2001). *The great psychotherapy debate: Models, methods and findings*. Hillsdale, NJ: Erlbaum.
12 There exist several different sources of this fascinating story. de Shazer himself testifies about it in his book Keys to solution in brief therapy (1985) Norton.
13 McKergow, M. & Korman, H. (2009). In between – neither inside nor outside. The radical simplicity of Solution focused Brief Therapy. *Journal of Systemic Therapy*, 28(2), 34–49.
14 de Shazer, S. (1994). Essential, non-essential: Vive la différence. In J. Zeig (Ed.), *Ericksonian Methods: The essence of the story* (pp. 240–258). New York: Brunner/Mazel.
15 Erickson, M.H. (1975). *Preface in Bandler and Grinder, patterns of the hypnotic techniques of Milton H. Erickson*. New York: Grune & Stratton.

16 https://www.erickson-foundation.org. Main source for all things Erickson.
17 Personal communication to Louis Cauffman in 1996.
18 de Shazer, S. (1990). What is it about brief therapy that works? In: Zeig, J.K & Gilligan, S. *Brief therapy. Myths, methods and metaphors. Proceedings of the Fourth International Congress on Ericksonian Approaches to Hypnosis and Psychotherapy*, held in San Francisco, CA, December 7–11, 1988 (pp. 90–99). New York: Brunner/Mazel.
19 An excellent overview of the gradual development of the theoretical thinking of de Shazer and his colleagues at the Brief Family Therapy Center can be found at: Korman, H. & De Jong, P. (2020). Steve de Shazer's theory development. *Journal of Solution Focused Practices*, 4(2), 47–70.
20 de Shazer, S. (1988). *Clues: Investigating solutions in brief therapy*. New York: Norton.
21 This theme is important in the development of de Shazer's thinking and is published in his groundbreaking from (1984). The Death of Resistance. *Family Process*, 23, 1–11. The concept will be discussed in detail in Chapter 6, page 131–132.
22 de Shazer, S. (1991). *Putting difference to work*. New York: Norton.
23 Bateson, G. (1972). *Steps to an ecology of mind*. New York: Ballantine Books, p. 465.
24 Whipple, J.L., et al. (2003). Improving the effects of psychotherapy. The use of early identification of treatment failure and problem-solving strategies in routine practice. *Journal of Therapy*, 50(1), 59–68.
25 Frank, J.D. & Frank, J.B. (1991). *Persuasion and healing: A comparative study of psychotherapy*. 3rd edition. Baltimore, MD: John Hopkins University Press.
26 Walsh, F. (2016). *Normal family processes, growing diversity and complexity*. 4th edition. Guilford Press.
27 Erickson, M.H. (ca. 1950). *Hypnosis in obstetrics: Utilizing experiential learnings*. Unpublished manuscript.
28 Professionals sometimes hear clients say, "What you are telling us is the same thing I have been telling my partner for months now. To me, he just doesn't listen". Now, we understand this phenomenon: meanings differ in the ritual context of a professional change conversation.
29 See what happens when a client seeks help for his efforts to be more successful in his work, while the practitioner is only interested in the possible traumas in the client's childhood....
30 Erickson, B.A. & Keeney, B. (2006). *Milton H. Erickson, an American healer*. Sedona, AZ: Ringing Rocks Press, p. 56.
31 *Retrieved from:* Singer, P.N. (2021). Galen. In Edward N. Zalta (Ed.), *The Stanford Encyclopedia of Philosophy* (Winter 2021 Edition), URL = <https://plato.stanford.edu/archives/win2021/entries/galen/>.
32 Lerner, B. & Fiske, D.W. (1973). Patient attributes and the eye of the beholder. *Journal of Consulting and Clinical Psychology, 40*, 272–277.
33 Erickson, M.H. (1954). Clinical note on indirect hypnotic therapy. *Journal of Clinical and Experimental Hypnosis, 2*, 171–174.
34 Chapters 5, 6, and 7 cover all the necessary, possible, and useful details, from the theory behind each intervention and mindset to the 'how-do-I-do-this-in-practice?'.

Chapter 3

The power of common sense

Living means constantly making decisions, day in and day out, all our lives. Knowledge, beliefs, misunderstandings, circumstances, chance, serendipity, other people, in short everything we encounter is at the root of that constant flow of decisions.

There are many roads to choose from in the landscape of our (co-)existence. Alfred Korzybski taught us that the map is not the territory.[1] We can never fully know the territory. We can only choose the best maps in the hope of getting us safe to where we want to be. But we must not forget that these maps inevitably reflect our opinions of the physical world. Remember the time when people thought that the Earth was flat, when it took courage to sail to the end of the Earth to look over the edge? The little man on the Moon could have easily told Magellan that our Earth is round instead of flat. Remember when the Universe was depicted with the Earth as its center? It was in fact dangerous to claim that the opposite. Until recently stomach ulcers were treated by therapists who specialized in stress relief, while internists Barry Marshall and Robin Warren cured Helicobacter pylori infections with antibiotics and won the 2005 Nobel Prize for their innovation.

Our physical environment is relatively stable and therefore easier to predict than the rational, emotional, and mental landscape we live in. Our thinking, acting, feeling, and interacting is modified by the thinking, acting, feeling, and interacting with our context, of which our fellowmen are a dominant factor. This way, the context in which we interact is changing and thus our thinking, acting, feeling, and interacting is changed by the context in which we ... ad aeternam.

Change facilitation is a process of interaction in which both parties involved continuously must make decisions. The client must decide what he says or does not say. The facilitator must decide what he asks or does not ask. In addition to that, there is an inevitable mutual influence that, on its turn, also decides what the client and therapist decide. To handle this complexity, people use decision rules of which they often are not aware, let alone that these decision rules are outspoken.

DOI: 10.4324/9781003320104-4

More than sharing and exchanging information, we exchange rules about how we handle information. In that way, we don't only exchange the content of what we're thinking of, but we change the thinking process itself.

The complexity makes your head spin. Life is complex and we must accept that our models only offer us a stylized version of reality. Precisely because life is so complex, it is best not to needlessly complicate it.

SoFAP developed decision rules to deal with complex matters in a simpler way. Those rules are neither map nor territory. They are tools that help you choose the exits that can be taken on the confusing road between problems and solutions.

Minimax

By rigorously applying the decision rules, as little energy as possible is consumed to elicit maximum results.

The decision rules

There was a time when the basic decision rules were short and therefore had the elegance of a haiku. The main drawback of this ultra-short version was that what you gained in brevity was lost in the lengthy explanations needed if you wanted to avoid misunderstandings.

The original solution-focused version reads as follows:

1 If not broken, do not fix it.
2 If it does not work, stop.
3 If it works, do more of it.

Today's SoFAP's version of the Basic Rules is more elaborate:

1 If something still works, do not repair it but show respect and appreciation for what still works.
2 If something does not or no longer or does not work well enough, after you have tried it for a while, stop and do not drone on but learn from this, and try something else.
3 If something works well enough, well, or better, keep doing it and/or do more of it.
4 If something works well enough, well, or better, learn it from someone else and/or offer it to someone else.

Rules are tools

This list of basic decision rules can be used as a checklist. Whenever you have the impression that your interventions are not catching on, there is a good chance that you are sinning against one or more of these basic rules. Maybe you are overlooking a rule, maybe you are putting too much emphasis on a rule, or maybe you are switching between rules too quickly without giving it a chance to catch on. If this is the case, use this list to adjust your interventions.

These rules seem self-evident. Yet, they have more depth than may appear at first glance. To get to the bottom of these seemingly simple rules, we deconstruct every rule and offer a detailed analysis below.

Deconstruction of the basic rules

Basic rule 1

If something still works, do not repair it but show respect and appreciation for what still works.

It often happens that people, therapists included, – usually with the best of intentions – go against this statement. The biggest pitfalls are the therapists' convictions and theories, to which he can be so attached that it can hamper the client. A couple therapist who recently followed a course in communication therapy can become convinced that couples can only function well when they communicate in a clear and transparent way, by – for example – letting each other finish their sentences. But in case of an elderly couple, where the wife says "cra..." and the husband immediately adds "she means crayons sir," it isn't evident that the husband should change his behavior.

Even in dire situations, there are always things that go well. Contrary to traditional types of therapy that focus on the (why of the) problems, SoFAP is not blind to the problems but has a keen eye for those things that still function well despite those problems. When the time is right,[2] you can ask for those things: "can I ask you a slightly different question? Despite all the suffering and misery that you just described, what are the things in your life that still go well enough so that you want to keep them?" It happens that the client is so despondent that he is not able to answer this question. Then the therapist searches for things that he assumes are important and still working good enough in the life of the client and he offers these issues in the form of a question: "Would you agree that X and Y in your life still works well?"

In a gentle, subtle, and yet incisive manner, the therapist helps the client to identify his resources. The therapist thereby shows respect and appreciation for the efforts of the client and for the resources that surface. This intervention often forms the base for later steps forward.

Basic rule 2

If something doesn't work or no longer works or doesn't work well enough after you have tried it for a while, just stop, learn from this, and try something else.

1 If something does not

One can offer an intervention once, twice but if the client does not respond, then it is better to let that intervention go. One of the most common mistakes is to drone on when an intervention, however well meant, does not work.

Some things the practitioner and/or the client does, just don't work and it is good to acknowledge this. Practitioners and/or clients sometimes seem to be "in love" with the things they keep on repeating without getting the desired effect. Bad habits are also included in this category.

2 Or no longer

Man is a creature of habit, and basically this is a good thing. Imagine returning from work, but instead of going home you walk into any random house... Routines, habits, fixed patterns may be useful in most situations, but there are exceptions. Some habits are rather counterproductive. What was helpful yesterday, may not work in today's changing circumstances. Certain psychological symptoms may once have had a function, but due to its repetitive and chronic character this function has been lost. The alcohol that may have helped a patient through a very stressful situation can turn into alcohol abuse (that becomes a stressor on itself, even when the original stressor has dissolved). Benzodiazepines may be useful in certain situations, but frequent use of this medication may lead to long-term abuse. In short, a client can continue doing something that no longer works and even worse, he now has an additional problem.

> Then why were there all the other symptoms? Did they serve some other purposes or relate to unrecognized significances? As in the case with other patients, the author simply does not know. Nor does he know of anybody who has ever really understood the variety and purposes of any one patient's multiple symptoms despite the tendency of many psychiatrists to hypothecate, to their own satisfaction, towering structures of explanation often as elaborate and bizarre as the patient's symptomatology.[3]
>
> Milton H. Erickson

3 Or does not work good enough

Some things the therapist and/or client do, are not sufficiently effective. One must notice and acknowledge this in time to avoid counterproductive obstinacy.

4 After you have tried it for while

Sometimes the therapist and/or client must show some persistence. A message, insight, suggestion does not always come across well from the start. If you give up immediately after a first attempt, you won't get very far in life.

5 Stop

Letting things go in due time is better than stubbornly push through. Continuing to push without the desired response can have the detrimental effect that the therapist may develop the idea that the client is "resisting" change. If you define resistance as directional cues or stage directions[4] that offer additional information, the client is only showing the therapist that he is not on the right track. Moreover, pushing on takes time and energy that can be put to better use.

6 Learn

A good next question is: what have you tried that hasn't worked? By asking this question, you show respect and consideration for the time and energy the client has already put into it, even if that effort has not helped. An additional benefit is that the therapist gets direct information about which things not to try again. Sometimes this question shows you that the client has good intentions but has handled it in a slightly wrong way.

7 Try something different

What the meaning of "different" is depends entirely on the context. To paraphrase Gregory Bateson: we are going to look for a difference that makes a difference. There are two categories of this "difference".

Category 1: Therapist's action

The therapist can do something different. For example, instead of allowing the customer to constantly talk about their complaints, you can suggest other topics in a polite and respectful manner. The following questions can be helpful: I understand how serious your problems feel and how frustrated you are because you seemingly can't do anything about them, but can I ask you the following question: Are there things that, in spite of this big issue that you're facing, are still going well in your life?

"What are things in your life you would definitely like to keep?" Here, we recognize the "continuation question"[5] which is based on the resource orientation that says that there are always some that are still going well. By asking this question we help the client to focus on those things that still work. Over time, this can help the client get rid of their problem-focused mindset.

Category 2: Client's action

You can ask the client if he wants to try something different instead of staying in a rut. In case the client agrees, he will give us his permission to try something different. By turning this suggestion into a question, the client can choose his own answer and thus become the owner of his answer.

To clarify this, we can use the following example: when it comes to housekeeping (or office work), clients sometimes complain that they have low energy levels. Often these clients have complaints like: "I can't go on", "I don't feel well", "I'm always tired" and other vague complaints. They talk about how one day they manage to do a lot of work, only to completely collapse afterwards and the next day feel guilty because they can't get up from the couch. Their approach is detrimental: one day they work too much and too hard, the next day their energy is wasted by hanging out on the couch all day swirling in guilt.

This behavioral pattern has become repetitive because, after a day on the coach the client forces himself to work at full throttle. Both working methods demand as much energy as running a marathon at sprinting speed. The change agent can help the client to deal with his energy and household chores in an alternative manner. "Would you be interested to see if there is a way to handle your energy in a slightly different way?"

He can suggest alternative working methods in the form of a question such as: working in phases, taking regular breaks, and making lists of what needs to be done. "Would it make a difference if you divided tomorrow's chores in small parts with regular breaks in between?" In short: by using suggestive questions you can help the client to do something that does work.

Basic rule 3

If something is working well (enough) or better, keep doing it and/or use it more often.

If something works well or works good enough

From rule 1, we learned to acknowledge and respect what does not need mending. Rule 3 goes one step further and teaches us to actively look out for what is working well enough so that these things can be used as a launching platform for further enhancements. These can be things that in our daily life are often overlooked because they seem evident. Healthy people have tendency to take their health for granted. It is only when something goes wrong, that we become aware of the preciousness of our health. "Count your blessings" became a cliché because it is the truth. Life isn't designed to be constantly happy. It is designed to be happy every now and again. It is a skill to be happy with what you've got and striving for perfection will usually leave you empty-handed. The same applies to our profession. You're better off asking your clients: "How do you find out if the facilitation process has helped you enough to figure it out on your own from now on?"

Or works better

The husband who's working from home is waiting in full anticipation of his wife returning from work. When she gets home, he immediately overwhelms her with all kinds of questions and news. His wife, however, has had a hard day at work and would rather have a break. They often have discussions because the husband thinks that his wife isn't interested in talking to him whereas she thinks her husband doesn't give her any space. If he would make her a cup of tea and engage in his own work for another half hour first, this cycle would soon be broken.

Just keep doing it

A General Practitioner is confronted with a hard-working patient who never allows himself a moment off and who complains of stress symptoms. The doctor cautiously advises him to have a 15-minute walk with his dog every evening. The patient follows this advice, but in a following session the doctor begins to wonder whether this is sufficient. Should the exercise be extended to 30 minutes or perhaps even an hour? Or, is it wise to simply congratulate the client on his daily exercise and encourage him to keep it up?

And/or do more of it

Physical exercise is beneficial for mind and body. If a client tells you he went to the gym for ten minutes in the past week, he should be encouraged to go more often. Ten minutes won't make a huge difference but may lay the groundwork lots of ten-minute workouts in the future. If we see actions that work, our automatic reaction should be to fully support and stimulate the client to do more of it. In this way, small improvements are likely to slowly grow into substantial progress.

Basic rule 4

If something is working well (enough) or even better, learn it from someone else, or teach it to someone else.

When something is working well (enough) or better

We have already discussed this in basic rules 2 and 3.

Learn it from someone else

You can be open to information and expertise from colleagues, literature, and refresher courses. When you've found out from your colleagues which interventions are efficient in certain circumstances, why wouldn't you make it easier for yourself and try similar methods? Of course, you should not copy these interventions mindlessly, but you also do not have to start from scratch. The client, by the way, is your main source of information, because he is constantly giving you stage directions that will help you better serve him.

And/or teach it to someone else

The same goes for useful interventions you've applied yourself: Is there any greater professional pleasure than sharing the things that work with your clients and colleagues? Think of the word team as the acronym "together each achieves more". Facilitating change processes is teamwork at its best because you are always a team with your client.

> In the relationship between patient and clinician, you have one goal in common. The patient wants some type of care, and you are prepared to give the desired care. There are two people joined together, working for a common goal – the welfare of the patient.[6]
>
> Milton H. Erickson

Taking a step back: a Darwinian algorithm

To avoid that the simplicity of the decision rules is reduced to simplism, we need to discuss the rules that regulate the use of rules:

1. The solution-focused decision rules have nothing to do with "you-should-do this or that".
2. The solution-focused rules aren't about the intervention by one single party, but about the interaction between parties.
3. The application of each solution-focused rule can relate to the actions of the change-agent, the client or both.
4. The result of each solution-focused rule can incite parties to use another rule.
5. All solution-focused rules are valid in all circumstances.
6. The solution-focused rules do not depict the truth.
7. The solution-focused rules are epistemological tools that can help (re) shape reality.
8. The solution-focused rules don't help to understand, but to change.
9. The solution-focused rules are contentless and only serve the interactional process.
10. Solution-oriented rules steer cooperation between the parties towards co-evolutionary processes.

Once you are aware of these decision rules, you will see them appear everywhere in your daily life and work. They are the thread that runs through all our decisions.

Conclusion

The solution-focused rules are smart ways to start a collaborative change process. When you study the basic rules, you will discover that they are universally applicable. These decision rules lead to changes that create a context in which solution-oriented ideas are accepted, adapted, adopted, and then allowed to spread like a benign virus.

Notes

1 Korzybski, A. (1933). *Science and sanity: an introduction to non-Aristotelian systems and general semantics*, (International Non-Aristotelian Library), 1e ed. 1933, 5e ed. 1994, ISBN 0937298018.
2 See Chapter 5 for details on how to decide when the time is right. This has to do with timing (sic) that can be learned but is difficult to teach.
3 Erickson, M.H. (1966). Experiential knowledge of hypnotic phenomena employed for hypnotherapy. *The American Journal of Clinical Hypnosis*, *8*, 299–309.
4 Reframing the concept of resistance as a stage direction, underlies the paradigm shift that is a major achievement of the thinker Steve de Shazer. This concept is explained in detail in Chapter 6 on pages 131–132.
5 Chapter 1 clarifies the basic axiom of resource-orientation and in Chapter 6. we explain how to use the continuation question in practice (p. 145).
6 Erickson, M.H. (1966). *A lecture by Milton H. Erickson*. Houston, February 18, Audio Recording No. cd/emh.66.2.18. Phoenix, AZ: Milton H. Erickson Foundation Archives.

Chapter 4

The three mandates

In this chapter, we discuss the three fundamental mandates from which we intervene as professionals: the leadership mandate, the facilitating mandate and the management or stewardship mandate.

On terminology

Merriam-Webster offers the following definitions of the used terms:

Leader: a person who has commanding authority or influence.

Facilitator: someone who helps bring about an outcome (such as learning, productivity, or communication) by providing indirect or unobtrusive assistance, guidance, or supervision. Depending on the professional field in which one is active, the terms "(psycho)therapist, coach or change agent" may be a substitute.

Manager: the art of conducting or supervising something or someone to accomplish an end. *Stewardship*: the conducting, supervising, or managing of something. Especially: the careful and responsible management of something or someone entrusted to one's care.

According to Merriam-Webster, the term 'management' has for synonym, the word 'stewardship'.

Throughout the book, we will use the term 'management' mandate as a synonym for 'stewardship'. We chose this option for reasons of simplicity, but we like to point out the close connection between the concepts of management and stewardship. Our working definition of management is 'the art of getting things done through other people'.

What is a mandate?

A mandate is the authority required to exercise a function. If we want to regulate traffic at a crossing, we must make sure that we have a mandate as a police officer. In the perception of the rushing drivers, we are allowed to

DOI: 10.4324/9781003320104-5

regulate the traffic because the (hired) uniform makes us look like a police officer. This means that a mandate is not something you 'have' but you need to earn it in the eyes of the client.

Three mandates

As a professional, we always hold three mandates at the same time. We have a leadership mandate (a) that allows us to take the lead in the interventions. We, at the same time, have a management or stewardship mandate (b) through which we apply our professional knowledge and make agreements with our clients. Our third mandate is our facilitating or coaching mandate (c) wherein we create a context in which we help the others to help themselves to obtain their goals by making use of their resources.

The three mandates are not static but are in constant movement between them. The essence of your mandate as a leader is to know precisely how and when to apply your mandates as a facilitator or as a steward. After all, it is you who decides – from your expertise, experience, and awareness of the current situation – whether you intervene as a facilitator or as a steward. It is important to choose the mandate that will yield the best possible results for your interventions. The interaction with the client who, without being aware, gives stage directions that the professional needs to decode. These cues guide the mandates from which the professional needs to intervene.

An example from clinical practice makes the concept of the three mandates immediately clear.

Ellen

Imagine that you are a therapist who works with adolescents. After a couple of sessions with 14-year-old Ellen, it looks like the problems she had at school, have been resolved. She's making such good progress that you think about ending the therapy sessions. Then Ellen comes back for another session. Everything seems to be going well at school, but when you ask if she wants to talk about something else, she bursts into tears. Apparently, her uncle has been sexually harassing her in the last couple of days.

What are your next steps as a therapist? Will you ignore Ellen's outburst and stick to the good results in school? Will you simply show your sympathy and ask how she feels? Of course, you will offer your sympathy but you will also offer other kinds of support.

These additional levels of intervention imply that SoFAP goes beyond the classical psychotherapy models that are often limited to therapeutic interventions sensu stricto that help the client grow towards his preferred future. All other interventions are not seen as part of the therapeutic process and are considered to be the responsibility of another professional, albeit the same person who acts from a different role.

SoFAP embraces the three different mandates simultaneously

Depending on the situation, one of the mandates is in the foreground while the others are in the background. It is never or-or-or but always and-and-and. The three mandates must be alternated to have the most appropriate and incisive effect on the situation at hand.

Ellen

The therapist must take the lead in ensuring that the abuse stops by exercising his authority as a steward. It is important that he does this in a way that does not create additional problems or a secondary trauma for Ellen. How to do this requires knowledge and intervention expertise which is also part of his stewardship/management mandate. At the same time, the facilitating mandate is used to help Ellen deal with this terrible situation in such a way that she gets over it, heals from it, and learns how to deal with this kind of inacceptable behavior in the future. All three mandates are at work, albeit in succession and with overlap (Figure 4.1).

Figure 4.1 Three mandates.

Leadership mandate

When using your leadership mandate, you take the initiative, you decide which questions to ask, which answers follow up on and which answers to leave aside. As the leader of the intervention process, you decide whom to invite, in what order and/or whether you involve other specialized instances.

Of course, you must earn this mandate. In other words, leadership is always bi-directional: the way you lead determines to a great extent if you are actually being followed or not. One can only lead people who choose to be led by you.

In SoFAP, the client is at the center of attention. This shows in the language we use. The question "correct me if I am wrong but is it correct that..." is a good example of this. The facilitator takes the lead by instructing the client to correct him if necessary. This way, the client becomes the leader of his own growth process. With suggestive questions like "have you ever thought about..." and "what would you think if..." we use our leadership mandate to make the client the owner of the content of the suggestion. Facilitation and coaching are always directive: the facilitator directs the client, who directs the facilitator, who directs....

One of the most important aspects of your leadership mandate is to decide when you access which another mandate. After all, thanks to your expertise, experience, and ability to take the current situation into account, as a leader you can decide to intervene as a facilitator or as a manager/steward.

Leadership also implies that in certain situations you must take decisions, decide what needs to happen and intervene in the reality. There is nothing wrong with this just as long as the decision is made from an ethical perspective. You use your leadership mandate in such a way that it will benefit your clients.

We started this chapter with Ellen who was sexually abused. Contrary to most traditional models of coaching and therapy in which interventions limit themselves to the mind and heart of the clients; in SoFAP we do intervene in the reality of the client. We use our leadership mandate and intervene to protect her.

Reach out or drown

A 40-year-old man has been in therapy for a serious drinking problem. Several hospitalizations were necessary. But now he has sworn to never let it happen again. When his wife suddenly decides that she wants a divorce, the man has a serious relapse. He calls his therapist.

CLIENT: I cannot take this any longer. I have not slept or eaten for three days now.
THERAPIST: It's good you called.
CLIENT: I cannot do this anymore. I am afraid I cannot keep myself under control for much longer.
THERAPIST: Do you need to be hospitalized?
CLIENT: I do not want to go to a hospital. It is useless. I have been there so often.
THERAPIST: My question is if you need to be taken to hospital, not whether you find it useful.
CLIENT: I do not have the time. The kids are coming over this weekend.
THERAPIST: Good. I know how important your kids are to you.
CLIENT: They are the only ones I have got left.
THERAPIST: What do you think you need to get through this period until they arrive?
CLIENT: I do not know. I am so exhausted. It is driving me crazy. I have not been outside all week.
THERAPIST: Are you prepared to try something to stop this downward spiral?
CLIENT: Sure. If I only knew how to do that. I cannot go on like this.
THERAPIST: Is there someone you can call? Or even better, someone you can go to?

CLIENT: My brother is a GP. I cannot go to him; he will send me to rehab.

THERAPIST: Not if you can assure him that you won't do anything stupid.

CLIENT: I am not going to commit suicide if that is what you mean. What about my children then?

THERAPIST: Despite your difficult situation, I am glad that you are focusing your energy on your children. Have you been to the store to buy food for the weekend?

CLIENT: No, but that is a good idea. Now I have a reason to shower and get dressed.

THERAPIST: I think it is really good that you are planning things with you children, even though you are exhausted.

CLIENT: Maybe it will distract me and keep me busy. I think it is better for me to walk there, that way I can catch some fresh air.

THERAPIST: Maybe you could walk to your brother before or after shopping, even if it is just for a cup of coffee. Maybe you can stay over for dinner. Going for a walk will help you. You will be physically tired and that is a lot better than being mentally exhausted.

CLIENT: Yes, I've noticed. I used to go for long walks before I got divorced. I would go for a walk when we had an argument, and I would feel better when I got back home. I'm going for a walk. Thank you for the good advice.

THERAPIST: Thank you for calling me. Good luck and take care. We will see each other next week.

CLIENT: Definitely.

We will never know how it would have ended if the therapist had limited his intervention to just listening and using your facilitating mandate. Putting the various mandates to work in the appropriate way at the right time is a professional intervention that is more encompassing than mere facilitation as a coach or therapist. In this example, the therapist chose to take leadership and suggested actions in the form of questions (that contain suggestions). Sometimes it is necessary to protect the client from himself and others. That is not paternalism or making the client dependent of the therapist. On the contrary, intervening in the reality of the client, albeit in the form of suggestive questions, can be necessary. Strictly speaking this is not using our facilitating mandate, or in the context of the example, doing a psychotherapeutic intervention. The three mandates are always present, even if one is in the foreground and the others are in the background.

Management or stewardship mandate

As the manager of the intervention, one has two closely related responsibilities.

The first is that you are responsible for creating and maintaining the necessary preconditions in which the intervention takes place:

- You must stay up to date with the latest developments in your field:
- Change is the only constant in our field. Professionals whose job it is to counsel, coach, or facilitate clients in whatever their context is, must continuously update their knowledge- and expertise base according to the latest developments so that they are able to offer the best practices in their field.
- You make appointments with the clients, and if necessary, also with other organizations.
- You make sure that everything is planned in time and runs smoothly.
- You take care of the paperwork, the health insurance documents, the treatment plan, diagnostic files (if required), billing procedure, quality assurance, etc.
- You make sure that the sessions take place under the right circumstances: nicely scheduled and on time.
- If you feel that the task at hand with this client is not up to your best possibilities, you make sure to refer your client to the best available professional.

If all these preconditions are met, peruse the simplest possible adagio while operating your management mandate: say what you do and do what you say.

The second responsibility in the management mandate that you stay updated on the latest developments in your work- and study field. And this is difficult for the simple reason that our field of expertise is vast. It touches on topics ranging from psychology to economy, from organizational science to sociological developments, etc. Yet you cannot and should not think you know it all. Such humility is OK, though, because it invites you to work on a team where the acronym T.E.A.M. stands for "Together Each Achieves More." And by that "Together" is meant not just your colleagues in the office, but the entire network of knowledge that surrounds our world of change management.

Facilitating mandate

It is your job as a facilitator, be it psychotherapist or be it coach, to create a context in which you help the client to (again) help himself and others to achieve his goals by (again) using their available resources. Simply put: your job is to help him get the best out of himself (together with and/or for the people around him). The essence of this facilitation mandate is that the client learns to deal with his feelings, thoughts, behavior and find the best way to interact with others. If the client, during this process, learns how to deal with future problems (or challenges), then he does not need more help. He becomes his own facilitator, which is the goal of facilitation process.

The way you use this mandate, depends on the position you hold. As a manager and coach, you work with people. All these people are part of the 'together each achieves more' chain in the organization. It is your job to coach these people so that they do their jobs better, more smoothly, more effectively and efficiently and with (more) pleasure. As a therapist, you talk to your clients to help them deal with their lives so that they suffer less from their problems and have easier access to their contentment. In both cases, you teach them how to (again)use their own resources.

Coaching versus psychotherapy

The professional fields of psychotherapy and coaching have overlaps and differences. The overlap is that in the facilitating mandate both professional activities have the same finality, namely: creating a context in which we help the other(s) to help (again) themselves to obtain their goals by making use of their resources. Yet they have important differences, notably in two perspectives that both belong to the management mandate. First, the goals of psychotherapy and coaching are different. Second, there is a different knowledge base needed for the different professions.

> The therapist's task should not be a proselytizing of the patient with his own beliefs and understandings. No patient can really understand the understandings of his therapist, nor does he need them. What is needed is the development of a therapeutic situation permitting the patient to use his own thinking, his own understandings, his own emotions in the way that best fits him in his scheme of life.[1]
>
> Milton H. Erickson

Rotating mandates

SoFAP is a tool that can be applied in many situations, and it is important to keep a broad and flexible perspective. SoFAP is not OR facilitating OR leading OR being a manager. It is and-and-and! SoFAP is applying all the three mandates at the same time, albeit with respect to the situation at hand. Exclusively applying a leadership mandate soon leads to bossy behavior. Exclusively applying a facilitating mandate soon leads to ineffective softness. Exclusively applying a stewardship mandate where you set objectives and make the client responsible for obtaining them turns you into a bureaucratic apparatchik who has no influence on the life of clients.

There is no mathematically fixed rule that can be drawn up that will unerringly indicate when to use which mandate, when which mandate gets the foreground while the other two temporarily remain in the background. There is no fixed rule that unerringly tells you when to switch to which mandate. There is only the fairly vague and rather unhelpful rule of thumb that says: "it depends". Let us try to offer some general guidelines.

The leadership mandate is what you use when you want to:

- Give direction to what is being discussed
- Invite people to participate in the intervention
- Guide the sequence of questions and answers
- Direct who gets to speak when
- Deploy your professional knowledge and expertise
- Invite people to consult with each other and with relevant third parties

The Facilitating Mandate is used when you want to:

- Help the client sharpen his/her focus
- Help the other to get access to and utilize his resources
- Invite the client to set and work on useful goals

The Management Mandate is used when you want to:

- Make appointments and agreements that smoothen the entire intervention process
- Check interim results of your agreements
- Expand your professional knowledge

A matter of life and death case

The different mandates are always present at the same time. Depending on the situation, there is always one mandate that comes to the forefront while the other two mandates remain present and available in the background. When things go smoothly, there is an easy link and an elegant transition between the three mandates. Yet, you will encounter situations in which your professional responsibilities oblige you to make choices that are not so smooth and elegant. In extreme situations, one of the mandates must prevail if you want to avoid making professional mistakes. Deciding which mandate to choose, can take dramatic forms.

Madam Bovary

A 40-year-old, childless woman decides to go into therapy because of an existential dilemma: she is married but she's got a lover. She got married at 18 to move out of her parents' house. She tells me her marriage is dead. The two have been living together like brother and sister for years. But the woman doesn't want to hurt her husband.

He is a civil servant who she describes as a gentle, sweet guy who has always given her enough opportunities to expand her business. Many years ago, she took over the shoe store where she had been working since her twenties. She turned that little shop into a famous shoe company. The woman describes herself as flamboyant and passionate and tells me she has been having an affair with her former boss's son for years.

When I told her, it took courage for her to tell me her story and emphasized that I'm a therapist, not a moralist, she calmed down. She passionately told me how she fell in love with her lover when she first met him at the shoe store. She was 20 and had just been married for two years. She decided to go into therapy because she thought it was now time to make a decision.

CLIENT: I cannot go on living a double life; it's taking its toll on me. I think my husband suspects something. When he finds out, I'm afraid he'll be hurt, or he might even kill himself. On the other hand, I'm afraid to lose my lover. I have tried to distance myself from him so many times already. Then I usually make a scene and break up with him. Afterwards I go to my husband to look for comfort and I just tell him I've been having business problems. My husband comforts me but I know that I'm lying to him, and it makes me feel bad. But then my lover calls me to go out for dinner or he sends flowers to the store. One time I even texted my lover that I was at a certain hotel in France when I was alone on holiday. The next day, he was standing at my hotel door with a bottle of champagne. I'm just addicted to that man. But I know we could never live together; we would destroy each other.

This woman clearly felt the need to talk about this complex situation. She told me that our conversations lifted a weight of her shoulders. Her husband nor her lover knew that she was in therapy, and she had decided it was none of their business.

CLIENT: Just hearing myself saying these things out loud already makes the situation a little more bearable to me. I obviously know that you, as a therapist, can't make my decisions for me.

Starting our next session, it immediately became clear that something terrible had happened to this woman. She looked awful and tears came into her eyes when she told me the bomb had fallen. For the umpteenth time, she had put her love affair to an end and afterwards her lover had called her husband who threw her out of the house. She went to her lover but another woman opened the door.

CLIENT: That's it, I'm so done with it. Now I have lost them both. Maybe it's better this way. Now I have no choice but to finally use my brain and make something of my life.

The woman was very calm and determined. She told me that she had to go abroad for a few days to visit a fair and that she would use that opportunity to figure things out. As her therapist, I told her I was quite worried about her, but the client assured me it was not necessary: 'You don't need to worry about me sir, I can take care of myself.'

She called me a few days later and I could hear from her voice that she was not doing well at all.

CLIENT: I'm calling you to thank you for what you have done for me. I finally reached a decision and I want to let you know that you are not responsible for it.

THERAPIST: I'm worried. Where are you?

CLIENT: I won't tell you. That's none of your business.

THERAPIST: All right, I'm sorry. How are you doing?

CLIENT: Very bad, but that will be over soon.

THERAPIST: What do you mean?

CLIENT: I have lost my husband, my lover, my house, and my passion. But it is my own fault. I should have done things differently over the past years. They both don't want to have anything to do with me anymore.

THERAPIST: I'm sorry, but I don't really understand what you are trying to say.

CLIENT: After our last conversation, I realized I can't go on anymore. I have had a good life, but I'm not proud of it.

THERAPIST: What choice did you make?

CLIENT: You are in no way responsible for this. I mixed some pills and whiskey. I'm ending it. The world is better off without me anyway. Now that they both dumped me, I don't have a future anymore. It's my own fault. I have arranged everything at work, so my employees will be able to continue their work.

Right at that moment, I knew it was a matter of life and death. I knew that I had to set aside my mandate as therapist and had to act as a manager. While I kept her talking, I ran to my computer because I was suspecting (and most of all hoping) that she would be in the apartment above her store. I looked up the address while we were talking about her career. How she started off, she had proven herself to be a real businesswoman. She had taken over a little shop and turned it into a successful enterprise in only a few years' time. We talked about how courageous she had been, taking the step towards therapy. I also showed my admiration for the business arrangements she had made for her staff.

I could clearly hear form her voice that she was slowly losing consciousness and I asked her to recall the happiest memories in her life to keep her talking. In the meantime, I grabbed my mobile phone and called the emergency services. Talking in an undertone, I quickly explained the situation and passed on her address. Then I just kept her talking.

Luckily, her store and the apartment were situated nearby a police station. Within just 10 minutes, I heard her doorbell ring, and at the same time, I received a phone call from a police officer. When he told me he saw light on the second floor, I knew I was right. I told him I still had her on the phone and that I had heard her doorbell ring.

CLIENT: Someone is ringing the doorbell. I won't open anyway.
THERAPIST: I understand, you're busy now.
CLIENT: I see two police officers standing outside! You sent them, didn't you? Bastard, you betrayed me!

The woman hung up. The police officer told me that they were going to force open the door. I told him to hurry up and to call me back after they had taken her to hospital. An hour later (believe me, it seemed ages) the officer called me back to tell me that my client underwent gastric lavage and was doing well, considering the circumstances. The police had also called her husband, who had come to the hospital immediately.

Afterwards, the woman was admitted to a mental hospital. Her psychiatrist called me a few days later to get some more information.

She told me that the woman was very mad at me. Six months passed and I didn't hear a word from her, until I received a postcard with only two words written on it: *Thank you.*

I have never talked to her, nor have I ever seen her again.

I had decided to switch mandates and act as a leader while still pretending that I was her therapist. This action has probably saved my client's life. But I do realize that I deceived her and that I could no longer be her therapist. What I did was not facilitating, let alone therapy. I deployed my leadership mandate to do a rather blunt managerial intervention. But that intervention needed to be done.

Rules of thumb in using the mandates

1. Develop an awareness for which mandate is best on the forefront while the others are in the background, but ready to be activated.
2. Gauge every situation you encounter in your professional dealings with the concept of the rotating mandates in the back of your mind.
3. The concept of the three mandates lays the foundation for how and when to apply all the other tools that are described in SoFAP.
4. Facilitate where possible and (re) direct where necessary.
5. The facilitation mandate is crucial when the receiver of your professional services needs learning, development, and growth.
6. The leadership mandate sets the context in which all interventions happen, especially when the professional has the skill to find ways to engage the client while employing his facilitating and stewardship mandate.
7. The management mandate creates the overall context in which respectful but incisive interventions aim to help the client achieve their goals, while the professional uses best practices that must be continually honed.
8. The leadership and the facilitating mandate are never freely given, let alone taken for granted, but must be constantly earned in the client's perception.
9. Your management mandate is not something you have to earn but is simply part of your job. You are expected to know your work, to make agreements and then to keep them (or have them kept). Your management mandate requires you to test the results of iterative interactions on a regular basis.
10. How professional change agents rotate the various mandates is more art than skill, but with experience, skillful use of the mandates becomes an art.

Conclusion

If we are aware of our three mandates and have learned to use them appropriately, we can switch fluidly between mandates, we can make one mandate larger than another as needed, and thus we become versatile in their use regardless of the variety of practice domains, each with its own rules and needs.

Note

1 Erickson, M.H. (1965). Use of symptoms as an integral part of hypnotherapy. *The American Journal of Clinical Hypnosis*, *8*, 57–65.

Chapter 5

The seven-step tango

Steve de Shazer taught us that we never know the meaning of a question until we get an answer. This lesson is an antidote to an all-knowing therapeutic hubris where the facilitator has the audacity to think he knows and understands everything from the moment the client walks in the door. Steve's lesson goes against the Bed of Procrustes method where the client must fit the therapeutic mold of the facilitator. Steve shows clearly that it takes two to tango and used to say: to know the meaning of a question, one needs the answer of the other; so (at least) two parties are involved.

Creativity

Since we never (can) know what clients will come up with, working with fixed scripts to structure sessions makes no sense. It is better to improvise in a creative way that suits the ever-changing and unpredictable conversations. The themes on which we improvise come mainly from the client and his situation. Yet, remembering the importance of our mandates, the professional, when necessary, uses his leadership mandate to guide the topics of conversation in the direction that he deems fit to serve the client's growth requirements more effectively. And, if need be, he intervenes from a management mandate to protect the client from counterproductive developments and/or to keep the focus on the made agreements. Yet, all of this works best if the client is offered maximal freedom of choosing his path to growth.

Bradford Keeney in his book The Creative Therapist[1] (2009, 3) states: "Creativity points toward a process of creating. It both originates in and emerges from a complex, circularly intertwined choreography that moves everything from the dancers to the audience, stage, and choreography itself." This sentence, in which every word counts, is both the perfect synopsis of and a hologram for the intervention process that fuels SoFAP. It is a dance from which a new reality emerges that affects the dancers (the involved parties, both the client and the professional), the audience (members of the ecosystem that are involved in the change process as both actors and bystanders), the stage (the context) and the choreography (the interaction

DOI: 10.4324/9781003320104-6

process itself). To avoid that creativity becomes a meaningless "new age-like concept", Keeney adds: "Creativity doesn't come out of thin air. It is not babbling noise. It always has deep roots in traditions of knowing and expressions". The corner stones of professional expertise and experience are the cornerstones that support the construction of the alternative reality.

The solution tango

SoFAP does not primarily seek to merely understand what happens. SoFAP seeks innovative ways to improve the efficacy of the change and growth-inducing interactions between the client(s) and the professional. To optimize this, we use the metaphor of a seven-step dance, the "process protocol" professionals use to deal in a flexible and creative way with what their clients bring up.

SoFAP, as you know, can be used in psychotherapy, coaching, counseling, mediation, organizational consulting, etc. In any endeavor where human interactions play a part, SoFAP is a helpful tool. So we again invite you to think of your own professional context and apply the SoFAP tool to your own situation.

SoFAP is like the tango: dramatic, passionate, precise yet unpredictable, repetitive yet always different, tender, and fierce, sometimes close together and then at a distance, leading and following where the leader steers and follows.... Like the tango, SoFAP interventions consist of a limited number of steps that can be combined endlessly. As dance partners, you move together as harmoniously as possible: you lead, you follow, you dance in different rhythms and combine different dance steps. A tango needs courtesy and elegance: you take care not to step on your partner's toes nor stumble over your own legs. Sometimes you are close to each other, then again there's some distance. Dancing is – together and separately – doing, enjoying, feeling, adapting and changing. It takes two to tango. Dancing the tango on your own is as absurd (or ridiculous) as coaching or practicing psychotherapy without a client.

The SoFAP tango is the dance of interactions on the music of life: love, suffering, hope, despair, expectations, disappointment, fear, joy, discovery, change, wonder....

This chapter explains the "SoFAP-tango" in which the professional and the client dance toward the latter's own solutions, growth, and well-being. There are seven basic steps. Some you will recognize, and chances are you already (unconsciously) use some of them (Figure 5.1).

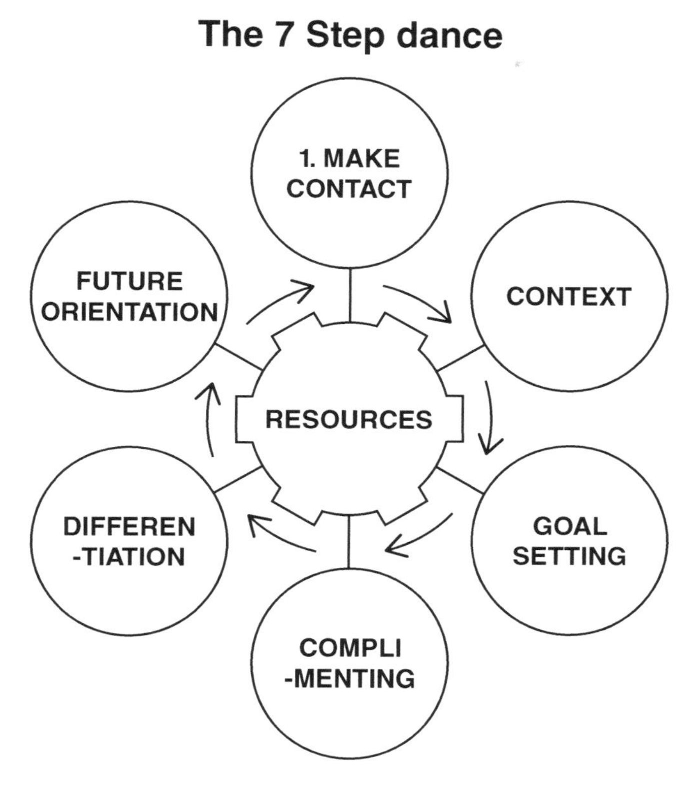

Figure 5.1 The 7 step dance.

Guidelines for the correct use of the SoFAP tango

- All the steps in the SoFAP tango are designed to facilitate a powerful relationship that can shape change and growth.
- The process protocol of the seven-step dance is an orderly and ever-changing way of working together with the client.
- The order in which the various steps are presented is a didactic aid in learning the seven-step dance. Experienced dancers may override this order and allow elegance to prevail.
- The schematic representation of the Solution Tango is designed in the form of a wheel. You notice that the only dance step that has a number is the first one, i.e., making contact. That step is always taken first, and we never stop doing it. After all, contact is the motor of change that gets the wheel of change moving and keeps it moving.

- The first step in the SoFAP tango is the invitation to the dance. Which step follows that first one depends on the situation. Of course, the order is never purely arbitrary; flexibility trumps all, and that flexibility comes mainly from "the leading party", the professional who uses his leadership mandate.
- Given the importance of the working relationship as a driver of change, the step of establishing and maintaining contact is present throughout the work cycle between professional and client.
- To accentuate the centrality of resources in the SoFAP approach, we present this resource orientation both as a separate step and as an ongoing process. Ergo its central position as the hub in the wheel of change.
- The SoFAP tango can be used in all circumstances where professionals are dealing with clients but also in collaboration with referring agencies, team members, family, coworkers, etc.
- Just like in the real tango, in the SoFAP tango you can make progress by moving sideways and even backwards. Except for step number one, making contact, you can dance backwards by using steps that you have already taken in previous moments in the interaction.

Overview of the seven-step SoFAP tango

- Establish contact
- Explore the context
- Goal setting
- Uncovering resources
- The Art of giving compliments
- Offer differentiation
- Future orientation

All steps are explained in detail and in a didactic order. Be aware that in the actual interaction process you will not use all the steps in this order, let alone all of them in every conversation. After all, you only take the steps that you consider useful at that time and in that situation.

Nevertheless, we always start with...

Step 1 Making contact

Making contact is an offer to get in touch with the person in the client by showing – through your actions and questions – that you are attentive to the person in the client and not just their problems or challenges.

Making contact is as easy to do, as it is easy to forget. Too often, professional change agents are so used to being in facilitation mode – it's their day job, after all – that they overlook the fact that entering a facilitative relationship is a new or – for some clients – a once-in-a-lifetime experience.

Making contact is very simple. You are friendly and courteous, show interest in the other person and offer yourself as an interlocutor at the service of the client.

Making contact is more than merely being friendly or acting nice all the time. Of course, there are myriad ways of socializing with other people. Just pick the ones that suit you the best, that you feel most comfortable with and that fit the client.

Establishing, ensuring, maintaining, and constantly updating an as good as possible contact creates the most constructive atmosphere of cooperation possible. This serves several purposes simultaneously. Besides the given that working in a positive atmosphere is enjoyable, a good relationship is more forgiving to the (unavoidable) glitches that we all make in human contact. Working toward change and growth can be difficult and requires, from time to time, tough decisions. Both taking, offering, and swallowing tough decisions is, however difficult, more acceptable if it happens in the context of a constructive working relationship.

The first meeting is important and sets the scene for the entire intervention. Contrary to the old belief that a working relationship requires time to build, SoFAP sees this differently and works on the relationship between the client and the professional from the very start.

Let's assume you meet a client for the first time. You can open the conversation with: "Welcome. Was it easy to find? Please, sit down. Allow me first to tell you a little about myself and the way I work. I will probably take some notes during our conversation, your name and address and some details. I'm not going to write down everything you tell me, because then we can't have an open conversation. And talking to each other is what our work here is all about. By the way, is this the first time you meet someone like me?"

In the first meeting, we have three possibilities.

CLIENT A: Yes. I have never met a professional like you. I find it quite exciting because I do not know what is going to happen.

PROFESSIONAL A: That is a big step you have taken, congratulations. The first step is often the hardest, but you have already taken it. Can I ask you some questions?

CLIENT B: No, not at all. I have already seen various professionals, but nothing has helped so far. I wonder if you can help me.

PROFESSIONAL B: Where do you get the courage to take the step to professional help again?

CLIENT B: I have no other choice. I am completely stuck.

PROFESSIONAL B: It is good that you have taken this courageous step again. Can I ask you some questions?

CLIENT C: If it were up to me, I would not be here at all, but my partner/boss/manager told me that refusing to talk to a professional would have serious negative consequences for me. There is nothing wrong with me. He is the one who is difficult.

PROFESSIONAL C: It is good that you are here, even if it is against your will. That is brave of you. Since you are here, can I ask you some questions?

The time to break the ice and establish contact does not have to be long. As a matter of fact, it happens in an instant.

A good working relationship is the motor for change.

As you remember from Chapter 2, where we explained what always works well, the working relationship accounts for 30% of the changes that occur in a professional encounter. Do I feel understood, respected as a person, being given the right amount of authentic attention that gives me the hope that change for the better is possible, are the determining factors that produce a beneficial outcome of every professional encounter which purpose it is to offer the client growth possibilities.

It is wise to invest time and energy to continuously monitor, hone, and strengthen the working relationship. By doing so, you open the SoFAP tango, and you demonstrate the style of the coming interactions without needing to explain your modus operandi.

Tips to enhance your working relationship

- Zoom in on the other's way of thinking and speaking and adjust to their language. If you seek effective communication with someone, it helps to speak the same language both verbally and nonverbally.
- Be quick, clear, and concise in your wordings.
- Show your commitment to the client, his resources and his needs for change and growth.
- Keep it simple. Reality is already complex enough.
- Build on whatever that you hear in the story of your interlocutor that is still or already working. All problem situations or challenges contain elements that can be built upon in constructive ways.
- Stay clear of the expert position where you (pretend to) know it all. Avoid the fantasy of being their savior ("Without me you can't do anything. I am indispensable because I am the key to your solutions."). Refrain from playing the role of an apostle ("I have seen the light, and if you do what I say you will be granted all thinkable successes."). Keep Carl Whitaker's famous words in mind: "Guard your missionary zeal or you will be eaten by the cannibals."

- Cooperate. You cannot work successfully in a vacuum. The professional always needs his client to build his own learning process. Thus, professional and client forge a T.E.A.M. that stands for: together everybody achieves more!
- Go slow and go with the flow. Take the time to allow your working relationship to develop from initial contact into ongoing cooperation.
- Evolution tops revolution.

Gradations in contact

When you say hello to your client in the parking lot, the intensity of your contact is different than when you talk to him in your office about his worries. Contact has a volume knob with which the intensity can be adjusted according to the circumstances. The needs of the client are the only deciding factor here and prevail over those of the professional. The more delicate, the more emotionally charged the situation, the higher the intensity. Careful attention to the signs of the client indicates the optimal intensity of your contact for these signs are his stage directions. Yet, more is not always better. The key is the appropriate intensity. Depending on the theme being discussed, this intensity can rise and fall during a conversation. The timing of this modulation is as important as the intensity of the contact.

Dr. Milton Erickson often said: "My voice will go with you". He obviously did not intent to say that he, as a person, was the guru that the client needed. The true meaning of this saying is that the voice of the professional, i.e., that what happened in the working relationship, can be incorporated in the resilience and the autonomy of the client. After a while, most clients forget the name of the professional while they remember what happened in their lives because of those encounters. And it is of no importance whether those memories are actually accurate or simply what the client chooses to remember.

> Furthermore, therapy should be a cooperative venture, the therapist contributing his skills and understandings and the patients contributing their own kind of responsiveness and their own capacities to utilize what can be proffered to aid them.[2]
>
> Milton H. Erickson

Step 2 Exploring the context

Nobody and nothing in life works in a vacuum. Everything and everyone we encounter; we encounter in a specific context. This context, determines, or at least greatly influences, how we perceive things. Even more, perception creates our reality: we (tend to) see what we believe, and we (tend to) believe what we see. When people are in trouble, their attention tends to narrow and move inwards.

Step 2 serves two purposes. First, by asking questions to explore the context, the client is invited to look outwards again and take notice of what is happening around him. This often is a first step out of the maelstrom of problem-fixation. Second, as we have seen in Chapter 1, where we discussed the axiom of systemic thinking, the context is the canvas on which life unrolls itself. The context influences and is influenced by whoever and whatever happens to play a part in it. Professionals, who use the SoFAP tools, are interested in this context because they know from the axiom of the resource orientation (Chapter 1) that the context shelters many useful elements that the client – with a little help from his friend the professional – can use to help himself.

After contact has been made (step 1), the following series of questions invites the client to focus outward and away from his problem-orientation and elicit information about his context. The attentive SoFAP professional listens to all answers with a keen ear for resources.

The basic context exploring question

> Can I ask you to tell me something about yourself first? How old are you? Are you single, married, in love, or engaged? Do you have children? What kind of work do you do? Just some information about you and your life.

Linguistic deconstruction of the basic context exploring question

Can I ask you	Permissive and invitational language
to first	"first" implicates that later there is room for other things
tell me something about yourself	"something" implicates that for the moment we expect little from the client and make it easy for him
How old are you? Are you single, married, in love, or engaged? Do you have children? What kind of work do you do?	For the client, this is factual knowledge that he has easily available. For the professional, these context elements contain resources
Just some information about you and your life.	Indicates that we are more interested in the factual world the client lives in than in his intrapsychic dynamics

Some clients will simply answer these questions. Some clients begin with a well-prepared litany about what all they are suffering from. That's not a problem. Their answer, like everything else they offer, contains a stage direction that tells us where their priorities are now. It makes it clear that they are motivated to offer the professional as much information as they think is relevant. It is respectful to allow the client the time to do this and – when the time is right – continue with: "You clearly are well prepared for this conversation. Very well! It's good of you to tell me how difficult it all is for you. Would you please be so kind to tell me something about yourself before we go on? Are you married or not? Do you have children? What kind of work do you do?".

Reassured by the word "first", all clients know that, when they feel the need to do so, there will be plenty of room to (continue to) talk about their problems later.

In fact, it does not matter how the client begins. This opening question is an indication that we are more interested in the person behind the client than in his problems. Since we know (from Chapter 2, What Always Works) that incorporating client factors and extra-therapeutic variables into the working relationship account for up to 70% of the change, we forge this working relationship by focusing on that information. That works better than being swept away – along with the client – by his problem analysis.

Some remarks:

- Working in a solution-focused mode by applying SoFAP should not allow the professional to become problem phobic, as this is disrespectful. Usually, their problems lead the client to talk to us, so it is natural for us to talk about their problems. Only we do it in a different way, with different perspectives and highlighting different aspects.
- In what is perhaps the most widely read book about solution-oriented therapy, "Interviewing for Solutions", the authors De Jong and Berg use the metaphor of an interview. This "interview" metaphor can lead to misunderstandings. It is quickly assumed that the therapist is taking a journalistic interview, collecting a lot of factual data, as is the case in a classical intake interview. Nothing could be less true! The SoFAP professional sees information as means for transformation: the process of change trumps the collection of facts.
- In a SoFAP conversation, questions and answers interweave: "Questions shape the answers you get that shape the questions you ask that…".
- This sequential cadence of question and answer creates a transformative dialogue.
- Problems are not solved by adding new information, but by rearranging what we already know.[3]

Step 3 Goal setting

The basic goal in SoFAP is not to diagnose, categorize, or create universal explanations for human psychological phenomena. The goal of SoFAP is to design and hone interventions that are useful for the client. Something is only useful if it presents the accomplishment of a goal. Without a goal, things can be nice to know, good to have, interesting to think about, challenging to explore. Such intellectual wanderings can, at best, prepare the ground for later useful developments but without a goal as teleological signpost, chances are slim that we arrive where we want to arrive. Forgetting to ask the goal setting question, or worse, thinking that it is not necessary to ask this fundamental question, will inevitably result in a trip that leads nowhere.

To paraphrase Steve de Shazer: "a conversation without a goal is like the ocean. The ocean is wide, deep, ever moving but going nowhere."

Which goals?

From the perspective of the facilitation mandate, the only goals that are worthwhile are the goals of the client. This is compatible with the basic axiom of the client orientation (Chapter 1).

These goals must, of course, remain within the bounds of what is permissible from a legal, deontological, ethical, medical, and public health perspective. Does this imply that the professional is not permitted to have his own goals? Of course, the professional has right to his own goals: he wants the sessions to start and end on time, that he doesn't waste time with clients who never show up, that the therapeutic agreements are met, that his administration is in order, etc. If the professional does not bother the client with his own goals, it is no problem to have them. But, as explained in Chapter 4, these are not facilitation goals but stem from his management mandate.

The basic goal setting question

The most basic and most powerful way to help the clients to turn their attention away from the quagmire of their problems and focus on what it is that they want for the future, is the following question:

> What do we need to talk about so that our conversation will be useful to you?

This question is a powerful tool for initiating goal setting. You can use this question at the beginning of each meeting to create focus on goals.

Linguistic deconstruction of the goal-setting question

The basic goal-setting question is simple. If we deconstruct the sentence, we discover its constructive components.

What do	Content and process
We	Collaboration as a T.E.A.M
Need	Imperative
To talk about	Language is our tool
So that	Indicates the direction
Our conversation	Action is in the interaction
Will	Future orientation and prediction
Be	Fixation
Useful	Utility value
To you	The client is the key person, the professional is a tool
? question mark	Answering the question creates ownership

The goal-setting question is a diamond with many facets:

- The question helps the client formulate and specify his goals
- The question puts the client where he belongs: in the center of the facilitation process
- The question helps the facilitator listen to the client rather than to his own good intentions
- What the client answers is important and useful because it forms the basis for the follow-up questions
- The follow-up questions invite the client to further specify and detail their goals
- During the cycle of questions and answers, the goals of the client become co-constructions of client and professional
- The answers to the goal setting question give the client responsibility over his goals

Useful goals checklist

SoFAP is an epistemological tool for the "lazy" professional who does not put his energy in finding solutions instead of his client but who puts all his energy in creating a context in which the client is facilitated to find his own strategies for achieving his own goals. Given the existence of two kinds of goals (useful and useless), SoFAP professionals prefer to concentrate on useful goals that, in contrast to useless goals, are:

1 Practical
2 Realistic
3 Realizable
4 Observable in behavioral terms
5 Preferably in a sequence from small to big

Whatever goals the client presents, the professional will ask questions to help the client improve the wordings of his goals so that they comply with the five characteristics of useful goals.

SMART versus solution-focused goals

The classic SMART stands for: Specific, Measurable, Acceptable or Achievable, Realistic and Time-bound.

The major difference between common SMART Goals and solution-focused Useful Goals is in the interpretation of the time-bound aspect. SMART is often used in organizational and/or managerial contexts where time is money and thus goals must be achieved within a certain period.

Solution-focused practice has to do with change in learning, or more profoundly, with change in learning-to-learn. A time limit often backfires in these situations. It is hard to set a time limit when you are striving for greater satisfaction, better working relationships, better responsiveness to changing circumstances in life and work, increasing resilience, etc.

Thus, within the working relationship that is based on contact (step 1) and with the information from the context (step 2), the professional's task is to accept whatever goal the client initially presents and then ask questions that help the client translate his original goals in terms of the Useful Goals checklist. When the client succeeds in doing this, this is change for the better and it immediately puts him on a promising road to change.

Though not all answers are useful, all answers are usable

Whatever the client answers to the goal-setting question, it always contains a stage direction that the professional can use to help the client to take the next step.

Basically, four possibilities arise in the answers.

First, the client simply says what his goal is. If he formulates his goals in theoretical, unrealistic, unrealizable, non-describable, and very large terms, this contains the stage direction: "ask me questions that help me translate what I strive for in terms of the useful goal checklist."

Second possibility is that the client responds with "I don't know". This can have several different meanings: I really don't know, I do not know yet, I do not want to tell you. Instead of interpreting this answer as resistance, we prefer to see it as a stage direction by which the client indicates that things may be moving a bit too fast for him and that he:

- needs more recognition about how difficult his situation is before he is ready to give a more substantial answer
- wants to tell a bit more about his context before he gets the impression of feeling understood
- does not know yet and that we should therefore ask more questions

Third, if he does not know (yet), the client sometimes answers the goal-setting question with very vague, cloud-like things like: "I'm not feeling OK. I'm stuck. I've tried everything and nothing seems to help. I'm spinning in circles. I have no self-confidence. I need to get to know myself better first. I want to be happy."

These answers contain a stage direction by which the client invites us to ask solution-building questions:

- What would be the smallest sign that you could notice that you were doing a little better? What would you think, do, feel differently then?
- If you had a little more self-confidence, how would those around you notice that?
- Are there moments when you are doing a tiny bit better? What is different then?
- What is the first sign that you will notice that you are getting to know yourself a little better?
- What could be the smallest sign so that you would notice that you are a little bit happy?
- What could be the next smallest step forward?

The fourth possible answer is also common. The generic version is: "I want to get rid of...". The professional then hears things like: I don't want any more arguing in my relationships, be it at home or at work. I don't want any more stress. I don't want to be jealous/aggressive/depressed anymore. I don't want to drink so much anymore. I don't want to be unhappy anymore. I no longer want this job. These are usable answers because they can easily be retranslated into useful goals. The basic question you can use here is, "What do you want *instead* of...?" We have numerous solution-building questions available on which many variations are possible:

- What would you want to happen in your relationship instead of arguing?
- What would you do differently if you experienced less stress?
- What will be different when you soon stop being so depressed and find satisfaction in your life again?

- By what would you like to replace that jealousy or aggressiveness?
- What will be different in your life if you drink less?
- When you are less unhappy, what will you do/think/feel differently?
- What other job would you like to embark on? Do you see another job opportunity in this company, or will you have to move on?

> The clinician should avoid fixating on what the client must stop doing. Growth-oriented therapy focuses on what the patient can start doing.[4]
>
> Milton H. Erickson

The client's answers guide the professional's next questions that help the client to articulate his vague goals in terms of the useful goals checklist. The fog of vagueness lifts. The way forward becomes visible. The client discovers concrete alternatives of what he does want instead of his problems. Hope then gives way to despair.

The co-creative question and answer cycle

The professional asks a question, and the client will answer. This answer determines the professional's next question. This question will then determine the client's subsequent answer.

This question-answer-question-answer cycle keeps unrolling itself, so that the goals of the client and the way toward them become co-constructions of the client and the professional.

As a result, both parties will find each other in the co-creative spiral we call "transformational dialogue" (Figure 5.2).

How to define a problem?

When you ask people to define a problem, you usually hear things like, "Something one wants to get rid of, something that bothers you, something that needs to be solved". Such a definition of a problem points to an existing situation and focuses the attention on what one does not want.

SoFAP prefers a different angle, asking, "What would you like instead?". The Formula-P tool, which defines a problem as a wish for change, operationalizes this approach. This wish for change may be expressed or tacit (for example, in the case of psychosomatic complaints). By asking the right solution-focused questions, the professional can help the client translate his wish for change into challenges. Each time a client formulates what problem

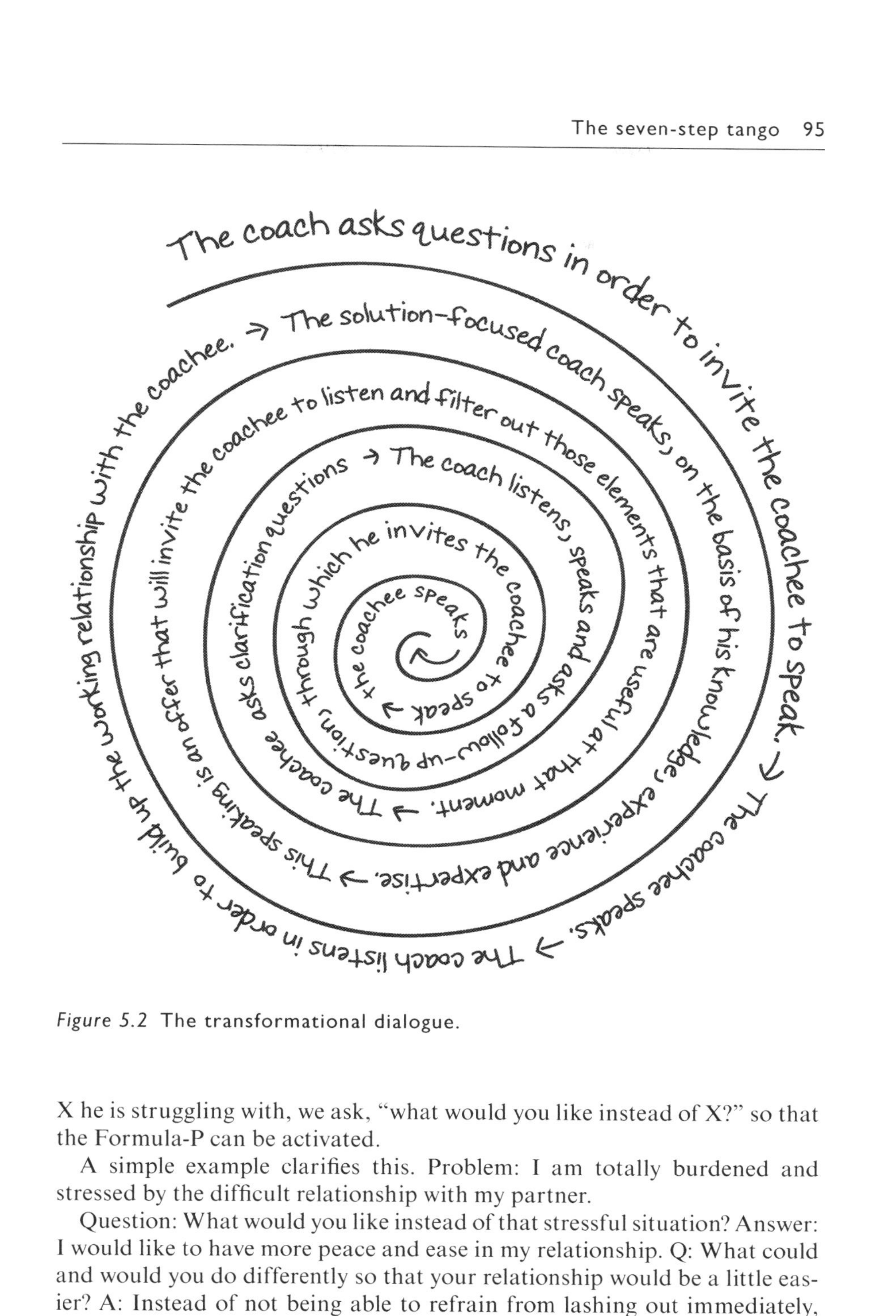

Figure 5.2 The transformational dialogue.

X he is struggling with, we ask, "what would you like instead of X?" so that the Formula-P can be activated.

A simple example clarifies this. Problem: I am totally burdened and stressed by the difficult relationship with my partner.

Question: What would you like instead of that stressful situation? Answer: I would like to have more peace and ease in my relationship. Q: What could and would you do differently so that your relationship would be a little easier? A: Instead of not being able to refrain from lashing out immediately, I would like to learn to take a few deep breaths first and then try to think of another way to respond. Q: What do you need to try this out? A: Maybe count to ten before I react and in the meantime think about whether there is no other response possible, even if that alternative is that I just leave the room for a few minutes.

By using Formula-P, we move from the initial problem (relational stress) through the "instead of" question about the wish for change (less stress by not acting in reflex) to the challenge (learning to use some time and distance).

This "Formula-P" is a tool for accepting problems as the client defines them without becoming mesmerized by them, then translating them into wishes for change that can finally be translated into challenges. The good news in this process is that problems are no longer annoying things to be avoided but are stepping-stones that lead to hopeful alternatives. In short, the more problems the better, because the more problems, the more desires for change and the more exciting the challenges.

The dynamics between goals and context

Goal setting is an interactive activity that doesn't happen in a single shot. On the contrary, goal setting is a continuous process. Every time a (partial) goal is reached or failed, the next line of goals is adapted according to this new information. Goal setting as a continuous process is an important idea because it helps us not to fall into the trap of thinking that once a goal is set, it's there to stay forever.

The clearer the goals are, the more visible the path to reaching them becomes. As you move toward your goal, the landscape through which you travel changes. In other words, the small steps toward the goals change the context in which the facilitation process takes place. Goal setting is an iterative process that continues to unfold along with the client's learning progress. In SoFAP work, there is a continuous alternation between the goal setting (step 3) and the context clarification (step 2). Once a goal is reached, other things from the context can become important and morph into another goal. The task of the professional is to help the client to learn from small partial solutions so that he becomes able to create his own broader solutions. The client learns to build solutions instead of merely solving problems. The facilitation can stop when the client has learned to learn.

> Long experience in psychotherapy has disclosed the wisdom of avoiding perfectionistic drives and wishes on the part of patients and of motivating them for the comfortable achievement of lesser goals. This then ensures not only the lesser goal but also makes more possible the easy output of effort that can lead to a greater goal. Of even more importance is that the greater accomplishment then becomes more satisfyingly the patient's own rather than a matter of obedience to the therapist.[5]
>
> Milton Erickson

More than facilitation

To avoid the trap of simplism, we must stress that we always have more mandates at the same time than just the facilitation mandate.

When the client indicates that he is not (yet) able or prepared to accept facilitation, the professional can, in specific cases, use his leadership and management mandate to suggest goals instead of the client. Please remember that when this is necessary, it has less to do with facilitation than, in the best of hope, it is preparing the scene to make facilitation possible. We explained the dynamics of the three mandates in Chapter 4 and return to them in Chapter 6, where we discuss what to do when the client does not formulate goals and thus has no help request.

The mother of all goals: growth, well-being and contentment

What is it that man expects from life? What is it that every person strives for? What is the purpose of our existence? These existential questions have captivated philosophers and religious leaders for centuries. If you boil down all the possible answers to these existential questions to their essence, perhaps the answer is: growth toward well-being and contentment. Growth as humans, both individually, as a group and as a society, gives meaning and significance to our existence. Well-being is the state of experiencing health, happiness, and prosperity. Contentment as in "count your blessings" is so much more rewarding than the constant happiness treadmill of ever-changing and ever-increasing desires.

> For Daddy [LC: Milton Erickson] the purpose of life is to be happy, healthy, and wealthy.[6]
>
> Betty Alice Erickson

We cannot strive for happiness directly, but the feelings of happiness, or rather, an increased sense of well-being, are epiphenomena when we live a more committed life full of meaning and purpose.

Realism please

SoFAP professionals are not happiness gurus who, dressed in a white robe and singing amidst a field of fragrant flowers, chant the code word for eternal bliss. SoFAP professionals are people of integrity whose job it is to *help* their clients find *their* way out of the quagmire of human problems by setting goals and leveraging their resources as building blocks for a meaningful life of well-being and contentment.

You want patients to realize that illness is only part of their total life experience. No matter what the illness, patients can always find something to appreciate about themselves. People are entitled to look upon their illness, or pain, as part of the meaningfulness of life. They ought not to feel that it is something to be frightened of. Why should any patient be frightened by any type of illness of disability? They have so much else to enjoy. In therapy, your approach should be to help them understand that they brought into your office a lot more than cancer, or arthritis, or any other type of problem. In talking to them you should convey to them an awareness of all other gifts they have.'[7]

Milton H. Erickson

Step 4 Uncovering resources

We detailed in Chapter 1 that the resource orientation is at the heart of SoFAP. Although described as a separate step, discovering resources happens all the time. As you can see in the drawing of the wheel of change, resources are the hub that connects all the steps of the solution tango.

The basic axiom, we repeat, is that every human system, be it an individual, a family, or a group of whatever constellations, always has resources at its disposal, even in times of trouble. Problem- oriented models run on the assumption that problems arise due to deficiencies. This is in stark contrast with SoFAP where problems are seen as an indication that the concerned parties have momentarily lost confidence in their own solution-focused possibilities, simply because they have lost the access to their own resources. You might say that they have (temporarily) lost their personal manual on "how to use our resources". The resources, that they always have available, need to be uncovered, discovered, or rediscovered.

The task of the SoFAP professional is to help the client(s) (re)discover their "forgotten" resources and/or to give them new tools for building solutions. In this context, we define "resources" as "every available tool that can be used to create solutions and support growth, well-being and contentment". Resources can be intangible such as intelligence, motivation, loyalty and warm relationships, experience and expertise, commitment, patience, resilience, introspective ability, social skills, etc. Resources can also be material things such as: a house, living (albeit rather uncomfortable) under a bridge, to have work or not, being single or in a relationship, a close family and friendship bond or isolation, sufficient wealth, access to the Internet, etc.

Remembering the story of the half-full and half-empty bottle, we know that things that at first glance seem purely negative can be retranslated into strengths. A personal loss, if properly processed, can be turned into acceptance; being temporarily unemployed can mean finally being able to pursue that education or devote more time to your family members; blind people usually hear and taste much better, etc. Weaknesses become strengths, threats become challenges, a crisis becomes an opportunity if you deal with it in the appropriate way.

A respectful attitude necessitates recognizing the pain that problems bring. Being human sometimes brings pain and every human being needs acknowledgment for his personal situation. Whether an elderly woman is grieving the loss of her lapdog or a young woman is grieving the loss of her child should make no difference in how the professional approaches her. Professionals who, out of personal belief, think the old lady's situation is less dire than the young woman's situation will have a hard time providing the old lady with the proper care she deserves, and he should refer that client to a professional who is able to give her the necessary support.

The absolute condition for professional care, therapy, coaching is to act with respect for each client, whatever his problems may be.

Understanding what resources are and appreciating their importance as the fuel for change, is the backbone of the solution-focused applied psychology approach.

Some remarks

- SoFAP professionals are only concerned with uncovering resources that – albeit under cover – are present. It makes no sense to try to talk the client into a resource that he does not have at all
- Nobody is able nor should strive to be able to use all his resources at any time in any circumstance. Reaching for perfection is futile
- Resources are especially useful when they fit the goal of the moment
- Nurture big dreams but put your energy into small goals
- What is a resource for Peter need not be one for Paul and vice versa

This resource-oriented attitude is a perfect antidote to a paralyzing problem fixation. By asking the right questions you can help the other person to (re) find the access to his resources. Sometimes you find resources in places that are so obvious that you forget to look for them.

Overview of the resource locations

1 The waiting list as a resource
2 Pre-session changes
3 Resources from the non-problematic context
4 Exceptions to the problems

The resource locations in detail

As you study these 4 locations, you will find that the first two locations precede the actual facilitation process and yet reveal interesting resources if one takes the trouble to question those pre-facilitation moments. Location 3 collects resources in locations that are peripheral to the coaching or therapy process. Location 4 describes the classical solution-focused approach that was the first intervention model that worked on the client's problems from a radically different perspective, namely from those moments when the problem was absent, less, or different.

The waiting list as a resource

For years, there's been a lot of commotion about the long waiting lists in our field. There are a lot of (inter)national studies on waiting lists, but the figures are not always comparable because of its political and social connotations. The numbers, although they vary from year to year and from subsector to subsector, remain impressive in negative terms. An example: in 2007, the average waiting period with the Dutch Association of Mental Health and Addiction Care[8] was (on average) three weeks from the first contact to the intake interview. And five weeks between the intake and the actual start of the treatment. This means that the average client, from the moment he mustered up the courage to contact someone, must wait 11 weeks before he can get help. And that is very long when you are struggling with problems.

When clients can eventually start their treatment after a waiting period of 11 weeks, a lot of them don't show up. These no-show-figures have never been researched in depth. Therefore, they vary from 75%[9] (which seems unrealistic) to only 10%[10] (which seems too optimistic). What the research clearly explains, is that most of these no-shows, gave up, simply because … (drum roll to mount the tension) it took too long. Researchers and policy-makers pay a lot of attention to the cost of these no-shows, the lost time of the professionals and the negative organizational impact on the mental health care providers. The result is that the organization becomes (even) less efficient and that clients must deal with the perverse effect of even longer waiting lists.

However, what we are interested in is what exactly happens to these no-shows. The little research that is available confirms our own experience: most of them are simply – and quite rightly so – disappointed. A large part reports that they have either sought help elsewhere (where it is faster available) or "they have tried to help themselves. Most no-shows put their own resilience to work and move on with their lives".[11]

To reduce the number of no-shows, the service provider must show some customer-friendliness. This can be done by simply keeping in touch. Studies of medical no-shows prove that numbers reduce drastically if clients are reminded of their appointment by a text, phone call, or letter. It gives them the feeling that the therapist on whom they pinned their hopes is concerned for the good of his clients, even when a lot of time passes before the "real" help starts.

What works even better is reducing the time between the first contact and the moment the therapy starts. In a private practice this is not difficult: you have your own schedule and method. In a big organization, it is often more difficult because a client first must go through four stages: "contact – intake – indication – treatment" before he can start working on his issues.

Instead of cursing this red tape, you had better do something more useful. What would happen if an organization decided to react as follows when a client contacts them for the first time: "Thank you for making the effort to call us. It's good that you took a step in the right direction to find help. We apologize for the approximately two weeks waiting time before your first appointment. Would you like to get started in the meantime? Would you mind checking whether there are some changes in your problems in the coming weeks? These can be small things, for example, moments when you have less problems or circumstances in which you don't attach too much importance to your problems. You could help us by taking notes, so we can discuss them during our first therapy session. Thank you and take care".

A Dutch organization that specializes in the treatment of addictions, experimented with a solution-focused protocol for clients during their waiting time.[12] This resulted in such a significant decline in no-shows that the organization decided to implement this "reduce-the-no-shows-through-solution-focused-simple-interventions"– exercise throughout the complete company. The results are significant on a variety of levels: financial improvement, higher client satisfaction, less idle time for the professionals, higher work motivation in the staff, less personnel turnover, less absenteeism.

When it comes to waiting lists, we adopt the rule: Avoid waiting lists when possible. If unavoidable, use what happens during the waiting time as a resource.

Pre-session changes

From the moment someone considers seeking help and thus becomes a client, self-motivation and self-care begins. In other words, their resilience kicks in. At that point, a virtual facilitation relationship is created.

Individuals who are so desperate that they do not even think about seeking help are often people who are convinced that help and/or change are not possible for them. These are ordinary people with a lot of problems. But they are not clients, because they do not seek contact with a therapist.

Once you have those people in your practice, they become clients. The therapeutic dance begins. Clients have already done some preliminary work: they realize that change is possible, they have already made the first step and – most of the time – thought about what they want to tell us. The average client thinks that the therapist is interested in a detailed description of "the how and why" of his complaints.

SoFAP therapists know that a waiting period can be a resource and zoom in on it by asking the *pre-session change question*: "Have you already noticed some changes between today and the moment you picked up the phone to make this appointment?"

Research shows that approximately 40% either say that nothing has changed or even that it got worse. This is not a problem as these clients simply want to show us that they are having a difficult time and they want to be recognized as such.

The other 60%[13] are surprised at first, but they will tell you what has already changed, even if it is only a little bit. In most cases, changes are small: we have been arguing less, the children knew we were coming to therapy and that may have calmed them down. Just the idea of me taking the step to come here has given me some courage, etcetera.

Clients who mention such "pre-session changes" have a better chance of a successful therapy. The wheel of change has already started turning and we just need to encourage these clients. Pre-session change is an excellent breeding ground for further change.

Resources from the non-problematic context

Resources can be found in situations where the client is functioning well despite his difficulties. Everyone has a life outside of his problems. In spite of occasional problems and hindrances, all clients have families, neighbors, friends, they are members of a club, they have colleagues at work, they meet people at the convenience store, they are members of a church, and so on. As do we professionals, for that matter. We all have resources at our disposal, which we use in all these circumstances. Yet, we often "forget" these resources when faced with overwhelming problem situations. If we ask the right questions when clarifying the context (step 2 of the Solution Tango), we can dig up a lot of resources that the client not only has available, but also actually uses, in non-problematic situations.[14]

To get access to these existing yet covered resources, we can use questions like:

- Would you be so kind as to tell me something that works well/good enough in your life?

- Despite all your problems, what are the things in life that you cherish and want to keep as they are?

Developing a keen eye for resources is like developing a keen eye when you are picking mushrooms in the wild. The untrained eye sees none, while the trained eye finds many. Once you know how to look for them, it is quite easy to find more and more.

If you share this skill with your clients, they too will develop the same keen eye. Despite being somewhat blinded by their problems, this will help your clients find resources in the folds of life.

You will be surprised how quickly the client starts using his resources (again) as soon as you point them out to him. In this way, you will create a virtuous cycle that will increase the client's self-confidence, with the result that the client will increasingly use his existing resources, even after his change agents is no longer needed or present.

Exceptions to the problems

There is no problem conceivable, except death or pregnancy – which are not problems but limitations – that presents itself 24/24–365/365 in the same way. Sometimes it is worse, sometimes it is less, sometimes it is different. Every problem has exceptions, times when the problem manifests itself in a slightly different way or not at all. Those exceptions interest us greatly because it is in those moments that the problem bearer produces partial solutions. These are the moments when he is apparently able to rediscover and reuse (at least part of) his resources. By asking the right exception questions, the resources are "uncovered". Asking follow-up questions creates a solution-building effect. Such questions help the other person to focus their attention on the "who, when, and how" of the exceptions. Further questioning though, makes this more concrete and we know: the more concrete, the better.

Useful solution-building questions are:

- What still works well/good enough despite your problems?
- What did you do differently when your problem was less/different/absent?
- Who in your relationship network did what differently when the problem wasn't as big as it is now?
- What would your partner/colleague/coworker say you do differently when your problem is less intense?
- What worked best when you solved a similar problem in the past?
- What were you doing differently during then?

The answers to these solution-building questions are filled to the brim with resources. When you systematically ask more and more details about the exception, you will find that these exceptions grow and thereby you enhance the chain reaction of intensifying solutions. Chances are high that the problem will dissolve itself.

Caveat: technique can become a hindrance

Strict adherence to the technical definition that something should only be considered a problem if there are exceptions to it can lead to solution-focused fundamentalism. When a professional succumbs to this fallacy, he no longer listens to the customer, but, with the best of intentions, gets in his way.

PROFESSIONAL: "Are there moments when you are less bothered by your problem?"
CLIENT: "No, it's a disaster and it's getting worse".
PROFESSIONAL: "Think carefully. There must be circumstances in which you have had a little less trouble in the past period".
CLIENT: "No way".
PROFESSIONAL: "Yes".
CLIENT: "No"...

As the professional becomes bogged down in his relentless search for exceptions, the client feels less and less understood and might even insist that it is becoming a bigger disaster by the minute.

The antidote to this fixation on exceptions is, as always, our constant alertness to the fact that everything our client offers us contains stage directions. In this case, the client is trying to tell us that he needs something else first before he will, can, or wants to talk about exceptions. First, the client needs recognition of the fact that he is in a difficult position that weighs heavily on him. When he feels understood after he has received sufficient recognition of his suffering, only then does it become possible to take the next step.

When this happens, we can take a step back to jump further and ask: "Have there been times in the past when things were even much worse than they are today?" The client, reassured that the professional is trying to understand him, answers, "Last Monday was a total catastrophe". Then invite the client to tell you something about that total catastrophe and continue with: "How did that lessen a little bit so that today it's a little more bearable?".

Alternatively, one could take a step back and return to context clarifying questions (step 2), pay attention to other resources (step 4), or consider whether the goal should not be set more sharply (step 3).

Step 5 Appreciation or the art of giving compliments

The basic SoFAP attitude is to emphasize the client's resources in an appreciative way and in the language of the client. By providing appropriate compliments on the resources the client can use to achieve their goals, you automatically strengthen the working relationship and help the client focus on steps toward solutions.

Words are magic

Compliments originates from the Latin "complere", meaning "to complete", over the Italian "complimento", meaning "expression of respect and civility" into the English "an expression of praise or admiration".

Appreciation originates from the Latin "appretiare" meaning "to set a price to", evolves from the French "appreciation" meaning "the act of estimating the quality and worth of something" into the English "appreciation" meaning "to set a just value on which implies the use of wise judgment or delicate perception".

In the SoFAP context, the meaning of the words appreciation and complementing is giving value to those things that are valuable to our clients.

Other languages have beautiful expressions for this. In German, the word for compliment is "Wertschätzung" that is composed of "Wert", meaning "value" and Schätzung meaning "estimation". In Dutch, the word is "waarderen" that is composed of "waarde" meaning value and "eren" meaning "to honor".

Compliments are tools for expressing our appreciation not only for who the client is as a person in his context, but also, and perhaps especially, for the client's behavior by which he demonstrates his ability and willingness to take responsibility for his life. We can define "taking responsibility for his life" as "learning to use his resources to find solutions to the infinite stream of problems (which can be translated into challenges) that life represents and thus achieve his goals, ranging from everyday problems to a meaningful life of well-being and contentment."

Why and how do compliments work?

Every person is sensitive to compliments. We all love a pat on the back, a word of encouragement, a sincere heartfelt comment on something that is important to us. Being kind and courteous feels nice, both for the person doing it and for the recipient of such behavior. It strengthens our relationships.

Careful examination of what makes complimenting such a powerful tool, leads us back to Chapter 2 (what always works) and Chapter 3 (Basic rules).

Authentic attention to our clients shows our commitment and that is a compliment with which we show them in word and behavior that we put them at the center of the working relationship. When we then also show the client that, in addition to acknowledging their difficulties and pain, we also pay attention to their resources by pointing them out, we direct their attention in that direction. Thus, we not only show our active engagement with them as human beings, but also honor the value of their strengths and what they can do with them to help themselves.

As professionals, we don't compliment clients in hopes of being seen as mister Nice Guy. If our clients like us, of course, that's a nice bonus, but that's not really the point. What really matters is that our compliments have a utility value for the clients: it helps them to keep doing what they are already doing that works and to do more of what works better.

Some of the active ingredients of complimenting are:

- You show the client that you pay attention to what he does that works well
- You distract the client's focus away from his problem fixation
- You build and expand a constructive working relationship
- You strengthen the client's self-image and self-confidence
- You nudge the client toward possible solutions
- You create a context and ambience of trust and cooperation
- You invite, help, and support the client to tap into his own resources to do more of what works

Necessary conditions for compliments

> One should not compliment patients for acting normal.[15]
>
> Milton H. Erickson

There are several capital important conditions that your compliments must meet if they are to be useful to clients:

- You must mean what you say and if you don't mean what you say, shut up. Compliments therefore must be sincere, authentic, and respectful.
- Your compliments must be relevant to the situation
- Your compliments, like resources, must be based on reality
- There is no point in exaggerating or smothering clients with compliments
- Compliments hit the mark best and thus have maximum efficacy when they are precisely tailored to the situation and the recipient.
- If the compliment is precisely tailored and appropriate, then more is always less and less is usually more (Figure 5.3).

What I see sometimes is the amateurs, so to speak – the beginners, who somehow think more is better and therefore, they give this endless stream of compliments and bore the client silly with them and therefore the client stops taking them seriously. That's one thing I see happen with beginners. There are just too damn many compliments and that will drive the client away.[16]

Steve de Shazer

Formula G-R-C

As important as compliments and showing appreciation are, they can only be a start. If they are not linked to resources that the client can use to obtain his goals, compliments disappear like smoke in the wind, leaving no trace.

To reinforce the Minimax motto (minimum effort for maximum output), we apply the G-R-C formula that creates change power by interlocking three SoFAP essences: **G**oals, **R**esources and **C**ompliments. The GRC Formula is a mnemotechnic tool that links the goals of the client with the specific

Figure 5.3 Formula G-R-C.

resources that will help him obtain his goals. In other words, compliments are only relevant when they activate the client's resources that will help him achieve his goals. All three components must be present and linked if your efforts are to lead to success.

Every relevant compliment pays a dividend.

So, if you encounter a situation where you have the impression that progress is absent, you can use the GRC Formula to determine in which component you are working sub-optimally and adjust accordingly.

In summary, Minimax will not work if:

- No clear goals = no clear direction
- No resources = no fuel in the motor of change
- No compliments = no ignition in the motor of change

In essence, Minimax will work if:

- Useful goals create a clear direction for change
- Resources appropriate to the purpose fuel the change
- Fitting compliments activate the resources

Giving compliments has nothing to do with:

- Flattery because it is unauthentic, unrespectful, and always counterproductive.
- Trivialization or minimization of the painful experiences with which you try to coerce the client to anesthetize his real problem.
- Blindly accepting whatever the client says or does while excluding giving due criticism.

Metaphor, not protocol

Before we go any further, let's remember that the solution tango is not a rigid protocol, but a metaphor in which creativity and customization determine which step you take and when.

Summary

Contact (step 1) is the motor of change, context (step 2) is the territory through which you travel together with the client, goal setting (step 3) is the satellite navigator, resources (step 4) are the fuel in the engine, and compliments (step 5) are the turbo that gives the engine of change and well-being more power.

To effect change, the professional and client must travel together in the vehicle of a constructive and cooperative working relationship. Clear directions show the shortest possible path to the goals. Since Alfred Korzybski, we know that the map is not the territory. So, we accept that even though the map shows the shortest path between two points as a straight line, the actual journey may be a curved, twisted, iterative, and recursive one. More fuel allows, if necessary or unavoidable, to make more detours, thus travel further and still arrive at the goal. Compliments are the turbo on the motor of change and when the change is in motion, one does not necessarily need a turbo.

These five steps reflect a basic SoFAP attitude and represent the solution-focused epistemology. The coming two steps, offering differentiation and future orientation contain more technical aspects of the SoFAP approach.

Step 6 Offering differentiation

People who feel they are in deep misery tend to think and speak in black and white terms. The tendency to think in extremes causes people to quickly fall into an "either-or" trap. One feels good or bad, one is perfectly happy or deathly unhappy, everything is going superbly or not at all. The light is on, or the light is off.

This binary thinking, of course, is not true; there is more under the sun than just good or bad. We know that life is not lived in black and white, but in a seemingly endless series of grays and colors: sometimes things get a little worse AND then they get a little better. Step 6 offers you a more differentiated way of thinking, where the concept of "and-and" replaces the "or-or" trap. This offers you greater freedom of thought, feeling, and action in dealing with self and others.

Indiscriminate black and white thinking quickly leads to the fallacy that a problem is not solved until it is eliminated. Unfortunately, it is not so simplistic. Haven't we all had to learn through trial and error that perfection is an illusion? The quest for perfect happiness that translates into a 100% problem-free life is an extremely frustrating endeavor that inevitably leads to failure.

> Perfection is not a human attribute.[17]
>
> Milton H. Erickson

Except for life or death, pregnant or not, most things in life are not or-or. We have several tools to help us find nuances in life:

1 Relativization
2 Differentiating questions
3 Scaling questions

Relativization

To relativize means to put something in relation to something else, so that it gets its proper proportions. In simpler language: putting things in perspective. Or even simpler: using common sense.

Examples of questions and comments that provoke relativization: "Are you sure you're not exaggerating a bit?" "Don't we all have difficult days from time to time?" "Wouldn't it be better to sleep on it first before making a drastic decision?" "Tomorrow there is another day!" "After rain comes sunshine".[18]

This is what family and friends do when they meet a relative in distress. They listen for a while and then offer a relativizing comment in the hope of putting things in perspective. It also happens at work. Imagine you are a new employee, and your boss gives you an unexpected snarl. Before long, someone on your new team will say: "Don't mind. When he is stressed, he always does that. You will see, soon he will come around and apologize".

If this method works, you are done. Unfortunately, in response to this commonsense intervention, many people react by stating that their problems are really very serious, and they feel the need to repeat their black and white ideas. The stage direction here is that they may have been offered these relativizing remarks many times before, without success. On the contrary, they do not feel understood by their interlocutor and therefore repeat their point of view. When you encounter this reaction, it is best to use basic rule number 1 from Chapter 3, "if something doesn't work, do something else."

Differentiating questions

This type of questions elicits answers that go beyond the binary "on or off". You can ask more detailed questions about each answer, allowing the client to clarify and elaborate on their own nuances, upon which the professional can proceed to ask follow-up questions.

Some examples:

- When did things go a little better than they do now?
- What was different then?
- What did you do differently then?
- How did your family members/colleagues/friends react when things were a little better?
- If I could ask them now, what would they tell me?
- Were there times when things were much worse than they are now?
- How did you deal with it then?
- What did you do to make it more bearable?

- When do you have times when things are going well in your life?
- What do you feel most comfortable with?

It is useful to deconstruct these questions, for then you will discover the operating principles behind their apparent obviousness.

- The client will feel more taken seriously because implicit in the questions is the acknowledgment of his difficulties and we know from Chapter 2 on "What always works" that this helps the client to feel understood.
- Answers to differentiating questions contain more useful information than the mere detailed description of misery.
- The questions invite your client to look at his situation from a different perspective and automatically focus his attention on what is going well or better.
- The answers inevitably imply the possibility of change in a constructive direction.

Differentiating questions become solution-building interventions. The professional is the architect of the questions, while the client is the builder of his own house of solutions and well-being.

Scaling questions

When the first two tools for offering differentiation do not produce results, or do not produce enough results to work with, one of the iconic techniques that the solution-focused approach has developed is the use of scaling questions.

Scaling questions, along with the Miracle Question that we will encounter later, are the iconic techniques in the classical solution-focused approach. Scaling questions and the Miracle Question are holograms of the solution-focused way of thinking and working. Unfortunately, it happens all too often that the entire solution-focused approach is reduced to these techniques. Then, these innovative techniques become tricks and the richness of the solution-focused epistemology evaporates. However, if the client reports that he is helped by these techniques because they match his needs and abilities, then the mere use of techniques, even if simplified to artifice, is sufficient. We must only be careful that simplism does not degenerate into naive foolishness: "if I push here, it hurts there. What to do? Do no longer push".

The basic scaling question goes like this: "Imagine if I asked you to give a number on a scale where the starting point, the zero, stands for X (to be filled in according to the specific situation and the specific scale you want to use) and the 10 stands for Y (ditto), where are you now?"

0-----------------------10

In Chapter 7, you will not only learn the many different types of scaling questions that are appropriate for many different situations, but you will also be introduced to the linguistic deconstruction of the change mechanism hidden in scaling questions.

Some salient points concerning the scaling questions

1 Steve de Shazer and Insoo Kim Berg used both techniques in every conversation, over and over. You can do the same, but you don't have to.
2 We prefer to define the starting point as "the worst thing you've ever experienced, the point at which you decided to go for help". We define the end point, as "then it's good enough so that you no longer need help, and you can handle things in life yourself".
3 Whatever number the client gives, accept, and ask, "what is already different so you can give yourself an X?". Proceed with follow-up questions to invite details.
4 Steve de Shazer said, "You can never know what is good, but you can always know what is better". We turn that into: "You can never know what is good, but you can always know what is different".
5 The number the client gives is not a mathematical expression of improvement but only a metaphor of difference. If you do use the numbers as a mathematical expression, then the numbers on a scaling question become grades on a scorecard: 0 is very bad and 10 is the maximum of the points. Scorecards are normalized, meaning that an external body has determined what is bad and good. In our professional context, there are no external bodies that standardize the result. It is the client, his progress and his satisfaction that is the evaluator. In fact, we help the client so that he does not impose standards on himself but learns to accept that good enough is "the norm".
6 Asking a scaling question implies that difference and therefore change is possible.
7 Scaling questions are contentless: the client himself only finds out what the given number means to him when we ask about it. Mindful of the motto that change works best on what is already there, we always ask first what is in the given number.
8 The subsequent magical "What else" – question elicits answers that:

- Invite the client to tell himself what is already different,
- Help the client to specify his original answer as concretely as possible and in vivid detail,
- Invite the client to discover the next possible step,
- Help the client become aware that his resilience is greater than he himself thinks,

- Give the client hope that there are alternative ways to move forward,
- Imply that, if the given number is higher than zero, something different is already present on which he can build further.
- Make it increasingly easy for the professional to acknowledge and compliment the client for (the use of) his own resources

9 The follow-up question, "what could be the smallest next step?" indicates that small steps are more likely to be achievable than large leaps.
10 Clients who already use differentiation and nuance in their lives do not need additional differentiation.

While problem-focused models all too often see black-and-white thinking clients as troublesome obstructionists, solution-focused change agents know that clients with binary visions of life are constantly giving us stage directions about how to help them think more differentially.

Step 7 Future orientation

Long live the future

SoFAP has several reasons to be more interested in the future than in the past:

1 Because the past is, well... past, it is a waste of time and energy to try to change it. One cannot rewrite pages in the Book of Life, let alone tear pages out of it. In this sense, the past is a limitation[19]: it is what it is, and you must deal with it.
2 How you deal with your past today and in the light of tomorrow is a problem for which a solution is conceivable. The Formula-P teaches us that a problem contains a wish for change that that can be turned into a challenge by asking the right questions.
3 The consequences of a limitation are a problem for which a solution is conceivable, while the limitation itself cannot be solved. An example: If you have become disabled because of an accident, you cannot get rid of that disability. However, you can learn to cope with the consequences of that disability, so that you suffer as little as possible.
4 Both for problems from the past and for those of today, the solutions are de facto hidden in the future. If we already had the solution now, what we encounter would not be a problem. Then we would not need to spend time and energy on it, and we could better use that time and energy to work on our growth, well-being, and contentment.
5 Asking future-oriented questions is an important marker that focuses the client's attention on the desired future rather than on analyzing past problems.

> We must be careful because what we don't ask is often more powerful than what we do ask. That is why in therapy it is dangerous when we do not ask patients about their future. This sends the message that they don't have one. And it is very difficult to defend yourself from a message of which you are not consciously aware.[20]
>
> Yvonne Dolan

Realism please

People who worry constantly and obsessively about problems that might crop up in the future are often unhappy brooders or hypochondriacs with low levels of well-being. It is better not to fixate on problems we might encounter in the future.

Nevertheless, it is wise to occasionally dwell on the unpleasant things that life may have in store for us. In this way we ensure that we always have our resilience ready, even if we don't need it at the time. After all, we also take out health insurance when we are healthy. Ditto for fire insurance, life insurance, and car insurance. Occasionally dwelling on the fact that on our life path we inevitably and periodically (will) encounter things that are unpleasant, can remind us how good we have it for the moment.

Solution-focused thinking is in stark contrast to positive thinking, a way of thinking that – if you really want it, if you love all people enough, and if you see the positive in everything – you can achieve anything. With positive thinking, you can win the Olympic marathon even if you are 99 years old. We don't believe in that, and neither does Milton Erickson:

> Erickson's original (future oriented, red.) formulation requires that the future imagined is a reflection of a nascent personal direction that already awaits fulfilment; not some unrealistic fantasy.[21]
>
> Ernie Rossi

Solution-focused applied psychology is not a denial of the negative we encounter in our lives, does not turn a blind eye to the badness in some people, and does not want to make our lives in this earthly vale of tears into a trip to a paradisiacal amusement park. What makes life difficult often precedes that which gives us the most satisfaction.

> So, I have discussed how our complex emotional experiences sometimes blend the positive and negative, how optimism is most meaningfully apparent when we think about setbacks and failures, how crises can reveal our strengths of character, how ongoing challenges are a prerequisite for us to experience flow in the moment and to achieve something important in a lifetime, and how relationships success is foreshadowed not by the absence of problems but by how we resolve those that arise.[22]
>
> Christopher Petterson

The past is a resource

More interest in the future than in the past does not, of course, preclude interest in the past. Whereas classical problem-oriented models consider the past as the hiding place of the problem causes, SoFAP takes a different perspective. So, what does interest us about the past?

1 From the systemic axiom (Chapter 1) and as discussed in step 2 of the solution tango (clarifying the context, page 99), we know that everything that happened in the past is an important part of the context in which we live today. We'd better not pretend that every day pops up out of nowhere. You can only reap today's day if it emerges from yesterday and grows toward tomorrow.
2 In the central step 4 of the solution tango (resource orientation), we learned that the past is a giant repository of resources and exceptions. If things go wrong today, it matters less what happened yesterday. What matters is what we learn from what went wrong yesterday so that we can address it more easily today.
3 Moreover and perhaps most importantly, the past contains more moments when things went well (enough) than it has peak moments or setbacks. Peaks are fun, setbacks are not, but both are part of life.

> Emphasis should be placed more upon what the patient does in the present and will do in the future than upon a mere understanding of why some long-past event occurred. The sine-qua-none of psychotherapy should be the present and the future adjustment of the patient, with only that amount of attention to the past necessary to prevent a continuance or a recurrence of past maladjustments.[23]
>
> Milton H. Erickson

Two major tools to offer future orientation

How do you help those who entrust themselves to your care to focus on their own desired future instead of remaining stuck in the past and the futile search for what caused the problems? How do you use the virtual reality of a desired future in today's reality?

Future orienting questions

The simplest way is by asking questions that allow the others to "retroject" possible solutions from the future into the reality of today.

The goal-setting question from step 3 forms the basis of this: "What do we need to discuss *today* so that this conversation *will* be useful to you?"

Some additional future orientation questions are:

- What would you like to see different and how will you notice that?
- What will be the first signs that you are making a little progress toward what you want to achieve?
- What will you then do, think, and feel differently?
- How will your friends, parents, colleagues notice?
- Imagine that a year has passed, and your problem has become manageable again – what will you do differently?

Some refinements

- What would you like to achieve in your life?
- What do you dream about?
- What do you expect from the future?
- What will make you notice that you are living the life that gives you satisfaction?
- How will you remind yourself in the future that good enough is better than best?
- What will you do to make those close to you feel good?
- What will you do today so that there is a good chance you will be satisfied with it?
- What can you do for someone else today so that that other person's satisfaction will make you satisfied yourself?
- What can you do so that there is a good chance that someone else will do something for you that you will be satisfied with?[24]

The Miracle Question

A wonderful technique for eliciting future orientation is the use of the Miracle Question. Along with the scaling questions, the Miracle Question is the second iconic technique in the classical solution-focused approach. It introduces a radically new way of looking at problems and dealing with them in an alternative way.

The basic Miracle Question goes like this:

> "Suppose that one night while you are sleeping, a miracle happens, and your problem is solved. How would you know that? What would be different? How will your husband know that without you telling him about it?"[25]

In Chapter 7, you will learn the history and the gradual development of this wonderful question. You will be introduced to the linguistic deconstruction of the change mechanism hidden in the Miracle Question, along with some practical suggestions to adapt this miraculous tool to the needs of your clients. At first sight, the Miracle Question is a seemingly simple and straightforward tool. In reality, many subtleties, complications, and nuances lie behind that apparent simplicity.

Some salient points concerning the Miracle Question

1. Steve de Shazer describes the result of the miracle as: "Your problem is gone; everything is perfect again". Mark McKergow speaks of "Future Perfect".[26] We prefer to define the result of the miracle as: "Good enough to get on with".[27]
2. Steve de Shazer and Insoo Kim Berg use the Miracle Question in every conversation, every time. We use the Miracle Question occasionally, namely when we think the client can use this detour to either get his goals clear or to see past his problem fixation.
3. Asking the Miracle Question is in itself trivial. The efficacy of the Miracle Question lies in the follow-up questioning of the client's answers.
4. Whatever the client answers, it is always useful, provided you ask the right follow-up questions.
5. If you estimate that the client cannot give a useful answer to the Miracle Question, simply do not ask it.
6. Our questions are midwives to the client's answers, and the client's answers guide the follow-up questions, so that this cadence of question and answer develops the transformational dialogue in which a new reality is co-created.
7. Paraphrasing each of the client's answers makes it seem as if you are simply repeating what he says while as a matter of fact you are giving each paraphrase a solution-oriented spin.
8. Follow-up questions help the client to visualize what he will think, feel, and do differently, and then to describe it concretely and vividly, so that this **de**scription becomes a **pre**scription of that alternative reality.
9. Each answer to the Miracle Question = change.

Conclusion

In this chapter, you've learned what you can do when interacting with your clients. Depending on the specific situation you are dealing with, there are endless combinatorial possibilities with these seven steps. And as with any dance, elegance comes from fluent movements in every possible direction. You can even dance backwards without having to retrace your steps. As you gain more and more experience in this solution-focused dance, you will find that it is not always necessary to use all the dance steps in every situation: the fewer steps to reach a solution, the better.

Notes

1 Keeney, B. (2015). *The creative therapist*. Taylor & Francis Ltd.
2 Erickson, M.H. (1973). Psychotherapy achieved by a reversal of the neurotic processes in a case of ejaculatio praecox. *The American Journal of Clinical Hypnosis, 15*, 217–222.
3 Wittgenstein, L. (1953). *Philosophical investigations*. Oxford: Basil Blackwell, 109.
4 Erickson, M.H. (1967). *Advanced techniques of hypnosis and therapy: Selected papers of Milton H. Erickson*. New York: Grune & Stratton.
5 Erickson, M.H. (1965). Hypnosis and examination panics. *The American Journal of Clinical Hypnosis, 7*, 356–358.
6 Personal communication to the author (2014).
7 Erickson, M.H. (1967). *A lecture by Milton H. Erickson*. Delaware; September 19, Audio Recording No. cd/emh.67.9.19 (Phoenix, AZ: Milton H. Erickson Foundation Archives).
8 Annual report of the Dutch Association of Mental Health and Addiction Care, 2009, 33–34.
9 Initial appointments are more frequently missed, less often rescheduled, and require more staff time than on-going visits (Kruse et al., 2002). In outpatient mental health settings, 30% to 75% of patients do not keep an initial appointment, and 20% to 60% fail to attend follow-up appointments for medical or psychological services (Westra et al., 2000). In perhaps the most comprehensive and scientifically rigorous study, a quantitative meta-analysis of randomized trials using both initial and follow-up appointments in both medical and mental health settings found an overall no-show rate of 42% (Macharia et al., 1992).
10 Korrelboom, C.W., et al. (2007). Wie zijn de no-shows en waarom blijven ze weg? *Psychiatry magazine, 49*, 623–628.
11 Of course, there are those for whom the waiting list makes their lives a total disaster, and at best they end up in the emergency room.
12 Offringa, K. (2013). Onderzoek naar de invloed op no-show binnen de ambulante verslavingszorg. (Investigating the influence of solution-focused working on no-shows within outpatient addiction care.) Master Thesis. Rijksuniversiteit Groningen, Holland. Retrieved from internet: https://pure.rug.nl/ws/portalfiles/portal/2389204/samenvatting.pdf
13 Weiner-Davis, M., Shazer, S. de & Gingerich, W. (1987). Building on pretreatment change to construct the therapeutic solution: An exploratory study. *Journal of Marital and Family Therapy, 13*, 359–334.
14 This refers to Chapter 2 where we explain about the importance of client factors and extra-therapeutic variables.
15 Haley J. (1994). Typically Erickson. In J. K. Zeig (Ed.), *Ericksonian methods: The essence of the story*, p. 11. Brunner/Mazel.
16 Hoyt, M.F. (2001). *Interviews with brief therapy experts*. New York: Routledge.
17 Erickson, M.H. (1973). A field investigation by hypnosis of sound loci importance in human behavior. *The American Journal of Clinical Hypnosis, 16*, 147–164.
18 Note the difference in effect of these questions as opposed to statements like: Don't exaggerate. Life is difficult for everybody. Sleep on it.
19 In Chapter 6 (The Flowchart), we will explain the concepts of limitations and problems. For now, it suffices to say that for a problem a solution is conceivable while for a limitation no possible solution is conceivable.
20 Dolan, Y. (2000). An interview with Yvonne Dolan, MSW, by Dan Short, *Milton H. Erickson Foundation Newsletter,* 20, 2. Phoenix, AZ: Milton H. Erickson Foundation Archives.

21 Erickson, M. & Rossi, E.L. (Eds.). (1980). *The collected papers of Milton H. Erickson on hypnosis: Vol. IV. Innovative hypnotherapy*. New York: Irvington.
22 Petterson, C. (2006). *A primer in positive psychology*. Oxford University Press, p. 305.
23 Erickson, M.H. (1954). Special techniques of brief hypnotherapy. *Journal of Clinical and Experimental Hypnosis, 2*, 109–129.
24 The last three future-oriented questions are my adaptation of Luc Isebaert's Three Questions on how to be Happy: 1. what did I do today that made me feel satisfied with myself?, 2. what did someone else do that made me feel satisfied, and how did I react to that in such a way that the chances have increased that this person will do something like that again? and 3. what else happened that made me feel satisfied, and how did I use that? (from: 'Praktijkboek Oplossingsgerichte Cognitieve Therapie', De Tijdstroom 2007, p. 108).
25 de Shazer, S. (1988). *Clues: Investigating solutions in brief therapy*. New York: Norton.
26 McKergow, M. & Jackson, Paul Z. (2007). *The solution focus: making coaching and change simple*. 2nd edition. London: Nicholas Brealey Publisher.
27 In a previous version, we used as a definition of the miracle: 'In the miracle all your problems are solved sufficiently so that you are less bothered by them'. The definition we now use is much more neutral and serves not only to think about problems and their solutions but also, and especially, to think about growth, well-being, and contentment. We now define the miracle as: 'just good enough to be able to take further steps forward'. As we delve deeper and deeper into the linguistic and epistemological mechanisms that lie hidden behind this, at first sight naive, question, the articulation of the Miracle Question will probably continue to develop.

Chapter 6

The flowchart

With the Seven Steps of Dance, you have learned *what* to do when interacting with your client. The flowchart[1] teaches you *when* to do what. The flowchart and the seven-step dance are two sides of the same coin.

Simple is not easy

We dance the seven steps of the solution tango and adapt our interventions to the appropriate quality of the working relationship. We do this against the basso continuo that enriches our SoFAP work by coupling the six basis axioms (Chapter 1) to the four elements (Chapter 2) that define if our collaboration is useful to the client. Added to this basso continuo are the constant intervention choices based on the four basic decision rules (Chapter 3) that steer from which mandate we intervene (Chapter 4). Activating all the components from Chapters 1 to 4 creates the background sound that adds a deepening dimension to what plays out in the foreground.

The interconnectedness of all the components described in the previous chapters, shines through between the lines of solution-focused conversations that at first glance are simple and straightforward. However, upon closer analysis, you will discover a multidimensional layer of meaning that points to a deeper epistemological richness. There is more than meets the eye when you consider what is behind each expression. On closer inspection, you will discover that the components from the previous chapters are silently at work. In that sense, studying change conversations is like discovering deeper meanings when you read world literature.

We will indicate the many cross-links with the material described in the other chapters of this book. The attentive reader will discover for himself many more cross-links.

The flowchart basics

The flowchart represents a decision tree by which you check the quality of your working relationship with the client and then deploy the appropriate

DOI: 10.4324/9781003320104-7

interventions. This tool shows you the shortest path to the most useful interventions when, as always, you aim for minimax, i.e., minimum effort and maximum effectiveness and efficiency. This flowchart follows an incremental, iterative, and recursive process that allows you to design interventions that are adapted to the ever-changing context and to the interim progress made.

The limited set of questions

Faced with the complexity of being human, we choose to keep life simple. To achieve this, we use four fundamental questions that probe for a difference that makes a difference.[2]

Each question has an answer; otherwise, it is not worth asking.

Each answer indicates the position where the working relationship we are gradually developing, is situated on the flowchart.

For each position, we have designed matching interventions that enable you, in cooperation with your client, to achieve maximum results with minimum effort.

1 Are we dealing with a problem or a limitation?
2 Is there a request for help?
3 Is that request for help workable?
4 Is the client able to use his own resources?

Because it is at least as important to do the right things at the right moment as it is to do things right, a correct positioning on the flowchart helps you to know what you should and should not do.

After distinguishing between problems and limitations, we arrive at the following positions:

1 The *non-committal working relationship* with clients who do not have a request for help
2 The *searching working relationship* with clients who have a request for help but where the request for help is unworkable
3 The *consulting working relationship* with clients who have a workable need for help but who are not able to use their own resources
4 The *co-expert working relationship* with clients who have a workable demand for help and can use their own resources

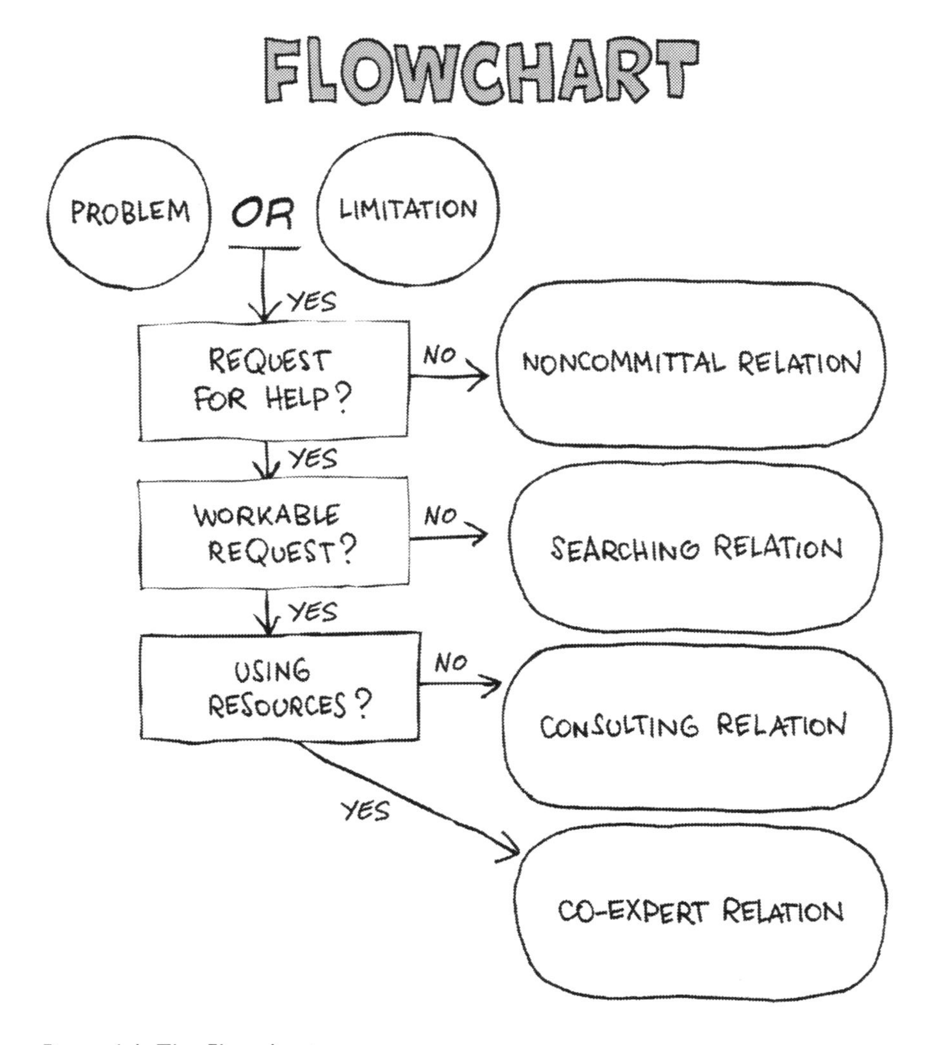

Figure 6.1 The Flowchart.

Notes on the use of the flowchart

- The type of working relationship is not determined by the intrinsic characteristics (or the intra-psychological make-up) of the client. Steve de Shazer and his team, in their book *Clues, Investigating Solutions in Brief Therapy* (Norton1988), described a first version of the flowchart. There they use the terms "visitors, complainers, and clients." Naming the positions on the flowchart with nouns suggests that the content of those

nouns are intrinsic properties of the clients in question. This is incorrect because it appears that the professional, as a neutral expert, is "diagnosing" that client based on their intrinsic characteristics. In reality, the professional co-creates the position on the flowchart with his client.
- The position on the flowchart is only an indication of the type of working relationship that you have, at time X and on topic Y, with your client.
- The flowchart indicates the mandate[3] that the client allows you to use and what you can do to enlarge that mandate.
- In essence, the flowchart is about the nature of our facilitation mandate but of course we need our leadership mandate to get the facilitation process going and, later in the process, to make the necessary adjustments. When we need to intervene in real life and/or apply our professional expertise, we use our leadership mandate to deploy our management mandate.
- There is no quality judgment about the different positions. Each working relationship is what it is; none is better than the other.
- We have chosen to give each position a name that is easy to remember and captures its essence.
- Reality and relationships are dynamic, never static. The same dynamic applies to the position on the flowchart, which is constantly changing depending on the issue you are discussing and the time you are doing so.
- Each position points you in the direction of the appropriate corresponding interventions; in this sense, the flowchart acts as a compass.
- The flowchart as a compass helps you design interventions that are the most appropriate for that theme at that time for this client in that context. Therefore, it is a meta-diagnostic tool that helps you design the co-creative process between client and professional.

Limitation or problem?

Faced with any situation, the first question we ask is: is it a problem or a limitation?

The definition of a limitation is that there is no conceivable solution to it. The condition is as it is. Examples of limitations are our age, our origin, our skin color, a disability or incurable disease, anything that has happened in the past. After all, we all realize that one cannot rewrite the pages of the book of life, nor tear pages out of it.

As professionals, we can only support our client to write additional pages in his book of life, preferably pages that describe well-being, growth, and satisfaction.

> A student at the university tells us that she was sexually abused during her childhood. That sexual abuse is not a problem, it is a limitation because it cannot be undone.

> For the professional athlete who has been forced into a wheelchair by an accident, his paralysis is not a problem, but a limitation.
>
> A girl may be hindered in her school performance by her parents' divorce, but the fact that her parents are divorced is a limitation.

The only thing you can do with limitations is to recognize them as such. The consequences that arise from the limitation are problems for which solutions are conceivable.

The definition of a problem is that there is a solution conceivable, perhaps difficult to implement – but conceivable.

> The way the student struggles with the consequences of her sexual abuse is a problem she can be helped to process, then put it behind her and build her life the way she wants to.
>
> The athlete in the wheelchair can be helped to learn to accept his handicap and from there discover new paths in his life.
>
> We can help the child to deal with her parents' divorce in a certain way, so that it will affect her school life less.

Thus, the very first intervention is to draw a clear and clarifying distinction between problems and limitations.

In the beginning there was distinction

Being aware of and helping your client to be aware of the distinction between problems and limitations is necessary for the following reasons:

- If you treat a limitation as if it were a problem, failure is unavoidable. No matter how great your arsenal of interventions and techniques, you will never, ever succeed in solving an impossibility. Oddly enough, it often happens that clients (or referrers or colleagues or we ourselves...) refuse to recognize that some things just can't be changed. The result is that an unnecessary amount of time and energy is spent (wasted?), while the failure (by the nature of the problem) is ingrained.
- If you treat a problem as if it were a limitation, you run the risk of lapsing into cynicism. If, as a therapist, you believe that clients with a cocaine addiction are nothing more than spoiled brats who leave themselves and you under the impression that they pretend to do something about it, but can't or won't do anything, you'd better refer those clients to a colleague who is open to offering constructive help.

Add lightness!

As the distinction between limitations and problems shows, problems are, in fact, defined by their possible solutions! Wonderful, and hopeful, because this implicitly indicates that for every problem a solution is conceivable – otherwise it would not be a problem (but a limitation).

Formula-P (pages 94–95) states that, if the professional asks the right questions, every problem can be seen as a wish for change that can be translated into a challenge. This adds lightness to problems that the client may perceive as unbearable.

For limitations, no solutions are conceivable. Yet, learning to deal with the consequences of a limitation is a problem for which solutions are thinkable. This insight lifts the crushing sense of impossibility and opens a hopeful perspective.

Acknowledgment facilitates acceptance

Limitations you suddenly face are often dramatic and require a tremendous effort to accept. A cerebral infarction resulting in paralysis or loss of speech, an accident where you lose an arm, blindness that strikes, post-polio syndrome that leaves you in a wheelchair, impaired hearing. You name it, the kinds of disability that can happen to you are all dramatic or sometimes even tragic.

> He [Dr. Erickson, red] felt that any amount of hard work was worth a result that was really wanted. He worked very hard to make the residuals of his paralysis from polio an inconvenience rather than a handicap. His neurologist examined him after what was originally diagnosed as a second bout with a different strain of infantile polio but what was actually understood later to be post-polio syndrome. The physician was astonished that Milton was able to stand so straight and with such level shoulders. He didn't know the hard work that Milton put into that achievement.[4]
>
> Mrs. Elizabeth Moore Erickson, spouse of Dr. Milton Erickson

Clients facing limitations are usually not served by platitudes such as "what does not kill you makes you stronger". Besides not being true, this statement, however well-meant, is disrespectful, rude, and insensitive. When you are confronted with a limitation, you need acknowledgment: "what you have to go through is a horror. I can hardly imagine what you feel but it must be a heavy and almost unbearable burden". Acknowledging the pain and sorrow helps the client to feel understood. This forms the foundation from which it then becomes possible to gradually take healing steps forward.

Acceptance opens possibilities

Once one has learned to accept that there are no conceivable solutions to limitations, new possibilities open.

> Once our professional athlete has processed his grief that he will never be able to run again, once he has accepted his limitation, he can pick up his life again. He can resume his studies in medicine, which he had set aside for his athletic career, and shift his specialization from surgery to rehabilitation medicine.

Accepting and learning to cope with (the consequences of) limitations is based on the concept of resilience as we explained in Chapter 1. This trait, one of the many gifts of Evolution, plays out on several levels: in an individual's reactions, in family relationships, between groups of people experiencing trauma together, and so on. Resilience also plays out on the physiological level. Just think of the blind person who develops a much sharper sense of hearing and a more refined sense of touch. The resilience in our brain (neural plasticity) after a cerebrovascular accident in which one region is damaged, allows those functions to be taken over by another brain region.

Accepting limitations and then learning to deal with the consequences of those limitations leads to recovery, activates new possibilities, and enables growth toward greater well-being. Human resilience activates resources that were hidden (or perhaps not present at all) before we were confronted with the limitation.

Realism please!

This argument for learning to accept limitations and deal with their consequences as constructively as possible has – again – nothing to do with "positive thinking", a poorly understood "new age" – like attitude or even the time-honored saying "where there is a will, there is a way". This last attitude is more an expression of megalomaniacal complacency than a demonstration of empathy with the person in trouble.

We again advocate realism: the glass is indeed half empty and the rest is just filled with air. We do not try to make the agony hidden in limitation look nice. On the contrary, our task is to support and encourage the other person to face the reality of the limitation and learn to deal with the consequences. In this way, and only in this way, namely by learning to see that every half-empty glass is also half-full at the same time, will there be room for new possibilities. But, make no mistake, coping with limitations is hard work.

Useful interventions checklist

With these hopeful insights about limitations and problems in mind, the following interventions are useful:

1 Draw a distinction
2 Accept the limitations

3 Focus on the consequences of the limitations
4 Create new opportunities by accepting the limitations

Draw a distinction

Situations where the distinction is rather obvious are easy. But in our profession, we often encounter complex situations where problems and limitations intermingle. That mix compels us to make clear distinctions, both for oneself as a professional and for your client.

> Tania, a twelve-year-old girl goes to a new school. During the first trimester she starts complaining about all sorts of (psycho) somatic ailments. After a conversation with the school psychologist, it becomes clear that Tania has ended up at a school that exceeds her intellectual capacity. Her limited intelligence is a limitation that we cannot change. Her choice of school, however, is a problem for which there is a solution: to follow a less demanding curriculum. Soon after switching to another school, her ailments disappeared, and Tania became again the lively and happy girl from before.

Accept the limitations

Easier said than done and yet there is no escaping it.

> Tania's parents are both successful lawyers. They find it hard to imagine, let alone accept, that their daughter does not have their intellectual capacity. Helping them in a delicate but determined way to accept their daughter's limited intelligence does not have to mean the end of their lives and ambitions.

Focus on the consequences of the limitations

Clients often tend to fixate on their limitations. This is easy to understand because the limitation limits their broad outlook on life. However, it makes much more sense to focus on the consequences of the limitation, because learning to deal with it differently is a problem for which solutions are conceivable.

> Tania, together with her parents, decided to transfer to another school with a less demanding curriculum. She is very happy about the fact that her classmates are making a concerted effort to help her keep up. Her first tests went well. Tania reports that she is now learning things at school that really interest her. The parents are relieved and very proud of their daughter's adaptability.

Create new opportunities by accepting the limitations

In life, sometimes you sometimes encounter things that you can't do anything about but endure them and (learn to) accept them. When you succeed in accepting the inevitable, when you stop trying to change the unchangeable, when you stop trying to break through a concrete wall – in other words: when you accept the limitations that irrevocably happen to you in life, a lot of energy is released. Then numerous opportunities can and most likely will present themselves that were previously invisible.

> Freedom and Happiness begin with a clear understanding of one principle: some things are within our control, and some things are not. It is only after you have faced up to this fundamental rule and learned to distinguish between what you can and can't control that inner tranquility and outer effectiveness become possible.[5]
>
> Epictetus (50–130 A.D.)

The non-committal working relationship

Having distinguished the limitations from the problems and having made the corresponding interventions, one then asks the second fundamental question: is there a demand for help? If the answer is negative, we are dealing with a non-committal working relationship. It is therefore obvious that someone who does not have a request for help will also not commit to doing anything with the help you offer him. In other words, he will not give you a mandate to act as a facilitator. So, the contact does not produce a commitment and is therefore non-committal.

However, it is good to keep in mind that there is contact and that this contact, even if it is of a non-committal nature, is the starting point from which we initiate our subsequent interventions. As you will learn, there are many different interventions possible for clients who do not have a request for help, provided the client feels understood, respected, and not forced into action.

Be careful not to rush in when not invited[6]

Careful simply means to be full of care so as not to take steps that might turn out to be detrimental to the working relationship. In a non-committal working relationship where the client does not have a request for help, it is advisable to be very careful with step three of the solution tango: setting goals. The fact that the client does not (yet) have a need for help related to the context of the conversation, i.e., facilitation, should be respected. That respect provides space to gently take step 1 (make contact) and step 2 (clarify context) of the solution tango. Bearing in mind Alexander Pope's famous lines: "Fools rush in where angels fear to tread", one avoids exposing oneself and one's client to well-intentioned "Sturm und Drang".

Clients without a request for help come in many colors

The first and most common type are the clients we never meet for the simple fact that they do not – willingly or under coercion – engage with a professional. The world is full of people who are able to use their own resources and resilience to help themselves and others to find ways to cope with life in a satisfying way. The world is full of people who benefit from a conversation with someone else, whether it's a neighbor or a chance encounter on the bus. The world is even fuller of people who have never heard of that strange species called professional facilitator, let alone talk to one. Since we will never meet them, we cannot or should not do much for them. What we can do for them, however, is to keep an open mind, ear, and heart. Whenever you think there is the slightest opening, you can offer your attention – gently, subtly, discreetly, and without any obligation from any party, but insistently if necessary – by reaching out to them. That is not meddling, that is good citizenship. Further interventions for this type: none.

Type 2 is the client who judges that he has no problem but comes because he must come from someone else.

Some examples clarify type 2:

- My partner/boss/parent has said that I must come and speak to you because they think that I drink too much/am too rebellious/do not do enough in the house/do not take care of myself enough (fill in the blank). There's nothing wrong with me but it's them who drink too much/are annoying/leave everything lying around the house/not taking care of themselves (fill in the blank).
- I come because my GP told me that I am a case for the psychologist, but I have no idea what she means by that.
- My husband has said that I am pathologically jealous and that he will divorce me if I don't get treatment for it. There is nothing wrong with me at all, but he can't stop flirting with other women.
- The judge has sentenced me to alcohol treatment because I have been repeatedly caught driving under influence, but that was by sheer happenstance because I am not an alcoholic at all.
- Children and adolescents often do not have a request for help but come for a consultation because they have to come from their concerned parents.
- My boss ordered me to talk with you about my leadership style, but it's only because she doesn't know how to deal with people herself.

- I don't have a communication problem, but my colleagues don't know how to consult.
- My coworkers say that I don't function well, but it is the office politics in the company that ruins everything.

In extreme cases you'll hear the client say: "I'm here because I was forced to come."

Type 3 is the client who has a problem but does not think we can provide the right help and therefore does not request our assistance. They only come to tell you that you are not the right person to help them.

Some examples clarify type 3:

- I don't know if you as a HR-manager will be able to help me because my problems are caused by the recent reorganization.
- I can't get my division to buy in into the new ERP software package because no one really backs it, and therefore, you as a director can't really do anything.
- I don't understand why my boss thinks I have to talk with you about this project management course. Sure, our three last projects were a bit late but that was obviously the fault of the subcontractors and surely not mine. So, there is nothing you can do for me.
- My general practitioner has referred me because he is convinced that my migraine has a psychological origin, but a brain scan seems more useful than a conversation with a psychologist.
- I was expecting a social worker, not a psychologist. I am not crazy and therefore do not need a psychologist but someone with whom I can discuss practical matters.
- I need a physiotherapist to teach me relaxation exercises, not a psychologist. A physiotherapist knows much better than a psychologist how the pain is structured.
- I've already had a lot of sessions with several physiotherapists. A psychologist who knows the psychological aspect of my pain would better serve me.

It is worth remembering that it is not only individuals who step into a non-committal working relationship. A married couple, a family, a team at work, an organization and even socio-cultural strata in society can also occupy that position on the flowchart.

How NOT to intervene?

In the classic problem-oriented approach, people without a request for help are (too) often seen as troublemakers, who are not motivated to do anything about their problems.

Those who do not have a request for help are often rejected with the following (usually tacit) arguments:

- If you don't ask for help or even refuse it, what are you doing here?
- If you don't know what you want, don't bother me.
- I have other things to do than fill my time with clients who come and whine about others.
- If you don't have intrinsic motivation to do something yourself, you can't be helped.
- If you don't have an insight into your problem, then you're impossible to work with.
- Fine, I won't bother you anymore. Don't think you can do it alone. It doesn't usually work that way. But if you think you know better, go ahead.

Such an attitude has no place at all in the SoFAP framework. It only produces non-helpful reproaches that result in wasted time and energy for both the client and the professional. In addition to producing zero results for the client, it may discourage the client from (ever) wanting to meet with another change agent.

Please note that the position on the flowchart is purely topographic and has no qualitative connotation. The working relationship they wish to enter at this time is just what it is. The client who does not have a request for help is no less (important) for it. There is nothing wrong with the colleague who would rather do their own thing than accept help from their fellow behavioral scientist. Judging is not helpful, condemning is out of the question, and reacting irritably is not respectful.

Death of resistance

Clients without a request for help, used to be labeled as clients who show resistance. In 1979, Steve de Shazer wrote a groundbreaking article on the subject. To put it mildly, this article was not initially met with much enthusiasm. After six revisions and 17 rejections (!), as de Shazer eloquently describes in his later article "Resistance Revisited,"[7] his article "Death of Resistance"[8] finally was accepted for publication in 1984. That this took so long had everything to do with the then (and unfortunately to this day) "scientific" belief that clients "resist" change and improvement for obscure (and different per school of thought) reasons. In this groundbreaking article, Steve counters the then-and, unfortunately, still now-widespread delusion that clients, consciously or unconsciously, don't want to get better because there are more benefits to continuing to wallow in their misery. Steve makes it clear that "resistance"[9] is a concept in the mind of the problem-oriented professional, and no more than a concept.

The SoFAP stance that sees what we used to call "resistance" as a stage direction obviously also stems from a concept, albeit one that is more useful than working with the bottle half-filled with "resistance".

Stage directions

Solution-focused professionals define "resistance" as: all interactions that at first glance do not seem helpful in achieving our goals, but through which we obtain useful information. In SoFAP speak: "resistance" provides additional information: the client is letting us know that what we are putting forward (or the way in which) is not very useful at that moment.

One can formulate it even more sharply and precisely. We state that everything the client does and says or does not do and does not say, are stage directions with which he helps us as professionals, so that we can help him better. Until proven otherwise, the client is constantly and (un)consciously trying to assist his professional with well-packaged advice. It is up to the professional to unwrap that help.

More aptly put, the more "resistance", the harder the client tries to help us. In its most succinct form: the more "resistance", the better.

Vivat the non-committal working relationship

Working with people without a request for help is difficult and challenging because they invite you to set aside, or at least question, much of your problem-oriented expertise. Clients, along with chronic patients, are the best trainers in our profession because they invite you to bring out all your professional skills as a facilitator and they require you to stay up to date with the latest best practices in the field.

While problem-oriented professionals tend to speculate about the question "why don't they show a request for help, what's hidden behind that", solution-focused professionals know that the "why" of not showing a request for help is usually not important. The only interesting question is, "What can we do anyway?"

If you use the right interventions in working with clients who do not (yet) have a request for help, then you can never do anything wrong. The worst that can happen is that you have worked on a constructive working relationship while the client does not (yet) want to use it. "Right" in this context means: "appropriate in the right way to what the client needs at this time and in this situation". The English word "fit" is a more accurate expression of what we mean, as in: "The key that fits the lock."

The set of seven interventions in general

In a non-committal working relationship, we can offer seven linked interventions. This series of seven is not an "either-or" but an "and-and" series.

We first offer this series of interrelated interventions in one sentence and then deconstruct each part of it.

We explicitly use the word "offer" because, in our work as facilitators, one cannot (and should not) force help on the other person without their consent.

If someone does not have a request for help, the following offers are helpful, preferably in the following order: 1/ offer no help *and* 2/ appreciate anything that can be appreciated *and* 3/ offer (if appropriate) additional information *and* 4/ offer (if appropriate) appreciation about the referrer *and* 5/ explore whether the client is willing and able to develop an alternative request for help *and*, if not, 6/ present the client with the consequences of not developing an alternative request for help *and*, if the client is unable to do anything with this either, 7/ respectfully wait and let time do its work.

The set of seven interventions in detail

Do not force help

If someone does not ask for help, do not offer help. This is the hardest part for people whose job it is to offer help. The client enters our store of solution possibilities, not to buy something, but to take shelter from the rain. Resist the temptation to force your well-intentioned help on him. Forcing unsolicited help on someone is neither very respectful nor very helpful. You cannot help someone against his will.

To avoid misunderstandings, let us clarify this intervention. "Do not offer help" does not equal "do nothing". The accurate description of "Do not offer help" is that you do not offer help that can be directly linked to the context in which the conversation takes place. If the client tells you that he is coming because he is obliged to do so by a third party because of problem X, then the context in which our conversation takes place is one in which problem X and its treatment must be discussed. If the client clearly tells us that he does not want to talk about that in the first place, for example, because he claims to be the victim of a misunderstanding, then we will not challenge this. We talk about other things first, so that we can develop a working relationship in which we can take the next steps in the set of interventions. We'll come back later to why the third party sent him for consultation.

AND

Show appreciation

The first step of the seven-step solution-focused dance is making contact. The client without a request for help is in front of us and we talk to each other. That is contact, that is already a working relationship. As a professional whose job it is to try to facilitate change with and for the client, it is difficult to resist the temptation to offer help, even if the client is clear that he has no need for it. It makes more sense to follow the client's stage direction: "Dear professional, please take your time. Currently, I do not have a help request regarding X, so please be kind enough not to offer me help regarding X. Before I am willing or able to develop a help request regarding X, I need to feel understood".

When we take this stage direction seriously, we demonstrate to the client that we respect their point of view. We know that a good working relationship encourages change, so we take every opportunity to strengthen that working relationship. You can do this by respecting that he is not asking for help, being attentive to all possible resources you can discover in the client and his context, and then expressing your authentic appreciation for anything that can be appreciated. In other words, don't offer help, just activate the non-specific factors from Chapter 2.

In short, don't focus your attention on the fact that there is no request for help. Instead, you focus your attention on what the other person is doing or has done and make positive and appreciative comments about it.

In practice, this means taking a little more time to ask context clarifying questions (step 2) about the client's life and experience. When you do that, you make a circumferential move that allows you to uncover even more resources (step 4), making it even easier to express appreciation. All of this strengthens your working relationship and makes the next step easier.

AND (if appropriate)

Provide information

Some people do not ask for help because they are convinced that help is impossible for them. Their stage direction, "I cannot be helped therefore I make myself believe that I have no problem", invites the intervention of offering information about their problem to help translate it into a challenge (See Formula-P). For all other clients who do not give us this stage direction, this intervention can be skipped.

This non-committal attitude can be understood from a lack of self-confidence, a lack of knowledge or a combination of both. In these cases, it is best to provide some additional information about the background of the problem. With the help of this additional information, the client may be willing to allow (the possibility of) change and have the courage to take small steps to develop a request for help.

An example: there are quite a few people with a hidden addiction problem. On the one hand, they are often ashamed of it and on the other hand, they often have the (false) idea that they are not able to get rid of their addiction. After all, they have tried so many times and they have never succeeded (until now). Hence, they do not ask for help. If for some reason (which may be the result of medical or physical problems) they encounter a health care professional, it is not wise to immediately grab these clients by the leash and confront them with their underlying addiction problem. The best thing you can do as a health worker is to take those medical problems seriously. In the meantime, you can provide information about how many percent of society is struggling with a similar hidden problem, about the consequences of addiction but especially about how quickly people recover when they stop drinking/smoking/blowing/gambling, and so on, about figures that indicate how great the chance of recovery is, about the average time needed to complete treatment, about the various possibilities for doing something about it, about the success stories of other clients. This may give them just enough hope to take the next step and it will, at least, not scare them away.

AND (if appropriate)

Give positive messages about the referring party

If someone does not have a request for help themselves but meets with us because they have been forced to do so by someone else, that is not pleasant for that client. But the fact that he shows up anyway, gives us the opportunity to do something. You only have to (gently) point out to the client that this referrer has a good reason to encourage (oblige) the client to contact us.

- Could it be that your partner, who sends you here because she is concerned about your alcohol consumption, would still like to stay married to you?
- I understand that you yourself don't know what to come and do, but apparently your family doctor, who has your best interests at heart, is concerned about you.
- Your mother would like you to come and talk to me, because she is worried about how to proceed with your studies.
- The fact that the judge is forcing you to come to treatment for those offenses, which you don't agree with, is very inconvenient, but apparently the judge wants to give you a chance.
- The fact that your boss told you to talk with an external coach about your leadership style shows that she wants to invest in your career.

AND

Develop an alternative request for help

Building on the appreciation you have expressed for a variety of things (aka resources) that are not directly related to the reason the client was sent, you can then test whether the client is willing to look at what they can do differently to satisfy their referrer.

- What would you be willing to do differently at home so that your partner is a little less anxious?
- What does your family doctor think should happen in our conversation so that he can be a little more reassured about you?
- What could you do so that your mother is a little less anxious about your studies?
- What do you think you should change so that the judge no longer thinks you need therapy?
- What could you do differently so that your boss no longer expects you to come and talk to me?

With this intervention, you can find out if the client is able and willing to work on a different goal than he was originally sent to you for.

If you succeed in helping the client develop an alternative request for help, then you can skip the next steps and move directly to the next fundamental question, "is this request for help workable?" (see infra page 150)

If you are unsuccessful in helping the client develop an alternative request for help, you can move on to the next intervention.

AND

Present the consequences of non-help demand

Every client has the right not to request help. If the client does not develop a request for help, it is good to dwell with him on the consequences this may have. Since he has been sent by someone else who has a request for help in his place, there is a good chance that there will be consequences if the client himself does not develop a request for help.

The general question that can be asked here is: "How will your referrer react if he notices that you have turned up for an interview but chooses not to do anything further with it?"

- Your partner wishes you to do something about your alcohol consumption but you say it is she who drinks too much? Would you like to stay married to her?
- How will your family doctor react if he finds that you don't share his concern that prompted him to refer you?
- If you don't feel like studying harder and getting better results, are you willing to accept not being allowed out on weekends, as your mother warned you?
- What sanctions will the judge impose if you will tell him that you are not willing to give therapy a chance?
- What might happen at work if you are not willing to comply with the demands of your boss?

AND

Take your time

If, after all the interventions mentioned above, the client indicates that he is still not ready to ask for help, all you need to do is wait. Sometimes the client comes for a follow-up interview and then he has had time to let things sink in. He has been able to think about the consequences of not asking for help and is possibly prepared to develop an (alternative) request for help. Sometimes the client accepts the consequences and acts accordingly. Sometimes the client goes to another professional at another time. Sometimes things happen that make him develop a demand for help: his partner effectively carries out her threat to leave, for example. Sometimes it remains a single session.

Interventions for the non-committal relationship as related to our mandates

When we intervene from our mandate as facilitators, and the client chooses not to accept or develop any form of help, we can use our leadership mandate to suspend collaboration temporarily or permanently with this client. Because we have respected him as a person, made sure as much as possible that he felt understood, and hopefully have provided him with a glimmer of hope that alternatives are possible, we have not harmed a possible future working relationship.

But when the client is at risk of doing things that are illegal, against deontology, unethical, or just plain bad for the (public) health of himself and/or those around him, we must take the lead and intervene from our management mandate as guardians of public health.

Checklist for the non-committal working relationship

1. if someone does not ask for help, do not force it on them.
2. show your appreciation and develop the most positive relationship possible.
3. when appropriate, provide information.
4. when appropriate, emphasize the positive intentions of the referring party.
5. explore whether an alternative request for help is acceptable.
6. present the client the consequences of not developing an (alternative) request for help and
7. wait, because perhaps the client will develop a request for help later or in another situation (for example, with another professional).

Metaphor for the non-committal working relationship

The Eskimo and the freezer

Imagine you are a salesman selling deep freezers and your sales region is the Arctic. You might not be able to sell a deep freezer to an Eskimo, but he may be interested in in an alternative product: a machine that stores their food in a hygienic way, protects it from predators and keeps it at a temperature of a few degrees Celsius. Even if you don't make the sale this year, if you behave in an appropriate, friendly, and respectful way, you can at least come back the following year and try again.

In a nutshell

The purpose of this set of seven interlinked interventions is to see if the non-committal working relationship can evolve into a committal working relationship.

If the set of seven interventions does not resonate with the client, then at least you have worked on the quality of your relationship. They will have to face the consequences of their non-committal attitude. Your appreciative attitude has not blocked the working relationship – which could happen if you were to impose help on the others without being asked. It is possible that they will come with a request for help at a later time. This may be with a different professional or with a changed context. Time is usually on the side of the professional who remains patient.

If the clients accept this offer, they accept the challenge and the responsibility to start changing something themselves: they accept a goal they want to work on.

From this point, you can move to the next position on the flowchart.

The searching working relationship

Having differentiated between limitations and problems and having helped the client to express a request for help, we can now move to the third fundamental question: Is that request for help workable? As we discussed in step 5, Goal Setting of the Seven Step Dance in Chapter 5 (page 90–91), we make a distinction between useful and useless goals. Useful goals are phrased in terms of the useful goals checklist: practical, realistic, achievable, observable in behavioral terms, and preferably from small to large.

If the request for help cannot be formulated in terms of this useful goal checklist, then we are faced with an unworkable request for help.

The client does have a help request and is therefore motivated to work on it. The only problem is that his request for help is so wrapped up that he can't get the package open. In the searching working relationship, the client enters our solution store, puts his package on the counter, tired and frustrated, and hopes that we will open it for him. This is not a matter of unwillingness from the client. Quite the contrary, it is a genuine request.

The client is constantly looking, but he is looking in the wrong way and in the wrong place. Our job is to help him unwrap his package by asking questions that will help him turn his unworkable help request into a workable help request. In other words, the practitioner's job is to translate the client's unworkable request for help into terms of the useful goals checklist.

Clients with an unworkable request for help come in many colors

People with unworkable requests for help come in a variety of subtypes. Their greatest common denominator is that they are open to help, even though they have no idea what they could do about it themselves.

We first describe the different types within searching work relationships and then explain the possibilities for appropriate intervention in detail.

"It's not me; it's the others"

Many clients have a clear picture of what should happen: it is the others who should change. They cannot see what they themselves could do differently but have a very good idea of what others in their immediate environment should change so that their lives become easier. Then you hear cries of distress like:

- If my husband does not change, then our marriage will go wrong even though I am trying so hard.
- As long as my mother-in-law is living in the house, I am not able to cope with the tension she causes.
- My 16-year-old daughter drives me crazy and gets under my skin to the point where I can't sleep.
- I can't go back to work if my colleagues keep bullying me.
- If no one makes sure that the neighbor's dog stops barking all night, I will never get rid of my sleeping problem.
- I can't feel comfortable in this chilly society.
- I can't be happy if none of my friends include me in their social life.
- How can I be happy with my life when my family members remain so malcontent?
- How can I possibly meet the standards when the company keeps moving them?

These clients hope that someone will come to their aid by influencing the other person or persons. The attitude of "it's not me, it's someone else" is common and has to do with feelings of powerlessness and dependence.

Vague and unclear goals

Sometimes clients articulate their problems in a kind of cloud-like blur that you can't do much with. Such a problem cloud is hard to blow away. Then we hear our clients say things like:

- It is no longer possible; I am exhausted.
- I am always just tired and lifeless.
- I have lost my self-confidence.
- I can't take it anymore.
- I am stuck.
- I would like to be myself.
- I want my life to be like it used to be when everything was perfect.
- I want to be happy.

When you ask that client what they mean by that, they often answer along the lines of:

- I don't know either, I can't explain it.
- I have no words for it – it's just a general feeling.
- If I knew that, my problem would be solved; that is exactly what I am coming to you for.

It goes without saying that goals that are formulated so vaguely and unclearly are very difficult to achieve.

Black-White thinkers

As we saw in Chapter 5, when people are in trouble, they tend to think in black and white: "'nothing ever works out for me, everything is disappointing, everyone is against me, I'm never lucky, I'm totally unhappy, I'm a complete failure, my life/work/relationship is a disaster and it's getting worse by the day, I'm watching the future and it is black", and so on. If their goal is then to achieve the opposite of their cited problem description, failure lies in wait.

Too many goals at once

Some people present so many problems (and therefore goals) at once that the whole of it becomes unworkable.

We quote verbatim what a desperate client once told at the beginning of a first consultation: "I am happy to talk to you about this. What desperately needs to change is my whole way of life. I am tired of drinking too much, of walking on tiptoe at work and of never daring to say 'no'. I would like to be able to concentrate better. My husband has been unemployed for so long now that it is causing us financial problems. That means we must continue living with my parents-in-law, even though the house is much too small for my family of three children and four adults. By the way, my oldest son is a real problem at school. I can't get rid of my cough, my blood pressure remains high, and I know that I should lose at least ten kilos and eat healthier. But I just don't have enough time to cook healthy meals because I also have to take care of my sick sister who lives next door. I feel lousy."

No wonder this lady feels lousy. You must be a superwoman to see the forest through that jungle of problems, let alone one tree.

As an aside, in the pre-solution-focused era, these families were called "multi-problem families." If you look at them with SoFAP glasses on, you will see that these families are, in fact, multi-goal families. With the right interventions, they can be helped to become multi-solution families. This adds lightness to both the families involved and the intervening professionals.

"I want to, but it's stronger than myself"

Here, we are dealing with a self-annihilating request for help. While the request for help is made, the solution is blocked. The generic variant of such self-annihilating request for help is: "I would like to…, but it is impossible because…".

Then, we hear the client say something along the lines of:

- I try my best, but then something snaps in my head, and I can't be held back.
- I know that I should stand up for myself a bit more and dare to say "no" more often, but I can't because I have never learned to do that.
- When I catch myself not being anxious for a moment, then my anxiety always strikes immediately.
- I realize that my concentration problem is the result of the fact that I always let myself be pushed around so much – I can't change that, because I was born that way.
- I would like to spend less time on the computer, but once I'm busy I can't stop.
- I would like to stop blowing/smoking/arguing/controlling but I can't because it's stronger than myself.
- I would like to stop those compulsions, but I can't because according to my psychiatrist, I have an obsessive-compulsive disorder.
- I realize that my relationship can't improve if I keep refusing to speak to my partner, but I can't help it either, too much bad things have happened, and it is impossible for me to open myself up to her.
- Mind you, I do my best! Every time I go home/office, I resolve to make up for it, but when I get home/to the office, it overwhelms me again and my good intentions are gone.

Clients trapped in such an unworkable request for help tend – often without realizing it themselves – to nip in the bud any attempt to find a possible way out. They have split off their problem from their normal daily life and therefore feel powerless to change anything.

General interventions in the searching working relationship

In general, you can say that the way complaints and problems are packaged always contain stage directions to useful interventions. Unpacking happens when you apply Formula-P in conjunction with the checklist of useful goals. Whatever problem the client presents in whatever form, there is always a goal in it that can be translated into a challenge. Through this translation, the problems presented can be formulated in terms of the useful goals checklist: practical, realistic, achievable, observable in behavioral terms and preferably from small to large. Helping the client make this translation is (the forebode of) change.

The cardinal question is: What would you like *instead* of your problem?

Specific interventions in the searching working relationship

By way of overview, this yields the following layers of intervention, which are closely linked and stacked:

1. If I understand you correctly, you are going through a very difficult period and there are so many things weighing on you that it is difficult to bear all of that. (offer acknowledgment)
2. It is good that you are persistent in your search to find a solution. (positive support)
3. What is the smallest thing you yourself could do differently? (stimulate own responsibility)
4. What are the things that, despite your problems, are going well enough for you to keep them? (focus on what goes well via the continuation question)
5. What is the smallest sign that you would notice that things are going a little better? What is the first thing you would then do/think/feel differently? (concretizing, differentiating, setting priorities)
6. Are there times when the problem doesn't occur or doesn't occur as much or is different? And what do you do differently then? (search for exceptions)

Asking solution-focused questions like these is the most effective method of helping clients to (re)gain confidence in their own abilities, (re)take responsibility for themselves and (re)tap into their own resources.

These interventions can be deconstructed into specific details to maximally meet the needs of the client.

Offer acknowledgment

The client's complaints indicate that he is struggling and having a hard time. This formulation includes the direction that he needs acknowledgement of his difficulties and how he is trying to address them before we can take next steps.

It is befitting to let the client hear and feel that you are compassionate: "Hearing you talk about all you have been through, I can well imagine that you are deeply distressed". Or: "Well, what a story. I can understand you saying that for the time being you don't know how to manage". Or: "What a predicament. How on earth are you coping with all this?"

We know by now how important the "feeling understood" factor is, which is why we take the time to make it clear to the client that we acknowledge the seriousness of their problems and the burdens that this entails. Only then is it appropriate to take the next step and express our appreciation for his efforts.

Acknowledgment is the most universal human currency.

Give positive support

People with an unworkable request for help are – by definition – motivated to work on their problems, otherwise they would not have a request for help in the first place. It is therefore helpful, respectful, and effective to express appreciation for that quest. That way you support them in their search. Our task as professionals is to teach the client in a searching working relationship how to use his energy in a different and more effective way so that he no longer tries to dig a hole in the water.

"From what you have told me I can clearly see that you are tired of trying so hard without any results. *However, I must congratulate you on your commitment. It's to your credit that you don't let up!* Would you be interest in working together to find a way to use your energy and commitment a little differently so that you will get better results?"

Encourage self-responsibility

People with an unworkable request for help often get bogged down in the idea that they are dependent on others to change their own behavior. This belief is sometimes false and always paralyzing. Most professionals know from experience that engaging in a rational discussion, in the hope that it will give the client insight into his own counterproductive attitude, is rarely productive. On the contrary, the stronger the well-intentioned argumentation, the less the client feels understood.

The professional who, no matter how well meant, tries to convince these clients that they need to change something themselves, often runs into a wall of rational arguments that starts with "Yes but (1) sir, you don't quite understand (2) me. As a professional you will agree (3) with me that..."

This line of arguments contains three interesting stage directions that must be addressed before one can successfully help clients embrace their own responsibility.

For starters, linguistically, the "but" (1) invalidates any statement that precedes it. I like you, but... You are doing a great job, but... we can try and change the "yes, but" into "yes, and".

Second, the client lets us know in the clearest of words that he does not feel understood (2). Ergo, we must take care that he does.

Third, the opening phrase (3) "you surely agree with me when I..." hides a linguistic booby-trap that must be recognized and defused. The statement implicates that the other party agrees with the statement. Clients use this opening phrase – often with the best of intentions and without being aware of its implications – to verify that the professional is on board. If you answer in the affirmative or even simply remain silent after the client uses this opening sentence, chances are, the client will get the impression that you agree with him. But precisely because the opening sentence "you will agree with me that..." is usually followed by a static description of a situation for which the client places the responsibility on someone else, it is not very useful to confirm him in this. This (unspoken) affirmation does not trigger change in the client. We know that you cannot change the others if you, both a client and as a professional, do not do something different.

A better answer is the question "What exactly do you mean by that?" with which you invite the client to think and dig up more details.

Then you can ask the next set of questions that will help the client take ownership of his life, step by step:

- Despite the bickering of your bosses/parents, what is the smallest thing you could do differently to focus a little better on your work/study?
- If your partner comes home from work late and stressed, that is probably not the best time for a meaningful conversation about the status of your relationship. What else could you do to have the most enjoyable evening possible together, so that there is room for that difficult conversation tomorrow?
- What is the smallest thing you could muster to do differently?
- Would you like to learn how to react in a different way so that you become less agitated?
- Would you like to discover what you could still do despite your tremendous fatigue that constantly overwhelms you?

Even if the client fails to answer those questions, you have at least planted the idea in his mind that he could do something different. This seed of self-responsibility is a necessary antidote to helplessness and hopelessness because the questions imply that there is hope for change.

Ask the continuation question

No matter how miserable life may be, no matter how despondent one may feel, no matter how hopeless one may look at life, there are always things that still work and are worthwhile. This working hypothesis stems from the assumption in SoFAP that resources are always available (Chapter 1, Basic axioms). Sometimes they are hidden under a thick layer of misery, sometimes the client simply is not aware of them, and sometimes they do not match up with the situation at hand. Yet, resources are always there. We reiterate our definition: a resource is any possible and conceivable means that can be used to generate solutions and promote well-being.

To surface those situations when and where clients do use their resources, we ask the continuation question: "What in your life, besides and in spite of the misery, is still going well, or at least well enough so that you want to keep that?"

If you deconstruct this continuation question linguistically, you will discover the following elements:

- Recognition of the fact that every normal life has elements of doom and gloom in it.
- Life is hard work[10] as B.A. Erickson used to say when quoting her father Dr. Milton Erickson.
- An invitation to look beyond the problem-fixation.
- There is always something worthwhile, why would you want to keep it otherwise?
- Things worth keeping are both the big important values and the small things of life.
- The continuation question activates the second basic rule: if something (good or good enough or better) works, continue doing it and/or do more of it.
- No matter how small the things are that one would like to keep, they often contain elements of possible solutions that, once noticed, can be built into larger solutions.

Concretize, differentiate, and prioritize

People in a searching relationship often articulate their request for help in vague or in black-and-white terms or they simultaneously list so many goals that they can no longer see the trees of their goals through the forest of their numerous problems. Knowing that the phrasing of their challenges offers stage directions for the way to deal with them, the interventions that fit here are straightforward: help the client to concretize his vague problems or to develop a differentiated goal or to set priorities for himself.

For solution-focused professionals, these are almost routine interventions. Yet there is a big difference with the classical problem-oriented method in which the professional as an expert prescribes to the client what he should do differently, counting on obedience and docility.

By asking solution-building questions, SoFAP professionals invite clients to do the heavy lifting themselves. *They do the sport; we do the support.*

HOW TO HELP CLIENTS CONCRETIZE THEIR CLOUD-LIKE GOALS

Vague cloud-like problems ("I don't feel well. I don't know what I want. There is something strange going on in my life. If only I knew what to do. My thoughts are racing like crazy") are initially just messages that do not involve a direct request for help. Using Formula P, we know that these messages encapsulate problems that can be reframed as desires for change that can be turned into challenges by asking the right questions. Behind these cloud-like messages, we hear the stage direction, "I can't articulate better what I'm struggling with at this time. Please give me recognition that this is difficult. Then, please ask me questions so that I can translate my vagueness into the terms of the useful goals checklist. Only then will I be willing and able to try to do something different".

Powerful translation questions are:

- What is the smallest thing you *could*[11] do differently if you no longer...?
- What is the smallest thing you *would* do differently if you no longer...?
- What is the smallest thing you *will* do differently if you no longer...?
- How would you notice if you were a little more... again?
- How would your partner/coworker notice that you are a little more... again?

HOW TO HELP BLACK-WHITE THINKERS DIFFERENTIATE

The black and white thinkers give us a clear stage direction: "Help me differentiate". In Step 6 of the Solution Tango (Chapter 5, page 109) we detailed all the adequate interventions, including the use of scaling questions to help the client take small steps.

HOW TO HELP CLIENTS WITH AN EXCESS OF GOALS

Clients who express a tidal wave of simultaneous requests for help give us the stage direction, "I want to address a lot of things at once. Please give me recognition that I am so motivated. I also recommend that you don't set priorities for me. If you just help me set my own priorities, I'm more likely to actually do something with them."

Useful solution-focused questions then are:

- "Of all those things you listed, what would be the smallest thing you could do differently so that, even all your problems are not solved, you find that you are taking a step in the right direction?"
- "And if you succeeded, what could be the next smallest step after that?"

Search for exceptions

When we discussed the central notion of the resource-orientation,[12] we explained that one of the locations where resources hide, is in the exceptions to the problem. In those moments of exception, the problem is absent, different, or less pronounced because the client can use his resources to produce (partial and/or temporary) solutions.

After asking "are there times when your problems are absent/different or less?" people may respond with a description of how massive and seemingly impenetrable their problems feel or they indicate a sense of not owning those exceptions or they describe a self-annihilating mindset that prevents them from being able to change. The stage direction in each formulation indicates which solution-focused questions are the best suited to help the client circumvent these objections, then expand these exceptions to use their resources more broadly.

HOW TO HELP PEOPLE WITH A MASSIVE AND IMPENETRABLE PROBLEM PRESENTATION

Formulating problems in massive form by ample use of the words "always, never, totally, absolutely..." ("I always feel bad, down, dejected; luck is never on my side; my life is a total disaster; it is absolutely true that I never ever have been able to do whatsoever correctly"), convinces the client that he is unable to do anything about them. The exception questions ("Have there been times in the past period when you felt a little better, less down, less dejected?" or "Have you ever experienced something similar? How did that stop then?") create an opening. Examples of relevant questions that you can follow up with "and what else?", are:

- Have there been times in the past days/weeks when you were doing a little better?

- What did you do differently then?
- What was different then and how did you notice?
- If I could ask your parents/friends/colleagues/classmates that same question, what would he/she/they tell me?
- What did the others see happening to you in those better moments?
- How did they show that to you?
- How did you respond to that in turn?

HOW TO HELP PEOPLE WHO FEEL NO OWNERSHIP OF THE EXCEPTIONS?

Some clients are convinced that they have no part in those exceptions to their problems. They assume that the exceptions have nothing to do with how they behave but are simply coincidences.

CLIENT: "Last week I had a good week while doing absolutely nothing different than I always do. It was nice weather though. After that long dark winter, there was finally some spring in the air. Could that have something to do with it?"

PROFESSIONAL: "Maybe so, maybe not. I'm just glad you can tell me you finally had a good week. Good on you for taking advantage of the good weather to have a better week. Most people that feel depressed,[13] don't even notice that the weather is nice. And indeed, after every dark winter, spring comes, and nature wakes up all over again.[14] Other than noticing this, are there any things that were a little different this past week?"

It is important to help clients attribute the changes that occur to something they themselves are doing or have done. Research[15] in social psychology shows that changes that clients attribute to internal factors, such as new coping skills or different behaviors, stick better. If the client attributes the change to external factors, that change tends not to be sustainable. This "locus of control," whether internal or external, tends to trigger self-fulfilling prophecies in the good and bad directions. Obviously, solution-focused change agents strive for eliciting good self-fulfilling prophecies.

HOW TO HELP PEOPLE WITH A SELF-ANNIHILATING MINDSET?

Clients with self-annihilating request for help (I want to, but I can't, it's stronger than me, I was born and raised that way) try to get out of their problems by constantly pushing against the door to their solutions. What they don't realize, however, is that they want to push open a door that opens inward. By asking for exceptions, they temporarily stop pushing, start thinking, and then the door might open a little on its own.

CLIENT: If I catch myself not being anxious for once, panic strikes immediately. I can't help it; it is stronger than myself.

PROFESSIONAL: Are there times when you find that you are not anxious and that you are able to do something that keeps the panic at bay?

CLIENT: I can only do this if I am so focused on my work and my colleagues that the panic doesn't have a chance.

PROFESSIONAL: How do you do that?

CLIENT: No idea, it's just like that.

PROFESSIONAL: So, if you manage to focus your attention on something other than your panic, you manage to exert a little control. Great!

CLIENT: Thank you. Do you think it's possible to achieve that even in my spare time?

PROFESSIONAL: Of course, but it will require a lot of effort from you.

CLIENT: Doesn't matter. Now I lose all that energy needlessly because of that panic. That energy would be better spent elsewhere if I only knew how.

PROFESSIONAL: Would you be interested to see how you are going to do that?

CLIENT: Of course.

Checklist for the searching working relationship

1 Offer acknowledgment
2 Give positive support
3 Encourage self-responsibility
4 Ask the continuation question
5 Concretize, differentiate, and prioritize.
6 Search for exceptions

Metaphor for the searching working relationship

The key under the streetlight

Suppose you wake up in the middle of the night to noise on the street. You hear someone across the street muttering to himself. After a while, your curiosity overcomes your fatigue, and you go to look. Across the street, under the streetlamp, you see your left-hand neighbor crawling around on all fours. You decide to get up and find out what is going on. Arriving at the lantern, you ask him what the matter is and if there is anything you can do for him. He replies I have lost my house key. Where did you lose it? I lost it at my front door. Then why are you searching for the key here across the street? Across the street is the only place with enough light.

In a nutshell

It is the task of the SoFAP professional to create a context in which clients gain hope that change is possible and then to help them figure out what small steps they can take to do so.

The consulting working relationship

We now come to the fourth and final fundamental question: is the client, who presents a workable request for help, able to make use of his resources? If the answer is "no," we enter a consulting working relationship. Those clients come to us for a consult[16] with the question how they can regain access to and (again) use their resources. In other words, they give us the mandate to help them on how to (re)discover and use their own resources.[17]

Clients without access to their resources come in many colors

People with workable requests for help but who indicate their loss of the manual on how to use their resources come in a variety of subtypes. Their greatest common denominator is that they are open to help, even though they have no idea how they could deal with their challenges.

The most common subtypes we encounter in the consulting working relationship are clients who:

- describe their problems in workable terms but indicate that they haven't got a clue on how to go about solving them: "I would like to … but I don't know how I to do this. Can you help me, please?"
- are simply unaware of the resources at their disposal: "In the morning, when I think of the day ahead, a feeling of helplessness already overwhelms me. I see the pile of work in the house/office looming up before me like a mountain. Although I used to deal with everything by tackling and solving one thing after another, now I don't see how that was ever possible".
- stop using the right tools too quickly before they get any results: "I really tried for a few days to plan my work a little better by dividing my energy better. But that didn't work either, after two days of hard work I had a relapse, and everything started all over again".
- don't use their resources well: "I've made so many priority lists, but that doesn't work because something always comes up".
- jumping too quickly from one technique to another: "I tried writing the agreements with my kids on the board in the kitchen, but they don't read it. Then I thought it would work better if I put a bill in their lunchbox, but apparently, they just throw that away. I even tried giving them a list of their chores at the table before I serve dinner, but they got mad about that. Nothing ever works.

These examples show that the client has resources but does not know or has forgotten or has simply overlooked how to use them properly.

General intervention for the consulting working relationship

The basic intervention in the consulting relationship is to create a context in which clients learn how to use their resources in a more useful and effective manner. As always, the SoFAP modus operandi of asking questions is a better way to build solutions than offering ready-made and off-the-shelf solutions: "Dear Reader, don't you think asking questions works better than prescribing what the other should do?".

Specific interventions for the consulting working relationship

One can apply the following six closely related and stacked interventions, or, depending on the situation choose one or more specific interventions from this list that seem exceptionally useful in a given situation.

Offer positive support and acknowledgment

As with any SoFAP intervention, to increase the likelihood of change, it is critical that clients feel recognized and understood. "It is clear from what you tell me that you are going through a rough patch. Despite this, you have already put a lot of effort into trying to do something about it yourself."

Analyze previous attempts at solutions

Take the time to interview the client about what he has already tried without success: "What have you tried so far that hasn't worked or hasn't worked well enough?"

When you linguistically deconstruct this question, there are several active ingredients hidden within it, all of which you activate with this one simple question.

- The answers provide information about what the client has already tried to do on his own, albeit without success. Consistent with basic rule 1 "if something does not work (well enough), after you have tried for a while, you stop, learn from it and do something else", this teaches you what you should not do. This paves the way for alternatives that might work better.
- The form and content of the answers give us a lot of information about the client's general thinking and actions. This will help the practitioner to act and speak in the language of the client.
- The question itself contains a compliment, which improves the working relationship and focuses the client on their resources rather than their problem fixation.

- With this respectful question, you make it clear to the client that you are more interested in his efforts to work on his problem than in the problem itself. More specifically, you show the client that you are more interested in him as a person with all his resources than in his problems.
- You show acceptance for the client's problems but prepare him to apply Formula-P by which you help the client translate his problems into challenges.

Once you have a good idea of what the client has tried to do, but what hasn't helped well (enough), you can offer him compliments on his efforts and move on to the next question.

Appreciate small success factors

"What have you already tried to do that has helped a little?"

This question elicits information about partial solutions that have proven helpful in the past. After learning firsthand how the client has short-circuited his own attempts at solution, the practitioner often finds things that can be made workable with some modification. Then it's just a matter of encouraging the client to use those things again, albeit in a slightly modified form.

A similar and equally useful question is: "How have you tackled this kind of problem in the past and what worked best then?" Somewhat adapted to changed circumstances, it almost always turns out that what worked in the past can be applied in the here and now.

If the client asks for advice, offer advice!

The client in a consulting working relationship has a request for help but he doesn't know how to use his resources. The client indicates that he is willing to accept help. He comes to consult with us and asks for advice. There is no reason why we should not give him advice.

The only condition you absolutely must meet when giving advice is that you only give advice when the client asks for it. To give advice to someone who has no request for help is not respectful.

Regardless of the widespread and politically correct misconception that giving advice is wrong, SoFAP professionals do not see why this should be the case. After all, giving advice is not the exclusive privilege of professionals. Clients are ordinary people with family members, partners, friends, acquaintances, and colleagues who constantly give each other advice. Some of the purists among solution-focused practitioners are terrified of giving advice. They justify this based on the completely outdated and old-fashioned idea that they would make their clients dependent on them. Exceptions aside, the average client is smarter than that. By the way, if you find your clients becoming temporarily dependent on your collaboration, there is nothing wrong with that. It just means that they want to continue to make use of our services and keep making progress. Of course, it is a different matter if the client becomes dependent on the practitioners as a person or if the practitioner deliberately keeps the client on a leash. Professional ethic, deontological guideline and in some cases even the law prohibits these malpractices.

Clients frequently ask us for tips. Tips on how to sleep better, how to communicate better, how to relax better, how to concentrate better, how to feel better, and so on. Countless self-help books and popular magazines are full of tips. And there is nothing wrong with that. On the contrary! We will never know how many people have been helped with "garden-variety" tips for the simple reason that those lucky people never end up in professional services. Unfortunately, by the time clients come to a professional for a consultation, they have often already received so many tips and tried them out without results. What is wrong with pointing out that tip of the veil: "Have you ever tried to...?"

If clients are very unsure of themselves or do not know what they could do, direct suggestions can be helpful. Suggestions are not guidelines or instructional commands. Suggestions are just suggestions, and the client can do what he wants with them. You can even distance yourself from them by attributing the suggestion to a third party: "I have known clients who found it useful to consult a lawyer in these circumstances".[18]

Many clients are genuinely grateful when we make direct suggestions to them, even more so when, in previous encounters with professionals, they have had to deal with colleagues who only listened and acted as a neutral sounding board.

There are two conditions you must absolutely meet when giving advice:

1 One only gives advice to a client who asks for it. Giving advice to a client who has no request for help is not respectful.
2 As you will see in the next section, advice works best when it is phrased as a question.

Give advice in the form of a question

When a client asks for advice, we are going to give it to him. Yet, we are always careful to do so in the form of a suggestion with a question mark behind it. After all, by answering our suggestive question that contains some advice, the client becomes the owner of the suggested possible solutions.

CLIENT: I have no idea what I could do to learn to deal more calmly with X. You are the expert I have come to consult. Can you help me with this?
PROFESSIONAL: Sure.[19]

CLIENT: What would you do if you were in my place?

PROFESSIONAL: I don't know because I'm not you. But what would you think of...? What if you were to...? Would it be useful to...? Do you think a... could be useful? Any idea if... helps? Can you imagine that another... would be beneficial? Have you ever thought about...? Should you try...? How would you feel about trying to...?

You can fill in the dots with what you think is useful for the client in relation to the situation at hand. It is best to give the client several options, so that he can choose what suits him best. You will find that the client often comes up with answers that you yourself would never have thought of!

By giving advice in the form of suggestive questions, you acknowledge the expertise of the client and give him (back) his responsibility.

> Focusing attention, facilitating as it does receptiveness and responsiveness to ideas, is of value in every aspect wherein instruction, advice, counsel, guidance, direction, reassurance, comfort, and all those manifold values of interpersonal relationships are so significant.[20]
>
> Milton H. Erickson

SoFAP is a meta-model

Because all insights from the Big Book of Knowledge of Psychology and Common Sense are useful in a consulting work relationship, we dare to state that Solution Focused Applied Psychology is a meta-model. All conceivable interventions and techniques that we derive from all kinds of other professional change models can be used, up to and including "Golden Tips".

Of course, you need to give these interventions a solution-focused twist.

Checklist for the consulting working relationship

1. Offer positive support and acknowledgment
2. Analyze previous attempts at solutions
3. Appreciate small success factors
4. If the client asks for advice, offer advice!
5. Give advice in the form of a question.
6. SoFAP is a meta-model.

Metaphor for the consulting working relationship

> Shopping
>
> Clients in a consulting relationship are like customers who are browsing the streets lined with solution shops. They enter our little shop of

solution manuals with their requests. They put their workable problems on the counter and ask. "Could you possibly help me? I'm stuck with a problem, and I have no idea how to tackle it. I'm sure you would know". Clients assume – quite rightly because we are professionals – that we know ways that they can use to solve their problems and/or initiate further growth in their well-being. What they are out to buy are tools that will help them solve their problems themselves. Sometimes they already have these tools available, but they have lost the manual on how to make the best use of their tools. Our task is not solving it for them, but to offer them ways to find their own manual again. We give them advice, preferably in the form of questions, so they can use their own resources optimally (again) and thus learn to help themselves.

In a nutshell

The more knowledge, experience, insights, and common sense you have available as a facilitator, the more flexible to specific circumstances and needs of the client, the more useful your services will be.

The co-expert relationship

When the request for help is clear, the goals are workable, and the client can use his resources, the answer to the fourth fundamental question is yes. Then client and practitioner find themselves in a working relationship between experts.

Clients who can use their resources come in many colors

1 A client may have gone through the previous phase(s) of the flowchart. Together you have moved from a non-committal, through a searching and a consulting relationship, into the co-expert mode. Now the client can (re)use his own resources to create solutions and has learned how to increase his well-being. If all goes well, you can now help that client to learn to do it all by himself in the future.

   Basic intervention: help the client to do more of what works.

2 It happens that the client is not aware of the fact that he already has what it takes to come to good and lasting solutions. Then he needs someone with expertise and mandate to confirm this and give him a gentle push in the back.

   Basic intervention: help the client to continue doing what works.

3 We meet co-experts when we are lucky enough to work with clients from whom we can learn as much as we can teach them.

   Basic intervention: **T**.ogether **E**.ach **A**.chieves **M**.ore

General interventions for the Co-expert relationship

When working with co-experts, your main task is to step aside, "applaud", and support your client in doing more of what works. Now, you have become a sounding board, inspirer, and supervisor who listen to the client's success story and only must encourage him.

Interventions at this level of the flowchart are quick and incisive because clients have learned to solve their own problems, or rather they have learned to learn. Once the client has mastered this skill, he will find his own way through the jungle of life.

Specific interventions for the Co-expert relationship

More of the same

The mantra for all previous positions on the flowchart is: stop doing what is not working and do something else instead.

The mantra for the co-expert relationship is: do more of what you are already doing, because it works.

Use everything

Every intervention, tip, trick, advice, insight, and technique that you can come up with together to move forward deserves encouragement. The most effective interventions come from the expert-client himself. As a professional, you are an expert in change and in learning processes. You can therefore act as a sounding board, provide additional information, and offer guidance and/or new tools.

Compliment the client on what works

Step aside and compliment the client on what he is already doing that works. By complimenting him on what he is doing well, we boost his self-confidence to keep going.

Help the client to help himself (and each other)

Metaphor for the Co-expert Relationships

Alpinism

A solution-focused change agent is like a trainer in mountaineering. When the client is ready to go up the mountain, he uses a special didactic method. He sits at the foot of the mountain, huddled warmly in a comfortable chair with a walkie-talkie in one hand and binoculars in the other. He gives the start signal and remains seated in his snug chair while the client begins his ascent. Because your client has done sufficient training beforehand, the solution-focused trainer is confident that he can handle this expedition all by himself. The trainer gets comfortable, stays warm, and most importantly stays down. All he has to do is keep an eye on the climber through his binoculars. Occasionally he uses his walkie-talkie to warn the climber about loose rocks, dangerous cliffs but also to correct him if he goes in a direction that leads nowhere. For the rest, all he must do is suggest to the athlete that he follow the path of least resistance and encourage him assiduously. He is the athlete, you the supporter.

In a nutshell

Reaching the position where client and practitioner become co-experts in the same endeavor is a joy of mutual learning. While the client and his/her relatives can enjoy the growth process to the full, the practitioner can celebrate with them, while remaining alert and ready to intervene should a setback occur.

Rules of thumb to maximize the effectiveness of the flowchart

1 More with less

With the help of the flowchart, you know exactly what you should and should not do. This helps to "minimax", to use minimum energy to achieve maximum results. You will quickly learn that you often achieve more by doing less. The flowchart shows the shortest route to a possible solution and helps to limit the number of interventions required.

2 Determining the correct position

Determine as precisely as possible to which category the working relationship with your client belongs. Once defined, limit yourself to the interventions that belong to that specific category.

If you make a mistake in determining the position, there is a good chance that your interventions will not work. For example, there is no point in giving advice to a client who is in a non-committal working relationship.

3 Follow the dynamics

Because of the constantly changing context in which we live and work, the changes in life we continuously encounter, and the complexity of our dynamic relationships with others, the position of the working relationship on the flowchart is in constant flux. Even within a single conversation, the position on the flowchart may vary depending on the topic that is discussed at each moment. This is perfectly normal. Accepting this flux as a given and pacing its dynamics keeps you alert and creative.

4 Multiple clients, multiple positions

When talking simultaneously to several clients, there is a good chance that the clients are in different positions on the flowchart with respect to certain themes. In that case, it is important to do the interventions with everyone corresponding to his/her position on the flowchart, and to avoid doing individual facilitation in the presence of the other interlocutors.

You do this by speaking to "the system-as-a-whole". Speaking with "the system as a whole" is, of course, a metaphor. What we mean is difficult to express on paper but let us try. For example, if you are working with a married couple, you can look at the husband while saying something to the wife about her husband. If you are talking to a family, you can say something to the parents about their parenting style, for example, while looking at the children. This way, you avoid giving the family the impression that you are talking to each family member individually while the others are in the room.

When you work with a team, chances are that not everyone is at the same level on the flowchart. Taking this into account, it is important to operate your leadership mandate to:

- make sure that every participant is invited to share his perspective,
- take the lead in the meeting so that no participant dominates the conversation
- make regular interim summaries to check if everyone is still on the same page
- leave room for dissenting views in such a way that they do not interfere with the smooth running of the meeting

5 The rule of caution

If you are not sure at what level your working relationship is, first do interventions that fit a position lower on the flowchart. For example, if you are not sure whether you are in a searching working relationship, it is better to start with interventions that fit a non-committal working relationship. You can quickly see from the way the client reacts whether you are right or wrong. That makes it possible to fine-tune your position.

Conclusion

In this chapter, we have explained the flowchart as a tool to find out what you should and should not do if you want maximum results with minimum use of energy. The correct reading of the position of your working relationship on the flowchart shows you the shortest route to the most useful interventions. The position indicates the quality of the mandate you receive from the clients and the working relationship fluctuates continuously between the different positions.

The essence of solution-focused work is not to be there, but to be underway.

Notes

1 We prefer to use the term "flowchart" instead of "decision tree". The "flow" in flowchart refers to the work of Mihaly Csikszentmihalyi (1934–2021) where he describes "flow" as the blissful state of maximum focus. The companion book, *Solution-Focused Applied Psychology, a Design Science Research Protocol* (SoFAP-P, Routledge 2023), written by Louis Cauffman and Mathieu Weggeman, provides a scientific rationale for best practices and solution-focused interventions. In it, a more sophisticated flowchart is presented, along with more than forty case studies.
2 In his 1972 book, *Steps to an ecology of mind*, Bateson developed his idea of a "difference that makes a difference" in his talk to Alfred Korzybski's Institute of General Semantics. The talk was entitled "Form, Substance, and Difference." Modern re-edition: University of Chicago Press; 1st edition (March 10, 2000).
3 The topic of the different mandates is extensively discussed in Chapter 4. Since mandates are an important issue in SoFAP and have great influence on the work, we advise a quick scan of Chapter 4 as a memory-refresher.
4 Betty Alice Erickson, Bradford Keeney. 'Milton H. Erickson, an American Healer'. Ringing Rock Books (2006). For information on the vital importance of Elisabeth Moore Erickson for the career of her husband, see the video on 'YouTube Bert Erickson'. Reference: https://www.youtube.com/watch?v=KC_qFUZmK4M
5 Epictetus. The Art of Living, HarperCollins 1994.
6 Here, you meet another cross connection between the seven-step dance of change and the non-committal position on flowchart.
7 de Shazer, S. (1989). *Contemporary Family Therapy, 11*(4), Winter 1989. This paper was presented April 14, 1989, at Ground Rounds, University of Texas, Southwest Medical Center, Department of Psychiatry, Dallas, Texas.
8 de Shazer, S. (1984). The death of resistance. *Family Process, 23*, 1–11.
9 We explicitly put the word "resistance" in parentheses to indicate that we are dealing here with a concept and not with "something that exists in reality." Gregory Bateson, the great epistemologist of systems thinking, emphasizes the danger that lies in reification, making into a "thing" what is no more than a concept. If you fall into that linguistic trap, you make the mistake of thinking that you have borderline like you have the flu, that there is a stone in your chest like you have a heart of stone, that you have a cold like you have a frozen shoulder (adhesive capsulitis), that you have resistance like you have a broken leg, and so on.
10 Personal communication 2009.
11 Linguistic connoisseurs will appreciate the subtle differences between would (conditional), could (potential), and will (actual). Words are Magic.
12 See Chapter 1 Basic Axioms and Chapter 5, step 4 of the Solution Tango (page 103).
13 The linguistically sensitive reader notices the difference between the client saying he is depressed and asking when he feels depressed.

14 Here, we make grateful use of what the client offers us. While the client describes the actual state of the weather, we turn it into a metaphor of change. This allows us to give him an indirect suggestion by which we 1/ normalize the good–bad cycle, 2/ compliment the client on his active effort, 3/ delicately point out to him that he is not among the depressed people because depressed people do not notice spring, 4/ point out to him his possibility, like nature, to wake up again. Words are magic.

15 For example: Weinberger, J. (1995). Common factors aren't so common: The common factors dilemma. *Clinical Psychology: Science and Practice*, *2*, 45–69.

16 According to Merriam-Webster, "to consult" means that the client asks for advice and counsel. The intransitive verb of the word means "to deliberate together".

17 Cross connection between the axiom of resource-orientation (Chapter 1), the three mandates (Chapter 4), step 4 "discovering resources" of the seven-step dance (Chapter 5), and the flowchart.

18 de Shazer, S. (2021). More than miracles. In S. de Shazer, Y. Dolan, H. Korman, T. Trepper, E. McCollum & I.K. Berg (Eds.), *The state of the art of solution-focused brief therapy*. Routledge, p. 155.

19 It goes without saying that you are transparent with the client and tell him if you do not know the answer to his question. You can always refer the client to someone else. The hallmark of a true professional: is that he knows his own limitations.

20 Milton H. Erickson, *Hypnosis in obstetrics: Utilizing experiential learning*. Unpublished manuscript, circa 1950s.

Chapter 7

The icons

The real innovation embedded in the solution-focused approach, was introduced by Steve de Shazer's paradigm shift that states that problems are of a different logical class than solutions.[1] This fundamental epistemological difference implies that one does not necessarily need problems to arrive at solutions. When one abandons the search for root causes and instead defines problems as possible golden signposts to alternatives, it opens new territory. In addition to the central role of resources as pivots for change, the direction provided by the client's goals, and the importance of the client's systemic context, there was the search for effectiveness and efficiency. The use of scaling questions and the Miracle Question were the most prominent and eye-catching innovations that carved out a niche in the already crowded world of psychotherapy models. Soon, these techniques became the icons of the solution-focused approach.

Simplism comes at a price. Too often the solution-focused approach is stripped of its epistemological richness and reduced to these techniques. When one makes the belief that the client is the expert of his own life into a credo and adds that giving compliments is the most important intervention imaginable, simplism can become naiveté. Techniques then turn into tricks.

Steve de Shazer and Insoo Kim Berg, along with the first generation of experts who further developed the solution-focused approach, did not adhere to naïve simplism, nor did they have the slightest interest in tricks. With these caveats in mind, this chapter explores the richness that lies within the two techniques and exposes the linguistic complexities behind what at first appear to be simple techniques.

Numbers on a scale, and particularly the difference between the numbers, are tools to help the client create differentiation. The conversation about the meaning of the differences between the numbers is what matters and makes the use of scaling questions less of a technique and more of a guide to the conversation.

The same is true of the future orientation that underlies the use of the Miracle Question. Here, the process of the unfolding conversational cycle

DOI: 10.4324/9781003320104-8

of questions and answers is more important than the mere content of the client's answers.

When, for the sake of ill-considered pragmatism and simplism, one reduces both interventions to seemingly simple and straightforward techniques, all the richness and complexity hidden in both interventions disappears into trivialities. This makes Steve and Insoo spin in their graves like perpetual mobiles. Because there is so much to discover in the folds of these seemingly simple techniques, the following pages unfold the practical complexities that promote deeper understanding and pay tribute to Steve and Insoo's gifts to the field.

Icon 1 scaling questions

The generic format of the scaling question goes like this: 'Imagine a scale where the starting point, the zero, stands for X (to be filled in according to the specific situation) and the 10 stands for Y (ditto), where are you now?'

Steve speaks

In his 1994 book, "Words were originally magic", de Shazer states: 'Our scales are primarily designed to facilitate treatment'.[2] In his last book, he writes: 'There are two major components of this [scaling] intervention. First, it is a solution-focused assessment device, that is, if used at each session, the therapist and the client have an on-going measurement of their progress. Second, it is a powerful intervention in and of itself, because it allows the therapist to focus on previous solutions and exceptions, and to punctuate new changes as they occur'.[3]

In Steve de Shazer's explanation, scale questions are seen as measurement tools that reveal on-going progress (or lack thereof). At the same time, scaling questions reveal past and/or partial solutions (a.k.a. exceptions to problems) and serve as pointers to alternatives (a.k.a. new and different behaviors).

In this respect, scaling questions are technical interventions that serve specific purposes, namely assessing progress and punctuating changes that generate partial solutions.

The difference between scales and scaling

de Shazer's distinction between the noun "cooperation" and the verb "cooperate" clarifies the distinction between reification (a noun denotes a state, a condition, something that just 'is', unmoving and thing-like) and the process of an on-going interaction between subsystems.[4] We paraphrase this linguistic subtlety when we prefer the verb "scaling" to the noun "scale" for the same reason. Scaling questions alludes to the activity of advancing to a particular position on a scale as a result of answering questions. The "ing" thus indicates an active and on-going process that takes place between interlocutors.

Scaling questions in relation to the SoFAP essentials

SoFAP goes beyond these original insights and connects the technique of scaling questions with the fundamental insights that underlie SoFAP.

The answers and follow-up questions unpack the content of whatever number on the scale the client provides. The details hereof increase the hope that change is possible, activate the client's resilience, and help him (re)gain access to their own resources. These are precisely the active ingredients that must always be present for professional facilitation to be successful (Chapter 2).

Offering differentiation is a tool that fully serves the client's efforts to achieve his – preferably workable – goals (step 3 goal setting in Chapter 5). Offering differentiation frees the client's resources and makes them usable for achieving goals. The future locked in a binary past is replaced by a future rich in colorful possibilities.

Numbers are magic

As an opener, we like to quote Steve de Shazer when he paraphrases Ludwig Wittgenstein:

> To paraphrase Wittgenstein (1958, #43): 'For a large class of topics or themes –though not for all – in which we employ scaling questions, the meaning of a number is its use and, more particular, its use in relationship to the other numbers on the scale'. As anyone who has played around with numbers knows, like words, numbers are magic.[5]

The quote clearly states that a particular number on itself means nothing. The implication is twofold. First, scaling questions are of a totally different order than the scales one usually uses to measure something based on a normative standard. The number the client chooses is not a mathematical expression of improvement,[6] like results expressed on a scorecard. *The number is a metaphor of difference.* Thus, it has nothing to do with how well or how poorly the client is functioning compared to a general standard. Second, and even more crucial, is the notion that one can only understand what a number means when the client is asked what is in the number and how what is in the given number relates to the content of the other numbers on the scale. Thus, the meaning of the number becomes clear only when it is used in relation to the other numbers on the scale.

The number given by the client is like a musical note on a musical bar: it only becomes music in relation to the other notes, the silences, the key in which the piece of music was written, the rhythm that connects all the notes, and the zeitgeist in which the piece was composed. Just as notes only become music when you deploy all those things, so numbers only come to life when you use them as tools to achieve something that, without the use of numbers as metaphor, remains hidden in the darkness of immobility.

By using numbers in this dynamic way, movement occurs as if by miracle. The client discovers what, compared to the starting point zero, he already does differently so that he can give the number X. Follow-up questions on the content of this X provide detailed information that is the stepping-stone to which he can add to get to the number X+1. Used in this way, the numbers of the scale become the steps of the ladder on which the client can move to get a different view of his own reality.

Scaling questions do not measure. Scaling questions change.

Scaling questions invite change

Scaling questions, follow-up questions, and the ensuing answers open and structure the dynamic dialogue between client and professional toward a solution-focused narrative. Starting from the given number, by asking questions we help the client unpack the content of the number they have chosen. This unpacking reveals the content of the difference packaged in the given number on the scale. Instead of the perception of a problematic reality frozen in black and white, the client is facilitated to uncover and thereby discover a new and more differentiated perception of reality. This is the starting point for change. Subsequent questions and answers explore the differences after the black/white blockage is lifted. During the conversation, a different reality develops. This promotes the emergence of new thoughts, feelings, and behaviors and can be continued beyond the professional relationship when the client enters the phase of self-healing and/or self-growth.

Scaling questions in practice

We opened this chapter with the simplest scaling question: 'Imagine a scale where the starting point, the zero, stands for X (to be filled in according to the specific situation) and the 10 stands for Y (ditto), where are you now?'

The opening word, "Imagine," invites and evokes a mental representation that makes it easier for the client to go along with it.

You can support your words in a nonverbal way by making hand movements that suggest difference. You can let the timbre of your voice slide from low to high as you move from the beginning point to the end point in your explanation of the scale. You can also visualize the scale by counting aloud from 0 to 10. At the same time, you can draw the scale on a sheet of paper. For clients who are in the pit, a vertically drawn scale fits better, while a horizontally drawn scale fits better when you talk about progress.

For young children and people who have no notion of numbers, the scale can be represented as follows:

You can use a scale from 0 or from 1, because a zero is just, well, nothing – to 10. For clients who are depressed or tell you they are down in the dumps, you can use a scale from −10 to 0.

Some clients are helped if they can visualize their scales. You can draw a scale on paper and ask them to circle themselves which number they choose.

Clients, who say they are down, are often better served by a vertically drawn scale. This provides a nonverbal hint that they can get out of the dip. Clients who are in a learning process or want to make progress, are best served by a scale drawn horizontally (in Western language culture, the scale runs best from left to right).

What doesn't work as well is a scale from −5 to +5: then clients have the socially desirable inclination to stick around 0 and that doesn't help.

There are interesting differences about the start and end numbers on each scale. The School of Milwaukee, the original institute of de Shazer and Berg, prefers that the continuum runs from 0 "a total disaster" to 10 "everything is perfect". Since we strongly believe that perfection is not of this world, we try to avoid these extremes. We prefer that 0 stands for "very difficult" and 10 for "good enough." The reader is invited to experiment at will.

A roadmap for using scaling questions

As you become versed with the underlying mechanism in the different types of scaling questions, you'll notice that there is a recurring pattern hidden within them that we've molded into a roadmap for your ease of use. As in any roadmap, you are free to choose different exits, detours, or shortcuts.

1 Prepare the client by asking permission to ask a scaling question.
2 Offer a scale where the starting point of the scale – for example, the 0 – stands for X and the end point – for example, the 10 – equals Y.
3 Then ask where the client is already on that scale.

4 Accept the number given, whatever it is.
5 Repeat this number, and validate it by complimenting it, "A 3, OK".
6 First, ask what is already different that enables the client to give this number.
7 Accept all answers and validate what the client brings in by repeating or paraphrasing it.
8 Make extensive use of the question "and what else?" to invite the client to describe in increasing detail what is already different compared to the starting point.
9 Broaden the perspective by asking triangular questions such as, "What would your partner/colleague/family/friend say if I asked him that same question?"
10 End with: 'What could be the smallest next step forward?'

Classification of scaling questions

The number of scaling questions you can think of is endless, because the content of the X and Y is different for each client and for each situation.

That said, we can distinguish several major types of scaling questions:

1 the scale of difference
2 the scale of progress
3 the scale of hope for change
4 the scale of motivation
5 the scale of usefulness
6 the scale of confidence
7 the scale of well-being

We present the different types of scaling questions in this order because this is the logical way to use them during a conversation or in a full facilitation process. It goes without saying that the situation determines which scale you use, and in which order you do so. Sometimes you use one type, sometimes you use several and sometimes – when the client is already functioning in a differentiated way – you do not use a scaling question at all.

The scale of difference

> May I ask you a question? Imagine, on a scale from 0 to 10, where the 0 represents "the moment you decided to pick up the phone and make an appointment" and the 10 represents "now it is good enough", where are you already?

The fact that the client comes in, voluntarily or forced by a third party, is already a difference. Asking the scale of difference is an invitation to expand on this. Questions that scale the difference that occurred in the period prior to the first session is a nuanced version of the pre-session change question that we discussed before.[7] This question focuses the attention of the client on small differences that can spawn real change.

The client can answer in four possible ways:

- *'I don't know'* contains the stage direction 'I don't understand your question, ask it again in a slightly different way' or 'I don't know yet, give me time to think'.
- A *'Zero'* contains the stage direction: 'Before I am ready for differentiation, I would like you to ask me how I got through the difficult situation, and I could use a compliment on that'.
- *'A minus 5,* because things are getting worse' contains the stage direction: ask me the coping question.[8]
- A *4 (or higher)'* contains the stage direction: 'I acknowledge a little difference already so now ask me questions so that I can expand on that 4'.

If the client can give a number that falls in the range of the scale, they are indicating that they have noticed a difference. Then we can ask questions to help build that difference into one that makes a real difference. That is change and is a steppingstone to the next scaling question.

The scale of progress

> Imagine a scale that goes from −10 to 0, where −10 stands for "the hardest thing you've ever experienced" and 0 for "not everything is solved, but I can get by. Where are you now[9]?

With this scaling question, you can not only help the client to think more differentiated, but also and especially help him to take steps forward by building on small changes. You can use this scaling question from the moment the client indicates small differences in a first session. The scale of progress can be used in each subsequent session.

The next question follows logically: "What is already different so that you can give yourself a 4?".

This question invites the client to explain what is wrapped up in the metaphor of the number 4. Whatever the client says, you accept it, repeat it in your own words whereby you do not avoid solution-focused suggestions. You then ask further questions that invite the client to provide as detailed a description as possible.

When the client is finished with each detailed description, ask "What else?" The "What else?" is a magic question because it packs a powerful intervention in just three components. The word "what" contains the invitation to (further) explain content, the word "else" suggests that there are more things wrapped up in the given number, and the "?" makes the client the owner of his answers.

If you feel[10] that the client has exhausted every possible detail, you can say, 'Fine. That's a lot already!'[11] Then follow up by asking, "What *could* be the smallest next step?"[12] This follow-up question invites the client to look ahead.

Now the client has several options:

- At the beginning of a facilitation process, a client sometimes says that he does not know (yet) what the next step might be. An elegant response then is, 'Fine. What do you need to be able to stay on a 3?'
- There are times when a client immediately wants to make large and probably unachievable quantum leaps. You can both compliment him on this eagerness and temper his probably counterproductive enthusiasm without disqualifying him, by saying, "What you're telling me all attests to your great commitment, motivation and belief in your own abilities. That's very good. Are you sure, however, that this is the smallbest possible step forward? Wouldn't it be safer to learn to walk first before you run?". Then ask: "Amidst all your motivation, abilities, and commitment, what could be the smallest possible first steps?".
- Clients who can give concrete examples of what the smallest next step forward might be, need only confirmation from the professional. After all, his answers are suggestions that the client gives to himself. All we need to do is paraphrase the client's answers in such a way that you help him translate his suggestions into concrete, realistic, realizable terms that can be expressed in behavioral terms. Now, the client's goals fit the useful goal checklist.[13]

The elegance of asking solution-building questions is that you don't have to tell the client what to do. Quite the opposite! If you ask the right questions at the right time, you will find that the client figures out for himself what his next steps are. As a result, he becomes the owner of his own progress. Our task is to lead from behind.

In a subsequent session, you can ask for the scale of progress again, albeit with a slight twist: "During our last conversation, we used a scale in which you showed me the small steps you have already taken. We are a while later now. Can I ask you that question again: "On a scale of 0 to 10, where 0 stands for 'worst ever' and 10 for 'good enough'? Where are you already today?".

The client's options now are:

- They will rarely give you an identical number. Even if the number itself is unimportant, they will usually give you a slightly higher number. This is understandable because the whole intervention is built around small steps forward that the clients have come up with themselves. People are simply more motivated to do something they have thought up themselves than something someone else has thought up for them. What the client then offers us is the material we use in this session to build on to make progress.

- In a second (or subsequent) conversation, clients sometimes say they are disappointed because they went backwards or got stuck: 'I'm sorry to say it didn't go well and I have to give today a 1' or 'I'm afraid I won't be able to make any progress because I got stuck where I was last time'.

No worries! That brings us to the next scaling question.

The scale of hope for change

> 'May I ask you a different kind of scale question? On a scale of 0 to 10, where the 0 represents "I have no hope that any change is possible for me" and the 10 represents "I am hopeful that, with the right effort, I can make a positive change," where do you stand now?'

People may experience things in their lives that make them feel powerless and despondent. This scale introduces the concept of hope. For the client, it can be the steppingstone to realizing that something can be done, albeit very small at first. Moreover, just by presenting this scaling question, the professional installs the idea that hope is possible. With some effort and persistence, the working relationship then does the rest.

The client's options now are:

- if the client answer with a zero or even a negative number, this is a stage direction that he needs something different first. This is a good moment to offer coping questions: "How do you keep that up? What kept you going? How did you come through that trial? etc." These coping questions not only offer recognition to the client's perception of despondency, but also help to uncover the client's resources that have helped him to get through it. The client's resilience,[14] is activated.
- If the client chooses a number that falls within the range of the scale, compliment him, and ask, "Good. What is already different that allows you to give yourself an X, where the X represents your hope that things can become different in your life?". Depending on the number the client gives, you can precede the word 'difference' with the words "very little, a lot, or enough."

The scale of motivation

> 'On a scale where 0 represents "I am in an impossible situation and I have zero motivation to do anything about it" and 10 represents "no matter how difficult it is, I am willing to do anything to address my problems," where are you now?'

The client chooses a zero: "I have no motivation to even try and do anything".

This zero may include the following possible stage directions that the client formulates like:

- Offering you a zero for motivation is my polite way of saying that I do not need nor want your help. Please don't push, dear professional, but offer me the interventions that fit the noncommittal working relationship on the flowchart.[15]
- Right now, I feel so despondent and powerless that being motivated won't help anyway, hence the zero. So, please, before you waste energy with futile attempts to motivate me, dear professional, return to the first five steps of the SoFAP dance (Chapter 5) to find a starting point.
- Before we can take further steps, I need to feel acknowledged for the difficult situation I am in.

Whatever number within the range of the motivation scale the client gives, compliment it, and ask for more, 'Your motivation to do something about your difficult situation is at a 2. OK. What gives you that 20 percent motivation?' And then, as always, ask for details, details, details.

When the client has exhaustively described these details, help him take the next step by asking, OK. Now, what do you need to increase your motivation a little bit? How are you going to notice that your motivation is increasing a little? What are you going to think, do, feel differently? How will people around you notice this?'

By asking follow-up questions and validating all answers, you encourage the client to take small steps forward. It is not the professional who dictates what the client should do. On the contrary, it is the client's own answers that propel him forward. He himself determines what it is that helps him move forward. In this way you do not have to pull and tug on the client, but give him small, friendly, and respectful nudges in the right direction.

The scale of usefulness

> 'May I now ask you a very different question? We have already discussed many things in our conversation. Imagine a scale where the 0 stands for "this is completely useless, this doesn't benefit me at all" and the 10 for "this really benefits me, this is very useful for me", where are we now?'

Note the "we." This scale and the series of subsequent questions are about the usefulness of what client and professional are doing together. Offering this scale and ending with the question "Where are you now?" is noncommittal on the part of the professional. Indeed, if the client gives himself a low number, he might get the impression that he is responsible for the conversation not being useful. The facilitation process is a joint effort by both parties, and the facilitator must assume his leadership mandate in this process, ergo, the "we".

The usefulness scale invites the client to a candid evaluation of the process. It gives both parties the opportunity to make immediate adjustments, if necessary, so that the facilitation process serves the client for the full 100 percent.

The client's answer options are:

- If the client replies, "Well… um… it's because you asked me and I hope you won't blame me, but… um… no, this isn't helping, so… sorry … a zero." Then you just accept this and move on to a renewed goal setting question[16] : "OK, good on you for being so clear about that. What do we need to talk about so that this conversation does become useful to you?".
- If the client chooses a number within the range, that number is an indication of their perceived usefulness. A 9 makes the process a little easier than a 2, but whatever the number is, it is always acceptable. "Well, I would give it a 4." Then you can say, "Excellent. What is it that we have discussed so far that is so useful that you are already giving it a 4?".
- It happens that clients are in such distress that they feel it necessary to give an extravagant negative number: 'Zero? Sorry, but last the week, I was at minus 27 and now it's going down. I appreciate what you're trying to do for me, but it's useless. I am useless. I hear myself talking and now I'm at minus 45.'

  Before you move to the coping question, you can try the following interaction:

  Professional: Well, that's terrible. How on earth do you keep up with that minus 45?

  Client (irritated): That's obvious, isn't it? I just can't do it. Don't you see what a catastrophe it is?

  Professional: Excuse me. I didn't mean it that way. I understand that it is indeed a terrible situation at those minus 45 moments. Can I still ask you a difficult question? Can you try to explain to me what is different when you are at minus 27 than at that minus 45? A minus 27 is still a disaster, but already a little more bearable than a minus 45. So, what is different? What do you do/think/say/feel differently then?

In other words, whatever the client says about his extremely negative figure, accept it, acknowledge him for his perception of his difficult situation, take him seriously, and work from there by asking solution-focused questions.

The scale of confidence

> 'On a scale where 0 stands for "I have absolutely no confidence in myself to address the issues in the right way" and 10 stands for "I am confident that I have everything I need to get out of this," where are you now?'

The following answers are possible:

- if the answer is zero, you can ask the coping question (see page 204).
- every other number deserves a little compliment and the follow-up question "Great. What is it that you are already doing differently so that you can give yourself a Y?".
- if the answer is "minus 10", the client deserves credit for coming to the session at all. After that, instead of insisting that the client gives an answer within the range, you better re-dance the first five steps of the SoFAP tango. This will give you more material to work with. But also, and most importantly, you show the client that you can be trusted with your offer of cooperation.
- if the client answers with a number that falls within the range, simply ask for more details and deploy the magic question "What else?" liberally.

The scale of well-being[17]

> 'On a scale where the 1 represents "I am totally dissatisfied with my life" and the 10 represents "perfection does not exist but I am satisfied with what I have in my life," where do you stand now?'

What is the purpose of facilitation other than to help the client, once his suffering has been alleviated, find access to a good life, and learn how to stay on that path all by himself? Why shouldn't it be possible to help a client build his well-being even if he (still) has problems? Who in their life is ever completely problem-free? As Martin Seligman said in a personal interview in 2009, "If you only take away the psychopathology of the patient, you will not get a happier person, but an empty one."

Each response on this well-being scale can be followed by questions that deepen the experience of satisfaction and fulfillment[18]:

- What is already there in your life and work that you are satisfied with?
- What could be the smallest step you could take to make life a tad easier?
- What do you need to learn so you can be satisfied faster?
- How can you remind yourself that how things are now is good (enough)?
- If you ask the people closest to you what number they would give for you on this scale, what would it be?
- If you are having a lesser day, what helps you the most to get back to a higher number?

Spice up each answer with "What else?".

Whatever the client answers when you invite him to provide details about the content of whatever number he chooses, these answers always contain building blocks to improve his situation, be it in the direction of solutions, be it in the direction of growth or greater well-being.

Special case: more clients at the same time

As professionals, we often talk to several people at once: couples, families, groups, clients together with third parties, concerned outsiders, stakeholders of all kinds, colleagues, teams, network partners, and so on. If you then present a scaling question, it is normal that not everyone is on the same number. That does not matter, because it is not a measuring instrument, but a means of differentiation and, from there, of gradual progress. How do you do this?

First, you can ask everyone individually what number they choose on the usefulness scale, where 0 stands for 'well-intentioned waste of time that doesn't benefit me' and 10 stands for 'if we continue to work together in this way, things will soon move in the right direction'.

First, ask each participant what has already been discussed during the meeting that allowed him to give his own number. This will give you, as the leader of the facilitation process, and all the participants a sense of the degree of usefulness of the work that has already been done.

Next you can have all the participants negotiate a common number and lead the discussion about what they have already done as a group to get to that common number. As always, it is important to ask for as much detail and concrete examples as possible.

You conclude by asking what is the next thing that would be useful to address and what number would then go with that. You can even end the discussion with the suggestive question, "Suppose that over the next two weeks you were all to experiment with all your useful suggestions, wouldn't it be interesting to know what number you will arrive at next time and what useful steps forward that will all entail?".

Ten tips for the optimal use of scaling questions

1 Respond positively.
2 Always ask *first* what goes into the number given.
2 Listen!
4 Practice neutral curiosity.
5 Treat the numbers as metaphors for difference.
6 Scaling questions in a follow-up interview.
7 Use triangular questions.
8 Treat the road as more important than the destination

9 Appreciate negative numbers as gifts
10 Experiment to your heart's content!

Respond positively

Whatever the client answers and whatever number on the scale he chooses, accept what he says and always respond positively:

- If the client says he is at a 1, respond with: 'Fine, that's already 10 percent progress. What is already different that allows you to give yourself that 1?'
- If the client gives another 1 at the next session, you can ask, 'Good, despite the difficult situation you are in, you managed to maintain that 10 percent progress. How did you do that?'
- It happens frequently that someone indicates that they have dropped on the scale. No problem, accept it and ask, 'Okay, last time you were at a 5 and now you are at a 3. What was different then? How did you manage to make sure you weren't on a 2? What do you need to get to a 4 and then back to the 5?'

Always ask first what goes into the number given

If the client gives himself number X on the scale, then he knows – per definition – what that number means to him, even though he may need answering our questions to find out. Therefore, we always ask first what is already different that has allowed him to give himself number X. This is a fail-safe intervention.

If the client gives himself a 5, it makes no sense to ask him immediately how he will arrive at a 6. After all, if he knew that, he would have given himself a 6 from the first time.

Listen!

The magic "What else?" question helps to get the client talking in more and more detail and helps the professional to stay quiet, making it easier for him to listen. Don't expect the client to be able to clearly explain what a particular number means right away. What happens much more often is that the client's answers contain resources and exceptions (read: partial solutions) that can be built upon.

Practice neutral curiosity

It is important to be curious about what the client has to say, but no more than that. Do not fall into the trap of the over-enthusiast who uses everything the client says to bombard him with 'wows' to convince him of his progress. It is well intentioned, but not wise to be more hopeful and optimistic than the client himself. Brian Cade, an Australian solution-focused therapist of the first hour, told us, "If the professional is more enthusiastic about the client's progress than the client himself, he is acting like a mother. And the clients all have mothers already!"

Professionals are like people, and people are curious. By listening only to those aspects of the client's story that you can use to maximize the client's feeling of being understood, you are activating that key non-specific factor. "Do I feel understood by my professional"[19] is the prerequisite for change. This is not the same as being a curious tourist in the client's life.

Treat the numbers as metaphors for difference

Because we so often encounter misunderstandings and reductionist simplifications when it comes to the use of scaling questions, we repeat again: numbers are metaphors for difference and not a mathematical expression of change, let alone improvement.

Scaling questions in a follow-up interview

As explained earlier, we do not use the numbers on the scaling questions as a measurement tool. Therefore, we do not confront the client with the number from the previous interview and we certainly will not ask him what (and certainly not why) his number is now more or less compared to the previous time. If we offer a scaling question again at all, we use the roadmap (see page 165) to do so and leave it to the client to fill in what they find useful as an answer in the current conversation. After all, last time's 4 could mean something very different from today's 4.

Use triangular questions

Triangular questions help the client put himself in the minds of relevant third parties. The answers he gives as if speaking from someone else's mind create a virtual reality that can be transformed into a usable reality with the right follow-up questions.

- What would your husband say if I asked him where you stand now on a scale where 0 stands for "very difficult" and 10 for "good enough"?
- Now that you can already put your pain symptoms at a 5, halfway between insufferable and bearable, how would your family members notice if you went to a 6?
- On a scale of 1 to 10 where the 1 stands for "things are just ordinary in my life" and the 10 stands for "perfection doesn't exist, but the way

my life is going right now, that's what I'm signing up for," what number would your partner give for you if I asked her?
- If you put yourself in the place of your spouse, what step would she recommend you take so that on the scale of well-being you would score a tad higher?
- What if you were to move up a notch on the well-being scale, how would the people around you notice? What will they see you doing, thinking, saying differently?

How come this virtual reality is so powerful?

Scientists indicate that the architecture of the mind has been constructed by evolution in such a way that much of the mental processes occur outside of conscious awareness. Timothy Wilson,[20] top researcher in the field of self-knowledge, argues that self-knowledge is less a matter of careful introspection than of learning to become an excellent observer of oneself. He claims that one of the most important means of doing this is to try to look at ourselves through the eyes of someone else. Ergo: the power of triangular questions.

> It takes two to know one.
>
> Gregory Bateson

Treat the road as more important than the destination

Defining the 10 as 'everything is perfect' invites the risk of getting stuck in solution-drivenness. We prefer to surf the waves of solution orientation and therefore define the 10 as 'good enough'. The scale question, "if zero stands for 'disaster' and 10 stands for 'good enough', where are you now?" implies a movement, where it is not reaching 10 that counts, but the road to it.

You can then offer the client the next scaling question: 'On a scale where 0 represents "how it was when you started this facilitation process" and 10 stands for "this is good enough for me," at what point do you think you no longer need help, and you can make steps forward by yourself?' Experience shows that most people consider their progress to be good enough when they average a 7.6. So, reaching for perfect 10 is like reaching for the moon: futile.

Appreciate negative numbers as gifts

If the client answers with a negative number, this is a stage direction that he needs something else first before a constructive dialogue can occur. The easiest manner to proceed now is to ask coping questions: 'How did you cope with that difficult situation? What kept you going? How did you get through that ordeal?' This line of questions makes clear that you accept the negative stance of the client, enhances the chance that he will feel understood and, at the same time, implies that the client has the resource of perseverance and resilience.

Experiment to your heart's content!

SoFAP is an attitude and an approach, not a model or protocol. This leaves practitioners free to play with all imaginable and possible subtleties and use their creativity to discover their own variations and variants. There is no right or wrong as in a protocolized method. Only usefulness or no usefulness to the client matters.

Beyond scaling questions

The use of scaling questions may give the client the impression that the practitioner is applying a stand-alone intervention that is somewhat separate from the rest of the solution-focused conversation. While there is nothing wrong with that, there are even more powerful and elegant ways to promote change in a more natural and almost imperceptible way.

The usefulness and coping questions can be innocuously inserted into the flow of the conversation, giving the client the impression that the collaboration requires no special effort, but feels like "just another conversation".

Beyond the scale of usefulness: the usefulness question

During a conversation, you can interject with: 'Can I ask you a question? Is what we've discussed so far useful?' Or more succinctly, 'Is it useful if we speak like this?' The usefulness question is a powerful and elegant way to invite the client to say something about what is happening in the working relationship from a meta-perspective.

Again, the client has several options that as always, contain stage directions:

- If he says "no, it is not useful", the stage direction is: "accept my no without discussing the why of it and ask me 'what should we talk about *instead* so that our conversation will be useful?'".
- If the practitioner gets the feeling that the client is answering in a rather superficial way and only wants to be nice to him, accept that and ask: "Thank you for your compliment. You make me curious. What is it precisely that we need to talk about so that our cooperation will be of further use to you?".
- II the client answers in a useful way, you just need to ask for more details first and then ask the magic question "What else?"[21] to elicit as

many details as possible. These details are excellent starting points to help the client discover his next steps toward solutions and growth.

The usefulness question comes in handy in many situations.

- It is a logical follow-up question to expand the answers on the usefulness scale.
- When the professional lost track of the conversation and doesn't know what his best next question might be.
- When the intensity of the conversation wanes, the usefulness question can bring life back into the discussion.

The elegance of the usefulness question is that it gives the client the impression that he is giving answers to the professional, when in fact he is giving those answers to himself through the intermediary of the professional.

Beyond the negative numbers on a scale: the coping question

It is rare for someone to exclaim, "On your scale where the 10 stands for good enough, I'm at 105". However, the opposite often happens. Clients may feel that they are in such deep trouble that they reply, "It's totally hopeless. My partner is threatening to leave me, I'm about to lose my job, and I'm getting more depressed by the day. I'm at −27".

What to do when the client gives a number that falls outside the range of the scale?

Don't panic! Accept what the client is saying and in an empathetic way, ask the coping question, "How do you cope?" The most common immediate response then is, "I'm not coping! It is a total disaster." Now is the moment to do what we are not good at namely remaining silent and waiting.

In this situation, one can make use of a law of human communication: when I ask something, you are supposed to answer. If I stay silent long enough while you don't answer, pressure builds up in you to say something. This is something professionals need to learn because they are so eager to actively help the client. And yet, at these times it is better to remain silent and give the client time and space to come up with his own ideas and thereby help himself.

At those moments, silence says more (or invites the interlocutor to say more) than words can express.

CLIENT: I really don't hold out anymore. It's unbearable and it's getting harder and harder.

PROFESSIONAL (LOOKS THE CLIENT IN THE EYE WITH A COMPASSIONATE EXPRESSION): – Client: I must. I can't let my children starve; they need to go to school in the morning.

PROFESSIONAL: – is silent and nods –.

CLIENT: I must go to work, otherwise they will throw me out. And if I let myself go too much, my partner becomes even more distant, and I don't want that. So, I gather all my energy to still function a little bit. I don't want to lose my relationship, I continue to take care of my family, and I desperately need the money I make from my work.

PROFESSIONAL (WHO HAS NOW HEARD ENOUGH TO BREAK THE SILENCE): So, if I understand you correctly, even though you are at breaking point and have a very hard time, you still manage to gather your last scraps of energy and persevere. With your last strength you manage to take care of your children, you drag yourself to work but you go and do your best so there should be no reason to fire you. You can prioritize the responsibility for your family over your own misery. And the relationship with your partner is important enough that you do your best for that too.

The coping question is a magical tool. If you linguistically deconstruct this powerful question, which consists of only four words and a question mark, you will see that the following elements are implied in it:

- It shows acknowledgment that the client is going through a very difficult time.
- The question implies that the client has the resources to keep going.
- The question contains a compliment because the professional tells the client that he is persevering despite the difficulties.
- This compliment is inescapable because it is packaged in the form of a question and therefore is not an opinion that the client can challenge.
- If you remain silent long enough, your silence gives the client the space to provide information about resources and exceptions to the problem, "I have to, because..."

In a nutshell

Practicing the solution-focused philosophy with the tenacity of a pit bull prevents clients and professionals from being sucked into the vortex of hopelessness. The SoFAP approach outlined here can therefore be called "hope in action".

Conclusion

Offering the right scaling question and continuing to ask follow-up questions that are precisely tailored to the client's needs, along with the usefulness and coping questions have a trance-forming and transformative effect: the client's attention is focused on nuances and possibilities, he learns to break free from the pull of problems, and the path to growth and well-being opens. The resources that are uncovered as result of the transformative conversation become drivers for positive change.

Icon 2 The Miracle Question

> "Suppose one night while you are sleeping a miracle happens that solves your problem. How would you notice that?"

The precursor to the Miracle Question

As de Shazer studied the work of Dr. Milton H. Erickson, he came across Erickson's 1954 article[22] describing the crystal ball technique. After Erickson put a patient into a trance, he asked her to visualize a crystal ball showing how she would solve her problem in the future. Then Erickson asked her to report on how her problem had disappeared. At first glance, this method is so simple that even modern researchers[23] fail to see the complexity behind its apparent simplicity and dismiss it as a "new-age-like" practice without any therapeutic relevance.

What mechanism did Dr. Erickson trigger when he used the crystal ball technique? It is a way of getting around the limitation of pure rationality and creating a future out of nothing by using, like soothsayers at fairs, the metaphor of a crystal ball to pretend to be able to see into the future.

The difference between the genius of Dr. Erickson and the soothsayers is that Erickson had the client report how she herself brought about those changes in the future: "Can you describe to me now as specifically as possible what you can see in the crystal ball that you are doing differently to address today's problems?"

Thus, solutions from an imaginary future become applicable in the present.

> It was observed through the mechanism of a crystal ball as if it were an objective event viewed from a distance. He [Erickson, lc] explains that this allows the client to have an experience of what that outcome would be like without the difficulties engendered by the actual experience of the target state.[24]
>
> Milton H. Erickson

Steve de Shazer was a researcher at heart and immediately understood the mechanism behind the crystal ball intervention.

The discovery of the Miracle Question

The tale goes that Insoo Kim Berg, one of de Shazer's associates and his wife, was talking to a client who in her desperation exclaimed, "Only a miracle can help me!" And promptly Insoo asked the archetypal Miracle Question: "Suppose one night while you are sleeping a miracle happens that solves your problem. How would you notice it? What would be different?[25]"

> As is our usual practice, we took a cue from some of our clients' spontaneous use of scales and developed ways to use scales [and miracles, LC] as a simple therapeutic tool[26].

This quote reveals a characteristic of de Shazer and Berg's modus operandi. They use whatever they get from the clients and fine-tune it into an epistemological and change-promoting instrument. Moreover, they always apply Occam's Razor and do not make things more complicated than necessary.

> Entia non sunt multiplicanda praeter necessitatem.[27]

Along with their writings on scaling questions, this miraculous question helped the rapid expansion and spread of awareness of the "Brief Family Therapy Centre, Home of Solutions."[28] The rest is history,[29] as they say.

The development of the Miracle Question

From that point on, de Shazer and his colleagues started experimenting with the Miracle Question. Over the years, different versions were developed with an ever-increasing refinement. Because of the great importance of the Miracle Question, it is instructive to present a small historical study of the different versions that have been brought into circulation.

Spoiler alert: The Miracle Question as such, however innovative and even now unexpected to most clients, is just a technique. Its essence lies in the unfolding dialogue that constructs new perspectives.

The 1994 version reads, "Suppose that tonight, after you have fallen asleep, a miracle happens, and with it the problems that prompted you to go into therapy are immediately resolved. But because you are asleep you do not notice that this miracle is happening. Tomorrow morning you will wake up. How will you discover that the miracle has occurred? How will other people, without you telling them, discover that a miracle has happened?[30]

In de Shazer's latest book (2007) this culminates in: "Is it all right if I ask you a strange question? Suppose after our conversation today you leave here and continue doing what you usually do on a day like today. As the day passes you continue what you usually do. Then you come home, you eat, you watch TV, and you continue doing what you usually do as the evening passes. It gets late, you get tired, go to bed, and fall asleep. And then... at night... while you're sleeping... a miracle happens. And not just any miracle! It's a miracle that causes the problems that brought you here today to be gone... Just like that. (Snaps fingers). But because the miracle happened while you were asleep, you didn't notice it. Then... you wake up in the morning. A miracle happened during the night. The problems that brought you here are gone, just like that. How do you discover that things have become different? What is the first thing you notice when you wake up?"[31]

Perhaps because of their habit of asking the Miracle Question over and over again in every session, and because the Miracle Question is a wonderfully ingenious linguistic tool for bringing about change in the client, the Miracle Question has become the icon of the solution-focused model.

Simplism comes with a price

In the circle of solution-focused purists, de Shazer and Berg's habit of asking the Miracle Question in every session is part of the canon. Many of today's practitioners solely focus on the model's practicalities and are not fully aware of the historical context in which the Miracle Question was developed.

First, de Shazer and Berg's ever-repeated use of the Miracle Question (and other solution-focused techniques) served to research the mechanism of this technique and its effectiveness. In doing research, it is useful to have some scientific rigor. Rigor is something quite different from rigidity, something of which one cannot accuse Steve and Insoo.

Second, we must consider the context of their work. In the last decades of their working lives, they spent most, if not all their time on stages, where students came to listen to the solution-focused trademark, the Miracle Question, from the mouths of its inventors.

The uncritical adoption of de Shazer and Insoo's habit has led to excesses that border on the absurd. During conferences and workshops, for example, where the praise of the Miracle Question sometimes degenerates into beatification, you regularly hear that you are not working in a solution-focused way if you do not ask the Miracle Question in every conversation.

Unfortunately, for well-intentioned didactic reasons, the complexity of the Miracle Question is often simplified to "while you are sleeping, a miracle happens that solves all your problems. How do you know that this miracle happened?"[32]

This simplistic version assumes that the client knows what his perfect future looks like and can effortlessly describe it. Out of a misplaced concern for ease of use, this simplistic version omits some essential linguistic components (that we will discuss below). We share the opinion of Matthias Varga von Kibéd where he states, "So, to reduce the process of asking the Miracle Question (for which many more essential differences could be and were pointed out by Steve) to a mere future perfect, although it is a smart didactic for beginners, would at the same time be a great loss for the SFBT approach."[33]

The SoFAP version of the Miracle Question

PROFESSIONAL: May I ask you an unusual question?[34]

CLIENT: Rather not. I have a hard enough time as it is.

PROFESSIONAL: Okay. Then may I ask you an ordinary question?

CLIENT: That's fine.

PROFESSIONAL: Today is Tuesday (yes[35]). It is almost four o'clock in the afternoon (yes). We are now sitting here together in my office (or: at your home) (yes). Soon our conversation will come to an end (yes). We will say goodbye to each other (yes) and then you (or: I) will leave here (yes). The rest of the day you do what you have to do and maybe you also do things you like to do. The evening comes and you spend the evening in your own way. At some point you decide to go to bed, maybe because you are tired from the day or just because you are disciplined and always go to sleep at that hour.[36]

CLIENT: Hm.

PROFESSIONAL: Let's suppose that while you're sleeping it's as if a miracle happens.

CLIENT: I don't believe in miracles.

PROFESSIONAL: I don't either, but let's suppose for a moment that it is as if a miracle happens.

CLIENT: Hm.

PROFESSIONAL: And in that miracle, the problems that you've told me about are solved in such a way that you have a little less trouble with them and that you can take a step forward in your life. Of course, you don't know that because you are asleep.

CLIENT: Hm.

PROFESSIONAL: Tomorrow morning you wake up. How would you notice that a miracle might have happened for you? What would you think, feel and do differently then?

CLIENT: I would wake up more refreshed because I would have slept through the night. My partner would be cheerful and finally recognize that I'm doing my best and wouldn't bully me anymore. As if by some miracle, our four kids at the breakfast table would behave decently instead of making a mess. But it would be a real miracle if my family members would listen to me.

PROFESSIONAL: Fine. So, if that miracle happened, you would sleep better, be better rested, and be able to handle the stresses of the day better. What difference would it make to you if your partner shows you know that he thinks you are trying to make the best of it?

CLIENT: Then it would be easier for me to stop being wary of him from the morning on.

PROFESSIONAL: How will he notice if you start the day a little more relaxed?

CLIENT: I would probably growl and snarl a little less and not immediately urge everyone to hurry up. Indeed, I will be a little more relaxed.

PROFESSIONAL: Fine. What will you do differently?

CLIENT: No idea... But believe me, for our four children to sit obedient and neat at the breakfast table... it takes several miracles, preferably all at once (laughs).

PROFESSIONAL: I can understand that. To get four young children through the morning rush hour, if that could be done without a hassle, well, it would take several miracles indeed (both laugh). What will be different now that you've managed to take it all a bit easier?

CLIENT: Well, I don't know... But if the day starts more smoothly, then perhaps what follows will also go more smoothly too, surely?

PROFESSIONAL: That is likely. How will it be different then?

CLIENT: There is a good chance that we will get the children to school on time and without fuss. Then hopefully I'll arrive at work a little less stressed.

PROFESSIONAL: How will your colleagues notice that things are different for you?

CLIENT: They will probably notice the same thing as my family members, namely that I start my working day more relaxed.

PROFESSIONAL: Excellent, what else will you do differently?

Etcetera...

The solution-focused cycle of questions and answers both supports the clients to access their resources, enables them to incrementally find alternative ways to address their problems, and thereby take steps forward. Going a step further, you can phrase this version of the Miracle Question as a well-being enhancer: "and in that miracle, you find ways to be more and easier satisfied with what life brings you."

Food for linguists

If you study our version of the Miracle Question carefully, you will notice that a curious interplay of "would" (irrealis), "could" (optativus), and "will" (realis) is used to enhance the effect.

At the beginning, when you ask follow-up questions to the client's initial answers to the solution-building Miracle Question, you use the irrealis, "would". With the use of the irrealis, the speaker (or questioner) expresses that, as far as is known, the action or condition mentioned has not (yet) occurred at the time of speaking. In order to increase the hypnotic[37] (or attention focusing) effect, we immediately add an optativus, "could" with which we represent an assumption that is theoretically possible. In our case, we even use a combination of irrealis and optativus in the question, "What *would* make you think that it is exactly as if a miracle *could* have happened for you?"

The conditional mode, "could", has the effect of presenting what has not yet happened (the miracle) as theoretically possible (for linguists: an optativus). The question "what could you do differently?" turns it into a possible option which can actually happen (for linguists: a potentialis).

Then we meticulously "pace" each answer that the client gives by asking the question, "What else?" At first glance, we are simply repeating the client's answers. Yet, we add a solution-focused paraphrase and, in reality, change the client's answer from an irrealis to a realis: "So if for you that miracle would have happened, then you will sleep better again, you will be more rested, and you can handle the stresses of the day again."

Once we notice that the client indicates in his answers that he is able and willing to speak from his own responsibility (what he himself would -->could -->will do differently), we switch to an indicativus (for the linguists: form of the realis that indicates future reality): "How will it be different then? What will you do differently then?"

Next, we take it a step forward by offering a triangular question: "How will your colleagues notice that things look different for you? What will they see you doing differently?"

The "What else?" question and the subsequent solution-focused paraphrases drive the trance/transformational cycle of questions and answers. This is the tool of choice for creating a context in which clients begin and continue to move forward.[38]

When using the Miracle Question for enhancing well-being, there is less need for complicated linguistic interventions to help the client break free from his problem fixation: "Let's suppose that, while you're sleeping, it's as if a miracle happens. And in that miracle, you find ways to be more and easier satisfied with what life brings you. What will you notice that you are doing differently?"

It is in both versions essential to introduce and frame the Miracle Question and the subsequent answers with "Let us suppose that..." and "as if...".

If you read the well-being Miracle Question with the help of this linguistic magnifying glass, you'll see that we can switch much faster from the irrealis and optativus to the indicativus.

This linguistic high-tech, gives the Miracle Question its full richness and complexity. It becomes clear what the Miracle Question, including the full series of subsequent questions, really is: the creation of a hypnotic framework in which the client's inner search processes have greater creative freedom than what takes place in his ordinary daily experiences.

Words are really magic.

> Hypnosis is not some mystical procedure, but rather a systematic utilization of experiential learnings – that is, the extensive learnings acquired through the process of living itself. All of us have a tremendous number of these generally unrecognized psychological and somatic

learnings and conditionings, and it is the intelligent use of these that constitutes an effectual use of hypnosis.[39]

Milton H. Erickson

A roadmap for using the Miracle Question

If you study the exact wording of the Miracle Question, you will recognize a pattern. Because the Miracle Question is seemingly simple, but not easy in practice, we offer a step-by-step roadmap to achieve maximum effectiveness. Of course, everyone is free to come up with one's own version.

The successive steps are:

1 Ask permission to ask an "unusual" question.
2 Use a "yes-set" to prime the question.
3 Ask the Miracle Question.
4 Meticulously define what is accomplished by the miracle.
5 Accept all the answers you get without discussing them, even if they are not very useful at first. Support the client by asking him what he himself would do, think, and feel differently after the miracle has taken place.
6 Elicit more and more details from the client by using the "What else" question.
7 Ask triangulation questions to invite the client to think and talk about how those around him would (and will) perceive that this miracle happened.
8 Repeat – with solution-focused paraphrasing – what the client has just said. Compliment on each useful answer. Useful answers are those in which the client himself suggests an alternative to the problem behavior and/or in which he indicates what concrete steps forward he is taking toward greater well-being.

The Miracle Question in plain language:

1 May I ask you an unusual question?
2 Today is Thursday (yes); it is eleven o'clock in the morning (yes); we are here in my office (yes); soon you will go home (yes) and do what you normally do the rest of the day (yes), later in the evening when you are tired you will go to sleep (yes).
3 Imagine that while you are sleeping, it is as if a miracle happens. But of course, you don't know that, because you are asleep.
4 And in that miracle, the problems that you told me about change such that they bother you less and/or you notice more acutely what you can

do differently to increase your well-being. Tomorrow morning you wake up without realizing what happened.

5 How would you know that it is as if this miracle happened? What would you think, do, feel differently?
6 Client: "I would... (Describes what would be different after the miracle)". Professional: Fine. What else could/would/will you do differently now that the miracle has happened?
7 How would your partner, your friends, children, parents, colleagues, clients, etc. notice that this miracle has happened for you? What will they notice you doing differently? What else? Okay, fine.
8 So now that the miracle has happened you would... (repeat what the client just said with a solution-focused twist and offer compliments on it).

What makes the Miracle Question work?

To answer this question, we will take a closer look at the active ingredients of the Miracle Question, which at first glance appears to be a simple, even naïve question, but on closer inspection hides an exquisite complexity.

1 Asking the client for permission to ask him an "unusual question" draws attention by arousing his curiosity.
2 Offering the yes-set focuses the client's attention further, while you elicit a cooperative thinking pattern because the questions have an obvious "yes" answer.
3 Asking permission and using the yes-set activates the working relationship and marks the beginning of a cooperative dialogue that will "co-create" a new reality. While both parties are important in this process, modesty is in order. The professional only listens and asks questions. This modesty is an excellent alternative to the conceit of the expert who knows better and comes up with solutions instead of the client.
4 Using the word "suppose" helps your client to exchange his rational and fixed thought patterns for an imaginary and virtual reality.
5 The word "miracle" gives your client permission to think about the broadest imaginable spectrum of possibilities: after all, miracles know no bounds.
6 The question bypasses any objection because miracles are not rationalizations and therefore there is no room for rational (counter) argumentation.
7 The Miracle Question invites the client to visualize a future in which his problem (challenge) is solved enough to make it less of a burden and/

or in which he has a sharper view of the skills he needs to enhance his well-being.

8 Further questioning is a means of eliciting details about possibilities that the client could not have imagined by logical reasoning.
9 Subsequent further questioning the answers leads to a future in which progress would first occur and then will occur.

10 It is an elegant way to help the client articulate workable goals,[40] making it easier to pursue them.
11 Helping the client articulate their goals in positive terms (what are you going to do *instead* of...?) creates hope, motivation, and future focus.[41]
12 By using solution-focused and well-being-enhancing questions, you help the client to give an increas-

ingly concrete description of his wished-for future. In this way, a map becomes visible on which the road to better care (for himself and his environment) and more well-being is easier to find.
13 The detailed description of concrete, realistic, and achievable steps toward that desired future becomes more or less automatically a

prescription for (more) efficient behavior. By describing assumed solutions to the professional, the client prescribes his own solutions to himself. Description becomes prescription.

The Miracle Question without the word 'miracle'

Clients do not always appreciate the word "miracle". In some cultures, the word "miracle" even has no place. Since we are great advocates of the maxim "speak your client's language," we suggest avoiding the word "miracle" if you have the impression that it might hinder collaboration. There are plenty of "ordinary" questions to help the client put words to their wished-for future, for example: "Suppose that by some favorable wind your problems were solved enough for you to be less bothered by them, what would you do, say, think, feel differently?"

Applying the linguistic magic, once the client is able to indicate in small steps what he could do differently, you can move on to what he would do, then to what he will do differently and end with what he does differently.

The miracle video

A picture says more than a thousand words and a video more than a whole encyclopaedia. How about the following version of the Miracle Question? "If I had a video recording of you the day after the miracle and one from the day before, both without sound, what differences would I see?[42]

Steve's final contribution

In his posthumously published book, "More Than Miracles," de Shazer's genius shines one last time when he introduces another innovation: the miracle scale.

> On a scale of 0 to 10, where the 0 means you decided to seek help and the 10 represents the day after the miracle happened, where would you say you are today?

The dialogue that follows the initial responses to the Miracle Question can shift to this miracle scale. This allows the client to deconstruct their miracle into smaller steps that follow the continuum from 0 to 10. As the dialogue progresses, you can use the sequence from "I would do" to "I could do" to "I will do" and help the client move from wishing to doing.

Closing consideration

Steve de Shazer once said at a conference in Heidelberg, "The Miracle Question does not exist, there is only the process of asking it."[43]

One might add, "The scaling question does not exist, there is only the process of asking it".

We translate these cryptic statements, entirely on our own responsibility, as, "Asking the scaling and Miracle Question is trivial. Their value is hidden in the linguistic ingredients that are activated by our use of language in further questioning the client's answers".

Discovering the subtlety and richness of the linguistic mechanism behind the scaling questions and the Miracle Question is an enduring tribute to Steve de Shazer and Insoo Kim Berg's genius gifts to our field.

Notes

1 de Shazer, S. (1982). Some conceptual distinctions are more useful than others. *Family Process*, *21*, 71–84.
2 de Shazer, S. (1994). *Words were originally magic*. Norton, p. 92.
3 de Shazer, S. & Dolan, Y. (2007). *More than miracles*. Routledge, pp. 7–8.
4 de Shazer, S. (1984). The death of resistance. *Family Process*, *23*, 1–11.
This article is such a pivotal moment in the development of solution-focused thinking and working that it is relevant to quote the full text of this epistemological shift. *(The term "cooperating" is used in an attempt to avoid reification, because the "ing" helps to keep the therapist thinking in terms of processes of continuing interaction between the subsystems, rather than the condition that might be implied using cooperation, which might describe a principle rather than a process. "Cooperation" tends to disconnect a "something" from its ground and makes it "thing-like": a likely process given the dominance of the old epistemology.)*
5 de Shazer, S. (1994). *Words were originally magic*. Norton, p. 92.
6 See Chapter 5, 'Some salient points concerning the scaling questions' on page 112.
7 See The 7-step Dance, Chapter 5, step 4 uncovering resources, page 102.
8 See page 178 for a detailed discussion on the mechanism of the coping question.
9 Words are magic. Please note the difference between the following questions and choose the most appropriate version if you want to promote change. Where are you *now*? Where are you *already*? Where are you *only now*?
10 "Feel" is the right word here. There is no watertight, always correct golden rule that indicates with mathematical accuracy when enough is sufficient. Of course, you can make this intervention fail-safe by first asking, "Are there any other things you would like to add?".
11 The alternative questions, "So, that's it?" or worse: "Is that all?", would not be supportive, respectful nor change inducing.
12 For explanation about the subtle differences between the verbs could/will/is, we refer to footnote 11 on page 146. "What is the next step?", "What will be the smallest next step?", and "How will you get from three to four? The follow-up question, "What do you need to get to ten?" is best avoided because it implies a large step that carries a high probability of failure.
13 For details, see chapter 5, step 3, page 91.

14 In Chapter 1, we detail the axiom of resilience as one of the foundations of the thinking behind the thinking of SoFAP.
15 In Chapter 6, The Flowchart explains all fitting interventions for the noncommittal working relationship, i.e., when the client has no request for help.
16 See: Chapter 5, Seven-step SoFAP dance, step 3 goal setting.
17 Chapter 1 clarifies the axiom of well-being and in Chapter 5, the 7-step dance we discuss in detail the importance of The Mother of All Goals: Growth, Wellbeing and Contentment.
18 Dear Reader, to experience the power of the scale of well-being, we invite you to think of your own answers as you read the questions below.
19 See Chapter 2 (What always works) on the importance of feeling understood on page 46.
20 Wilson, T.D. (2009). Know thyself. *Perspectives on Psychological Science*, 4(4), 384–389.
21 As you know by now, dear Reader, this is one of our favorite questions. We explained the hidden implications of this versatile question on page 113 (chapter 5, step 6.)
22 Erickson, M.H. (1954). Pseudo-orientation in time as a hypnotic procedure. *Journal of Clinical and Experimental Hypnosis, 2*, 261–283.
23 Eyes wide shut and unencumbered by any knowledge of the complexities of Milton H. Erickson's work have fallen into this trap, the trio: Norcross, J.C., Koocher, G. & Garafalo, A. (2006). Discredited psychological treatments and tests. A Delphi survey. *Professional Psychology: Research and Practice, 37*, 515–522.
24 Erickson, M.H. & Rossi, L.L. (red). *The collected papers of Milton H. Erickson on Hypnosis: Vol. IV. Innovative hypnotherapy*. New York: Irvington, p. 396.
25 de Shazer, S. (1988). *Clues: Investigating solutions in brief therapy*. WW Norton.
26 de Shazer, S. (1994). *Words were originally magic*. Norton, p. 92.
27 Famous line attributed to William of Ockham (circa 1287–1347), a medieval English Franciscan friar. To avoid simplicity, the words "than necessary" are crucial.
28 This was both the name and the logo of their institute.
29 For an overview of the history of the solution-focused approach, we refer to: McKergow, M. (2021). *The next generation of solution focused practice*. Routledge.
30 de Shazer, S. (1994). *Words were originally magic*. New York: Norton, p. 95.
31 de Shazer, S. (2007). *More than miracles*. Routledge. (Text combined from pages 42 and 43 by LC).
32 Let there be no misunderstanding: this is NOT how this book's author uses (or is it 'abuses') the Miracle Question.
33 Varga von Kibéd, M. (2006). Solution-focused transverbality. How to keep the essence of the solution-focused approach by extending it. In: Lueger & Korn (red.), *Solution-focused management*, Band 1. München/Mering: Rainer Hampp, p. 46.
34 Asking permission to ask an unusual question makes the client curious and focuses his attention.
35 To bring the client into a "yes" state, one asks questions about truisms to which the answer is so evidently a "yes" that the client does not even have to utter the yes. This is the beginning of focusing the client's attention (also called trance) which can be deepened by adding the Miracle Question. When the working relationship is sufficiently developed, one can skip this introduction.
36 Notice the compliment that is wrapped up in this sentence.

37 de Shazer, S. & Dolan, Y. (2007). *More than miracles.* Routledge. On page 43, de Shazer describes in exact words what a trance-like state represents, without using the word "trance". "Over the years we have observed that at this point our clients' bodies typically become very still and their breathing deepens and slows. Their eyes seem to dilate a bit and lose focus. Usually they continue to stare off into space or look down at the floor for a moment or two while they are composing their answers. Oftentimes they even close their eyes for a few seconds."
38 Cross connection with Chapter 4 Mandates: the leadership mandate is used to activate the facilitation mandate.
39 Erickson, M. & Rossi, L.L (Ed.) (1980). *The collected papers of Milton H. Erickson on hypnosis: Vol. IV. Innovative hypnotherapy.* New York: Irvington, p. 224.
40 Cross connection: see Chapter 5, Seven-step dance, step 3 goal setting.
41 Cross connection: see Chapter 2, What always works in good therapy?
42 de Shazer, S. (2021). More than miracles. In S. de Shazer, Y. Dolan, H. Korman, T. Trepper, E. McCollum & I.K. Berg (Eds.), *The state of the art of solution-focused brief therapy.* Routledge, p. 58.
43 Personal communication with Matthias Varga von Kibéd (Vienna, May 2006).

Consulted Literature

Bachelor, A. (1995). Client's perception of the therapeutic alliance: A qualitative analysis. *Journal of Counseling Psychology, 42*, 323–337.

Bargh, J. (2006). What have we been priming all these years? On the development, mechanisms and ecology of non-conscious social behavior. *European Journal of Social Psychology, 36*, 147–168.

Bargh, J. & Chartrand, T. (1998). *The mind in the middle. A practical guide to priming and automaticity.* Retrieved from http://projectimplicit.net/nosek/teaching/761/auto- maticity_and_priming.pdf.

Bargh, J.A., Chen, M. & Burrows, L. (1996). Automaticity of social behavior: Direct effects of trait construct and stereotype activation on action. *Journal of Personality and Social Psychology, 71*, 230–244.

Bargh, J. & Morsella, E. (2008). The unconscious mind. *Perspectives on Psychological Science, 3*, 73–79.

Bateson, G. (1972). *Steps to an ecology of mind.* New York: Ballantine Books.

Cauffman, L. (2006). *The solution Tango: Seven simple steps to solutions in management.* London: Marshall Cavendish Limited.

Cauffman, L. (2022). *Developing and sustaining a successful family business: a solution-focused guide.* Oxford: Routledge.

Cauffman, L. & Weggeman, M. (2023), *Solution-Focused Applied Psychology, a Design Science Research Protocol (SoFAP-P).* Oxford: Routledge.

Clark, H. (1996). *Using language.* New York: Cambridge Press.

Damasio, A. (1994). *Descartes' error: Emotion, reason, and the human brain.* New York: Avon Books.

de Jong, P. & Berg, I.K. (2001). *Interviewing for solutions.* San Francisco, CA: Brooks/Cole.

de Shazer, S. (1984). The death of resistance. *Family Process, 23*, 1–11.

de Shazer, S. (1985). *Keys to solution in brief therapy.* New York: W.W. Norton.

de Shazer, S. (1988). *Clues: Investigating solutions in brief therapy.* New York: W.W. Norton.

de Shazer, S. (1994). Essential, non-essential: Vive la différence. In J. Zeig, *Ericksonian Methods: The essence of the story* (pp. 240–258). New York: Brunner/Mazel.

de Shazer, S. (1994). *Words were originally magic.* New York: W.W. Norton.

de Shazer, S. & Dolan, Y. (2007). *More than miracles.* New York: Haworth.

de Shazer, S. & Molnar, A. (1984). Four useful interventions in brief family therapy. *Journal of Marital and Family Therapy, 10*, 297–304.

Dolan, Y. (2000). An interview with Yvonne Dolan, MSW, by Dan Short. *Milton H. Erickson Foundation Newsletter, 20*, 2.

Duncan, B. (2002). The founder of common factors. A conversation with Saul Rozenzweig. *Journal of Psychotherapy Integration*, *12*, 10–31.
Duncan, B., Miller, S. & Sparks, J. (2004). *The heroic client*. San Francisco, CA: Jossey-Bass.
Duncan, B., Miller, S., Wampold, B.E. & Hubble, M.A. (2010). *The Heart and Soul of Change: Delivering what works in Therapy*, 2nd edition. American Psychology Association.
Dweck, C. (2006). *Mindset: The new psychology of success*. New York: Random House.
Epictetus (1994). *The art of living*. London: Harper Collins.
Erickson, M.H. & Cauffman, L. (2016). *The Canoe Diary. Two Volumes*. Cauffman Books, http://www.miltonericksoncanoediary.com.
Erickson, B.A. & Keeney, B. (2006). *Milton H. Erickson, an American healer*. Sedona, AZ: Ringing Rocks Press.
Erickson, M.H. & Rossi, E.L. (Eds.) (1980). *The collected papers of Milton H. Erickson on hypnosis. Vol. IV. Innovative hypnotherapy*. New York: Irvington.
Erickson, M.H. (ca. 1950). *Hypnosis in obstetrics: Utilizing experiential learnings*. Unpublished manuscript.
Erickson, M.H. (1954). Clinical note on indirect hypnotic therapy. *Journal of Clinical and Experimental Hypnosis*, *2*, 171–174.
Erickson, M.H. (1954). Special techniques of brief hypnotherapy. *Journal of Clinical and Experimental Hypnosis*, *2*, 109–129.
Erickson, M.H. (1954). Pseudo-orientation in time as a hypnotic procedure. *Journal of Clinical and Experimental Hypnosis*, *2*, 261–283.
Erickson, M.H. (1965). Hypnosis and examination panics. *The American Journal of Clinical Hypnosis*, *7*, 356–358.
Erickson, M.H. (1965). Use of symptoms as an integral part of hypnotherapy. *The American Journal of Clinical Hypnosis*, *8*, 57–65.
Erickson, M.H. (1966). Experiential knowledge of hypnotic phenomena employed for hypnotherapy. *The American Journal of Clinical Hypnosis*, *8*, 299–309.
Erickson, M.H. (1966). *A lecture by Milton H. Erickson*. Houston, February 18, Audio Recording No. cd/emh.66.2.18. Phoenix, AZ: Milton H. Erickson Foundation Archives.
Erickson, M.H. (1967). *A lecture by Milton H. Erickson*. Delaware, September 19, Audio Recording No. cd/emh.67.9.19. Phoenix, AZ: Milton H. Erickson Foundation Archives.
Erickson, M.H. (1973). A field investigation by hypnosis of sound loci importance in human behavior. *The American Journal of Clinical Hypnosis*, *16*, 147–164.
Erickson, M.H. (1973). Psychotherapy achieved by a reversal of the neurotic processes in a case of ejaculatio praecox. *The American Journal of Clinical Hypnosis*, *15*, 217–222.
Erickson, M.H. (1975). *Preface in Bandler en Grinder: Patterns of the hypnotic techniques of Milton H. Erickson*. New York: Grune & Stratton.
Erickson, M.H. & Rosen, H. (1954). Hypnotic and hypnotherapeutic investigation and determination of symptom function. *Journal of Clinical and Experimental Hypnosis*, *2*, 201–219.
Fraenkel, P. (1998). Time and couples, part II: The sixty second pleasure point. In T. Nelson & T. Trepper (Eds.), *101 interventions in family therapy, volume II* (pp. 145–149). West Hazleton, PA: Haworth Press.

Frank, J.D. & Frank, J.B. (1991). *Persuasion and healing: A comparative study of psychotherapy* (3rd edition). Baltimore, MD: John Hopkins University Press.

Grawe, K. (2004). *Neuropsychotherapie*. Göttigen: Hogrefe.

Haley, J. (1994). Typically Erickson. In J.K. Zeig, *Ericksonian methods: The essence of the story* (p. 11). New York: Brunner/Mazel.

Hoyt, M.F. (2001). *Interviews with brief therapy experts*. New York: Routledge.

Hubble, M.A., Duncan, B.L. & Miller, S.D. (2009). *The heart and soul of change: What works in psychotherapy*. Washington, DC: APA.

Keeney, B.P. (1983). *The aesthetics of change*. New York: The Guilford Press.

Keeney, B. (2015). *The creative therapist*. New York: Taylor & Francis Ltd.

Kennedy, J. & Eberhart, R. (2003). *Swarm intelligence*. San Francisco, CA: Morgan Kaufmann.

Lakoff, G. & Johnson, M. (2003). *Metaphors we live by*. Chicago, IL: University of Chicago Press.

Lerner, B. & Fiske, D.W. (1973). Patient attributes and the eye of the beholder. *Journal of Consulting and Clinical Psychology, 40*, 272–277.

McDonald, A. (2007). *Solution-focused therapy*. London: Sage.

McKergow, M. & Jackson, P.Z. (2007). *The solution focus: Making coaching and change simple*. London: Nicholas Brealey.

McKergow, M. & Korman, H. (2009). In between – neither inside nor out – side: The radical simplicity of Solution-Focused Brief Therapy. *Journal of Systemic Therapy, 28*(2), 34–49.

McKergow, M. (2021). *The next generation of solution focused practice*. Oxford: Routledge.

Norcross, J.C., Koocher, G. & Garafalo, A. (2006). Discredited psychological treatments and tests: A Delphi poll. *Professional Psychology: Research and Practice, 37*, 515–522.

Petterson, C. (2006). *A primer in positive psychology*. Oxford: Oxford University Press.

Pinker, D. (1998). *How the mind works*. London: Penguin.

Reynolds, C. (1987). Flocks, herds and schools: A distributed behaviour model. *Computer Graphics, 21*(4), 5–34.

Rosen, S. (1982). *My voice will go with you. The teaching tales of Milton H. Erickson*. New York: W.W. Norton.

Rosenthal, R. & Jacobson, L. (1968). *Pygmalion in the classroom*. New York: W.W. Norton.

Rosenzweig, S. (1936). Some implicit common factors in diverse methods of psychotherapy. *American Journal of Orthopsychiatry, 6*, 412–415.

Seligman, M.E.P. (2003), *Authentic happiness: Using the new positive psychology to realize your potential for lasting fulfilment*. New York: Free Press.

Seligman, M.E., Steen, T.A., Park, N. & Peterson, C. (2005). Positive psychology progress: Empirical validation of interventions. *American Psychologist, 60*, 410–412.

Varga von Kibéd, M. (2006). Solution-focused transverbality: How to keep the essence of the solution-focused approach by extending it. In G. Lueger & H. Korn (Eds.), *Solution-focused management, Band 1*. München/Mering: Rainer Hampp.

Walsh, F. (2016). *Normal family processes, growing diversity and complexity*, 4th edition. Guilford Press.

Wampold, B.E. (2001). *The great psychotherapy debate: Models, methods and findings*. Hillsdale, NJ: Erlbaum.

Weinberger, J. (1995). Common factors aren't so common: The common factors dilemma. *Clinical Psychology: Science and Practice*, *2*, 45–69.

Weiner-Davis, M., Shazer, S. de & Gingerich, W. (1987). Building on pretreatment change to construct the therapeutic solution: An exploratory study. *Journal of Marital and Family Therapy*, *13*, 359–334.

Whipple, J.L. et al. (2003). Improving the effects of psychotherapy: The use of early identification of treatment failure and problem-solving strategies in routine practice. *Journal of Counseling*, *50*(1), 59–68.

Williams, E. & Bargh, J.A. (2008). Experiencing physical warmth promotes interpersonal warmth. *Science*, 322, 606.

Wilson, T.D. (2009). Know thyself. *Perspectives on Psychological Science*, *4*, 384–389.

Wittgenstein, L. (1953), *Philosophical investigations*. Oxford: Basil Blackwell.

Wright, R. (2000). *Nonzero: History, evolution & human cooperation*. London: Abacus.

Zeig, J. (1980). *A Teaching Seminar with Milton H. Erickson*. New York: Brunner/Mazel.

Index

Note: *Italic* page numbers refer to figures and page numbers followed by "n" denote endnotes.

Printed in the United States
by Baker & Taylor Publisher Services